THE FIVE-MINUTE DEVOTIONAL

Jan Silvious

ZondervanPublishingHouse

Grand Rapids, Michigan

A Division of HarperCollinsPublishers

The Five-Minute Devotional
Copyright © 1991 by Jan Silvious

Requests for information should be addressed to:
Zondervan Publishing House
Grand Rapids, Michigan 49530

Library of Congress Cataloging-in-Publication Data

Silvious, Jan 1944–
    The five-minute devotional: devotions for the busy woman / Jan Silvious
      p. cm.
    ISBN 0-310-34401-8
    1. Devotional calendars.   I. Title
    BV4811.S3785 1991
    242'.2—dc20

90-35210
CIP
Rev.

Edited by Anne Severance
Interior design by Louise Bauer
Cover design by Lecy Design

Printed in the United States of America

95 96 97 98 99 00 01 02 03 / DH / 13 12 11 10 9 8 7 6 5

ACKNOWLEDGMENTS

This book, written with women in mind, has come about through the encouragement of some special men. I thank each of you for the role you have played in challenging, teaching, enduring, and laughing with me.

My dad, Jay Fulgham, who loves me and tells me so.

My husband, Charlie Silvious, who is my lifelong companion and friend.

My sons, David, Jonathan, and Aaron, who keep me "in touch with reality." We have learned unconditional love together.

My pastor, Wayne Barber, who has shown me the beauty of humility wrapped in a smile.

My colleague, Dr. Mark Womack, who has shown me a heart that hurts deeply for hurting people.

The men of WMBW, Dean Sippel, Gordon Hall, and Jay Johnson, who believed in me enough to say, "Let's give it a try." As a result, "Jan's Journal" is on the air, and *The Five-Minute Devotional* is a reality.

I couldn't close a list of men who have encouraged me without making one exception for my mom, Verna Fulgham. She's every bit a lady . . . with the courage of the strongest man.

INTRODUCTION

My heart's desire is that you might be encouraged in your walk as a follower of Jesus Christ. I know that five minutes a day is hardly enough to establish you in your faith, but five minutes a day can get your mind working, can stir some thoughts, or touch a tender spot.

I pray that in the time you spend meditating on each day's devotions you will discover more about you, more about your feelings and behavior, but more than anything I pray you will discover more about our God. As your thoughts are directed toward Him, may you learn to love Him, trust Him, and depend on Him as never before. He is wonderful.

Yours and His,

Jan Silvious

Jan Silvious

Is winter a difficult time of the year for you?

For many people, this drab and dreary season shapes up to be an endurance contest. Despite the dreamy pictures of cozy fires and families eating popcorn and playing games by the hearthside, the reality is that winter forces us to face the elements with a determination to survive.

Think about these words from *Lord, Don't You Love Me Anymore?* by Ruth Harms Calkin:

> *O God,*
> *On this cold January morning*
> *I am like a lonely tree*
> *On a distant mountaintop—*
> *Leafless, brittle, trembling.*
>
> *Howling winds twist me mercilessly.*
> *How long must I wait, dear Lord*
> *For the brilliant sun*
> *To melt the heavy-packed snow?*
> *And when will you prove*
> *To my aching heart*
> *That one lonely tree*
> *On top of a snow-covered mountain*
> *Has purpose wherever it grows!*
> *As I stand against the forceful elements*
> *I pray, I watch, I wait.*
> *I long to see streams of water*
> *Flowing down soft, rolling hills.*
> *Perhaps I shall be productive again*
> *When the long, long winter is past.*[1]

Sometimes I feel like a lone tree facing the howling winds of criticism and self-doubt, not always sure I can stand firm. For you, this winter may bring the painful gusts of grief. You will enter the season without someone you have loved, and your temptation is to give in to self-pity and depression.

It's at times like these that the Scriptures can bring indescribable comfort and wisdom.

Psalm 1 says: "Blessed is the man who does not walk in the counsel of the wicked or stand in the way of sinners or sit in the seat of mockers. But his delight is in the law of the Lord, and on his law he meditates day and night. He is like a tree planted by streams of water, which yields its fruit in season and whose leaf does not wither. Whatever he does prospers" (vv. 1–3).

If the cold winds are blowing in your life and you feel like a lone tree, God has a plan for your success. The plan is constant meditation on His Word. That may seem a little ethereal, but it's simple really. You make a choice to read, believe, live and breathe God's Word. Instead of concentrating on the criticism or self-doubt, take the time to go to the Word of God and look for His perspective. Then when the icy blast of self-pity and depression overtakes you, not only will you be able to stand, but you will actually prosper and bear fruit.

There have been times when I have felt like the last tree on the last hill, being buffeted by the strongest wind that could blow. Yet those solitary times have proved to be the times of greatest growth as I have been forced to search for God's perspective.

Amy Carmichael, a favorite writer of mine, was a lone tree on a windy hilltop for over fifty years, first as a missionary to India and then as an invalid, bedfast for twenty years. These are her words:

> Before the winds that blow do cease,
> Teach me to dwell within Thy calm:
> Before the pain has passed in peace,
> Give me, my God, to sing a psalm.
> Let me not lose the chance to prove
> The fullness of enabling love.
> O love of God, do this for me:
> Maintain a constant victory.[2]

My friend, we are all lone trees, whether battling the elements on the mountaintop or in a great forest. But God says we don't have to be uprooted or destroyed in these chilly, cold days of winter. We can bring forth fruit in due season if we plant our faith deep in Him.

WEEK 1 — TUESDAY
STARTING OVER

> I wish there were some wonderful place
> Called the Land of Beginning Again,
> Where all our mistakes and
> All our heartaches
> And all of our selfish grief
> Could be dropped like a shabby old coat at the door,
> And never be put on again.[3]
>
> —Louise Fletcher

I have read these words over and over, knowing that the heart cry of the author is the same as yours and mine. Who among us would not like to begin again?

That's what New Year's resolutions are all about. That's why birth—with its potential for one who has never been touched by hurt, pain, mistakes, or sin—is such an awesome wonder, and why we look at fresh-faced youth with such longing.

Would you like to relive your wedding day? To be able to take back all the careless words you have thrown at your mate since then?

Would you like to live your teenage years over? To please your mom and dad rather than alienate them?

Would you like to be confident that the words you have screamed at your child in frustration were really forgotten when the scene ended?

Though each of us yearns for new beginnings, the Land of Beginning Again is only a dream. Time, circumstances, and experience are all marks that can never be erased from the board on which we write the history of our lives.

With God, however, it is possible to start over!

Psalm 32 was written by a man who had every reason to want to begin again. David writes: "Blessed is he whose transgressions are forgiven, whose sins are covered" (v. 1).

8

This is the description of the clean slate, the place to begin again. And in the next verses David gives us the key for entering this place with God: "When I kept silent, my bones wasted away. . . . Then I acknowledged my sin to you and did not cover up my iniquity. I said, 'I will confess my transgressions to the Lord'—and you forgave the guilt of my sin" (vv. 3, 5).

Admitting that we have sinned—that we have really blown it—is the first step to starting over with God. He tells us that if we will agree with Him about our sin and choose to go in another direction (repentance), we can know the freedom of a clean slate. "As far as the east is from the west, so far has he removed our transgressions from us" (Ps. 103:12).

There is a luxury that comes with a clean slate. It is the luxury of beginning again with no fear that the past will ever be thrown in our faces. There will be only the joy of perfect freedom, knowing that God is not holding anything against us.

Have you been wishing for a Land of Beginning Again? There is such a place. That place is in the heart of God!

WEEK 1 — WEDNESDAY
ONLY FIVE MINUTES

I was convinced long ago that people who get things done know how to use every scrap of time they have rather than excusing their inaction by saying, "Well, I only had five minutes."

In commenting on the format of my daily radio program, ".Jan's Journal," people have often said, "Maybe someday you will have a fifteen-minute program." I'm sure they mean well, but to me, five minutes is a gold mine.

How do *you* feel about a short span of time? Is a few minutes here and there about like finding a penny—you don't even bother to pick it up because of its small value? Or have you learned that even pennies add up?

Time, like money, can be squandered or wasted or not properly valued. Each of us has been given the same number of minutes in an hour, the same number of hours in a day. Those who excel have simply learned to squeeze out of their time just a little bit more.

One of the best books I've ever read on this subject is Ted Engstrom's *The Pursuit of Excellence*. This little volume gets down to the basics of why some folks excel and some folks don't. Ted writes:

> Someone has said that the difference between an amateur and a professional is about five minutes more.
>
> Just five minutes more of reading toward your goal.
>
> Just five minutes more of working out a communication problem with your spouse.
>
> Just five minutes more with a son or daughter who may be having difficulties in school.
>
> Just five minutes more of asking God to give you the special guidance you so desperately need.
>
> Are you an amateur or are you a professional? Are you willing to give it that extra five minutes? Are you determined to strain your muscles until they cry out for relief, to keep on trying when you want to quit?[4]

In our "instant society," five minutes can seem like an eternity. I get anxious when I have to microwave something longer than five minutes. The quicker, the better for me.

But God says, "Whatever your hand finds to do, do it with all your might" (Eccl. 9:10). Sometimes it takes five minutes more to do it right.

How about you? Been slacking up a little? Have you slipped to amateur status when you really want to be a professional? Maybe you need to invest just five minutes more.

WEEK 1 — THURSDAY
THINGS

How important are "things" to you? And what are you working for? More "things"?

God has blessed us abundantly here in America. But some people never seem to have enough and think they should keep accumulating more and more. Isn't that really why some of us go to work? To subsidize a greedy spirit? Of course, some things are necessities—food, clothing, a roof over our heads. But what about the things we put out of reach of small hands? What about the things we store in vaults? What about the things that own us instead of our owning them?

There's a warning in Scripture that addresses the person who is owned by things: "It is easier for a camel to go through the eye of a needle than for a rich man to enter the kingdom of God" (Matt. 19:24).

"But I'm not rich," you may argue. Well, maybe by your standards, you're not. But if you're like me, you have more than you need, and if you are like me, you *want* to have more than you need. In fact, you work to keep a little extra padding, then hang on tight if anyone suggests that you let go of a little.

This reminds me of the story of some natives who wanted to catch monkeys in the jungle. Knowing the monkey's fondness for sweet beans, the natives put some beans in jars and set them out where the little creatures would find them. Before long, the monkeys, catching a whiff of the beans, put their paws in the narrow necks of the jars, made a fist around the beans, and refused to let go. Their obstinance made them easy prey for the hunters. They became captives because of what they had; the beans had the monkeys instead of the monkeys having the beans.

Speaking at a college commencement, Rudyard Kipling told the students, "Someday you will meet a man who cares for none of these things. Then you will know how poor you are." That man was born nearly two thousand years ago. Jesus Christ had nowhere to lay His head, no earthly place to call His home, yet He came to bring eternal life—something no money can buy.

Leona Helmsley, the hotel magnate, probably doesn't know the first thing about eternal values. She was recently sentenced to four years in jail and fined seven million dollars for tax evasion. The prosecution claimed her crime was greed. At sixty-nine years of age, Mrs. Helmsley has spent an entire lifetime going after things only to find that, in the end, she never owned them at all; *they* owned *her*.

What owns you? Are you fretful over your house? Your furniture? Your clothes? Your jewelry?

No one can answer those questions for you. Only you know if you've put your hand into a jar and fallen captive to the things you're holding onto. And only you know if you are willing to let go.

WEEK 1 — FRIDAY
QUIET AND LITTLE

Hudson Taylor, the great missionary to China, once said, "When God wants to do His great works, He trains somebody to be quiet enough and little enough, then He uses that person."

I don't think Taylor is talking "timid and fearful." I think he's saying that only when we know where our strength comes from, only when we realize that we really are weak apart from the strength of God in us, do we become fully usable.

Each time I go into the studio to cut my weekly program, I am freshly aware of my weakness. With a five-minute format, I must watch the clock closely, and sometimes I have to rush to get everything in before the end of the segment. So my words get tangled. Somehow, though, in spite of the flaws, many of you have written, "You said just what I needed to hear." Only God could take an imperfect person with an imperfect script and make it what lots of others "need to hear."

Then there are those who feel "too quiet" and "too little," frighteningly inadequate and vulnerable to the big guns, the power people, the stronger personalities who tend to run over others.

If you have ever been victimized by one of these, God has good news for you: "My grace is sufficient for you, for my power is made perfect in weakness" (2 Cor. 12:9).

God is at work in a variety of people who depend upon His strength. Two young men have recently come to my attention. David Ring, despite cerebral palsy and other related afflictions, is a powerful evangelist. David's speech is slurred and halting, and you wouldn't look at him twice if you passed him on the street, but God is using him mightily to reach the lost. Darryl Gilyard is a young black man who was abandoned early in life and grew up without a home. For no reason that is apparent to the onlooker, God has sovereignly chosen to bless Darryl's life. Remember, "[God's] strength is perfected in weakness."

Are you feeling weak and vulnerable today, *too* quiet . . . and *too* little? Do you feel that though God is obviously at work in others, He could never use someone like you?

Actually you may be just "quiet and little enough" for God's purposes. Why not give Him an opportunity to show what He can do through you? He delights in exalting His servants who know they can do nothing without Him.

WEEK 2 — MONDAY
AT HOME ON THIS EARTH

Malcolm Muggeridge once said, "The ultimate disaster that can befall us is to feel ourselves at home on this earth."

Why is this the ultimate disaster? Because making plans and priorities based on what we see removes the element of believing God for the unseen.

11

When we become too earthbound, we're asking for trouble—worry, depression, panic, fear, and greed. And the list goes on and on. All of these emotions deal with holding on to the people and possessions that are part of life on this earth. So this is a message for those who own citizenship in another world, since only those of us who see ourselves as sojourners on earth have any inkling that we are not permanent residents here, that we are just camping out!

The average newscast usually mentions something about our world that is wearing out or being used up, along with the name of some person or group who is willing to go to extreme measures to save the planet from destruction. These people are to be commended for their efforts, though the Bible tells us that their cause is only temporary. "The world and its desires pass away . . ." (1 John 2:17). Since we know it's all going to go up in smoke someday, believers need to keep their bags packed and their tent pegs loose if we want to stay emotionally healthy, spiritually tuned in, and ready for a new heaven and a new earth.

"Don't be too earthbound" is a popular piece of advice. "Great," you say. "But how do I avoid it?"

Try these suggestions for living like a stranger on the earth:

1. *Each morning, wake up determined to take God at His word, no matter what happens.* He has told us that He is in control. If your citizenship is in heaven, you can bow to His sovereignty and believe that no matter how chaotic and bizarre circumstances may seem, our God reigns.
2. *Don't try to measure God's fairness by what happens.* It wasn't fair for Jesus to have to hang on a cross, but we know now that there was a purpose far beyond what could be seen. Jesus Himself gave the whole situation to "God who judges righteously" (1 Pet. 2:23 NASB). The last chapter hasn't been written, but justice will prevail.
3. *Keep reading His Word.* That's where God gives us a glimpse of the other land of which we are citizens and of the kingdom where He reigns. It's almost like reading a travel book before visiting a foreign country.

If you are feeling too much at home on earth and you are worried, depressed, and panicky, maybe you should take some time to ponder the Book and think about the wonderful journey we will all soon be taking.

WEEK 2 — TUESDAY
HE HAS A NAME

How important is your name to you?

My name is pretty important to me. It gives me an identity that sets me apart from other people. It brings either a negative or positive response from others, depending on what their interactions with me have been. It is a representation of the person I am.

We don't appreciate people messing with our names. My mom recently had someone use her name to get a government agency to do something. Without asking permission, these people wrote a note and signed it with what they claimed was her signature. Needless to say, she was livid. You can get by with a lot of things, but when you misuse a person's name, you have stepped over the line.

That's why I'm concerned. I've done a lot of work with people trapped in dependencies and addictions. Many find help in support groups and twelve-step programs which often skirt the issue of identifying the ultimate Source of help. These programs refer to a "Higher Power," "God, as you know Him," or "Universal Force" instead of using His real name, Jesus Christ.

Acts 4:12 tells us plainly that "salvation is found in no one else, for there is no other name under heaven given to men by which we must be saved." Salvation (of the soul and wholeness of the total being) comes only through Jesus. There is power in His name because it speaks of who He is.

An unknown author has said, "Today, whenever you feel a need, just whisper His name—'Jesus, Jesus, Jesus.' You will find the power to handle the circumstance."

I once saw a woman hit by a car and was the first on the scene to offer help. She was conscious and overly excited. When I repeated the name of Jesus over and over and prayed aloud for His peace, I could see immediately that this had a calming effect on her. I don't know if the woman knew Jesus personally, but she recognized the power of His name.

I could have been "tolerant" and said, "Let's call on God as you know Him . . ." or I could have prayed, "O Higher Power, we make an appeal for your peace . . ." But that would be like my husband calling me on the phone and addressing me as "Woman" or "Wife" instead of using my name that is personal and very specific.

The name of Jesus is personal and very specific. Some Christians may not call on Him by name because they're so afraid they will violate someone else's rights or offend their "significant other." But I think these believers are *too* tolerant. It's time to speak up and boldly declare, "As for me, I will serve the Lord and His name is Jesus Christ!"

WEEK 2 — WEDNESDAY
THE RESTLESS HEART

"You have made us for yourself, O Lord, and our heart is restless until it finds its rest in you."

These are the words of St. Augustine, a man who, by all accounts, was a real rascal. He ran from God for a long time before he finally surrendered his will and found rest in Him.

When I speak at conferences, I usually end up counseling with people who are searching for answers to all kinds of problems—problems with relationships, the past, sin in their lives, and many others. But for the majority, the bottom line is the same as for St. Augustine—a restless heart.

Everyone has this "God-shaped vacuum." Romans 1:19 confirms that the reality of God is known to every person. And even though people may suppress the truth or look in many other places to satisfy that knowledge, the truth is still the truth—that God exists and can be known.

Recently I watched a television talk show featuring two young men who were incredible specimens of manhood—handsome, articulate, sensitive. But they were consumed with their homosexual relationship. As I listened to them, I was reminded once again of the restlessness of the human spirit apart from

13

God. Though these young men think they have found someone to fill up the hole in their hearts, the truth is that only God can satisfy.

Unless you have found your rest in Christ, you know what that emptiness is all about. I experienced it for over twenty-six years. Though I was in church faithfully and went through the motions, it was not until I realized how empty my life was without a personal relationship with Christ that I found peace.

Peace with God means giving all you know of you to all you know of Him. The Bible says . . .

1. We know that God exists (built-in knowledge).
2. Nature confirms His existence.
3. The Scriptures bear the historical record of His existence.

But knowing *about* God is not the same as knowing *God*. Rest comes when you decide to "give up all of you to all of Him." Once you have turned over the controls of your life to the Lord, the Holy Spirit will come in to teach you, to walk with you through the rough spots, to lead you into all truth, and to be your guarantee of heaven.

I invite you to find out today what it means to experience God's rest. Don't run from Him any longer. Admit that you have sinned and give the controls of your life to Him. Let Him provide the peace that passes understanding, the rest St. Augustine described. Let Him fill the empty place in your heart with Himself!

WEEK 2 — THURSDAY
THE WORD BECAME FLESH

A certain verse in the gospel of John brings back vivid memories for me: "The Word became flesh and made his dwelling among us. We have seen his glory, the glory of the One and Only, who came from the Father" (John 1:14).

Several years ago I was asked to substitute as a teacher for a large Bible class of about sixteen hundred members. Most of them attended regularly and dearly loved their teacher, so to find that I was going to teach was no great thrill for them.

I had never spoken before so large a group, so I studied for weeks. Since I was teaching from John 1, I had picked this verse to be the springboard: "The word became flesh. . . ." That statement spun around and around in my dreams, and I had to wonder what I could possibly add to this great truth.

That was over fifteen years ago, and every time I read that verse, I still wonder if it is possible to fathom its depths: The Creator God actually came to earth in human flesh to live among us so that we could see what He was really like in terms we could understand.

Carroll Simcox has said, "Christ is God's self-disclosure. He is God showing Himself to us in such a way that he leaves no room for doubt or error in our minds as to what God is like. That is why we call him the Word of God. A word is a true word only as it reveals him who speaks it. In Christ we do not see all that there is of God; but all that we see in him is God and it is enough for our present need."[1]

When I think of present need, I'm reminded of my helplessness on that long-ago day when I had to teach. I needed help and read: "The Lord is my helper. I will not be afraid. What can man do to me?" (Heb. 13:6). I needed peace and He told me: "My peace I give you" (John 14:27). I needed strength, so Jesus promised to give me His: "I can do all things through [Christ] who strengthens me" (Phil. 4:13 NASB).

I still remember my overwhelming sense of inadequacy as I stood up to teach. I was perspiring, shaking, and dizzy. The only words that came to mind were, "The Word became flesh and dwelt among us. . . ."

As I prayed, using the time to steady my nerves and to get used to the sound of my voice over the microphone, I realized I had everything I needed at my disposal, through the Holy Spirit. Since that time, I have come to rely on the fact that the qualities I see in Jesus Christ are the same qualities that belong to my God. As Jesus dwelt among men then, so He still dwells among us today in the form of His Spirit.

What challenges are you facing? Do you have to give a speech or talk to someone who intimidates you? Are you in a position of having to correct or take correction? Is some dreaded happening on the horizon?

Then this truth is for you: Jesus, the Word made flesh, went about doing good—helping the weak, healing the sick, giving hope to the hopeless, binding up broken hearts. He's the same today, and He is here for you.

WEEK 2 — FRIDAY
SAME IN THE DARK AS IN THE LIGHT

Through the news media, we're hearing of some unthinkable acts that are becoming frighteningly routine—torture chambers, satanic rituals, child pornography. We shake our heads in horror at this evidence of gross sin and darkness.

But maybe it's time to ask ourselves some questions: What sort of behavior do I engage in when nobody is around? Am I the same in the dark as I am in the light?

This sameness is not to be confused with airing one's dirty laundry in public. There's no virtue in that. Rather, I'm speaking of integrity—the desire for consistency under the scrutiny of God.

At the end of the book of Ecclesiastes, Solomon summarizes his thoughts: "Here is the conclusion of the matter: Fear God and keep his commandments, for this is the whole duty of man. For God will bring every deed into judgment, including every hidden thing, whether it is good or evil" (12:13–14).

One thing seems clear. Someday every "hidden thing" will be brought out into the light.

In his book, Solomon covers all the inconsistencies of life. He squarely confronts the contradictions that cause us to excuse behavior that is displeasing to God. To be honest, haven't we all, at one time or another, been tempted to say something like: "But you don't know what kind of background I have," or "I was a victim of my parent's addictions," or "I never learned to trust anybody," or "I just can't believe that God loves me"? Each point has validity, but when we stand before God, I'm afraid most of them will look like excuses to Him.

All of the hidden behaviors that come from excuses will one day be judged, and there won't be any more pretending that things are okay . . . in the light or in the dark.

I know of a situation in another state where a pastor has had to move his family to protect his son from sexual abuse at the hands of some prominent people in town. Because of the political climate in the town and in his church, and the power of the people involved, the deeds that went on in the dark have never come out. But someday, everyone who participated in this atrocity will have to give an account. The sad part is that while some of these people are highly respected, their respectability has not carried over into their secret life.

Are you willing to confront your own behavior? Is the pattern consistent? Would you allow the Lord to put His finger on any darkness in your life in order that you might seek His forgiveness and His cleansing?

Again, I ask: Are you the same in the dark as you are in the light? If not, pray for forgiveness and consistency.

WEEK 3 — MONDAY
COMMUNICATION

Each of us differs from one another in our style of communication, but the biggest difference seems to be between men and women.

Since my radio program, "Jan's Journal," has been on the air, I've received mail from an equal number of men and women. Inevitably, the men are more direct and make a concise statement or ask a straightforward question, while the women usually try to establish some kind of relationship first. Some of them go into great detail, telling me where we have met or mentioning a program that has meant something to them. Only then do they get around to their purpose in writing.

These differences between men and women and the way they communicate are partly rooted in the fact that most men are goal-oriented and most women are relationship-oriented. Communication can be frustrating if you don't know that.

I recently read this excerpt from a book called *On Your Own Terms: A Woman's Guide to Working with Men* by Kathryn Stechert:

> Males like to talk about things and activity; females prefer to talk about people and feelings. Those distinctions show up at very early ages. Even in preschool, psychologists have found boys are already talking about the physical environment and about activity. They talk about what they're building or the games they're playing. Their talk is auxiliary to activity. For little girls, talk often is the activity. Girls tend to play in twos, using shared secrets to establish and maintain friendships.[1]

So what does this mean for you as you go about your day's activities?

1. *For the woman who wants more communication with the man in her life, don't complain about it or demand it.* Try to understand how he perceives things. If you want him to share on a more emotional level, draw him out with a direct question: "What do you think about the crisis in the Persian Gulf? How do you feel about the way we have handled the political situation in Romania? What is your reaction to the fall of the Berlin Wall?"

   Women are often disappointed in conversations with men because we expect them to communicate the way our best girlfriends do. Remember, for you and your women friends, talk is often the tie that binds the relationship.

16

2. *For men, try to tell the woman who matters to you how you feel about a situation.* Let her get to know you apart from your activity. Let her know how you feel about your job, not just the facts of what you do. Another guy may be fascinated with how you make a motor work. But she wants to know how you *feel* about working on motors.

God made us distinctively different. Let's celebrate the differences, not complain about them. Understanding the communication style of the opposite sex is what God calls "bearing with one another in love."

WEEK 3 — TUESDAY
GRATEFUL FOR GOD

Have you ever wondered what life would be without God?

E. Stanley Jones once told the story of a little girl who prayed: "God bless Mama and Papa, my brothers and sisters, and all my friends. And now, God, do take care of Yourself, for if anything should happen to You, we'd be in the soup!"

From the looks of things in our world, we'd be in the soup without God. How does this fact affect your daily walk, your conversation?

When you are among people who don't profess to be Christians, do you freely refer to God, or are you afraid of what they might think of you? Do you watch the news with one eye on the eastern sky in the belief that the Messiah is really coming back soon, or have you written this off as an event that couldn't possibly happen in your lifetime? Are you willing to talk about world events in the light of Scripture, or do you just keep quiet, letting others speak of coincidence and troubled times?

And how do you operate over the holidays when you are with unbelieving family members? Are you a bold witness? Do you speak confidently of what God has done for you? Or are you afraid of being ridiculed as the family fanatic? And what about the cynics at work? When they sit around and second-guess the government and the powers that be, can you give a strong word for the Unseen Hand?

Kids, too, have a chance to speak up. Try looking for a good opening in a discussion among your friends at school, and then say, "The world may be in turmoil, but I know Who's in charge!"

One of the hardest tests believers face is speaking confidently about how God is moving in the world when we are with unbelievers. It's painful to be laughed at, to hold the minority opinion.

But in 2 Timothy Paul gives us a promise to hang on to: "I have fought the good fight, I have finished the race, I have kept the faith. Now there is in store for me the crown of righteousness, which the Lord, the righteous Judge, will award to me on that day—and not only to me, but also to all who have longed for his appearing" (4:7–8).

No matter what happens in this world, no matter what goes on, we can know beyond a shadow of doubt that our God reigns. Why not take some time today to thank Him for being a God we can trust . . . for being a God who is not limited by time, space or imagination . . . for keeping His hand on the controls of the world. "Lord, I'm so grateful that You are in charge!"

WEEK 3 — WEDNESDAY
FEAR AND ITS RESULTS

Fear seems to be a big issue in the lives of many people I meet—fear of the future, fear of financial disaster, fear of rejection, fear of failure, and so on.

Fear is an expectation of danger, a feeling that something bad is going to happen. But if you are fearful, you may be sure of one thing: Your fear is not from God! The Scriptures tell us that "God did not give us a spirit of timidity [fear], but a spirit of power, of love and of self-discipline" (2 Tim. 1:7).

I have trained myself to examine my fears and remind myself when I am afraid that the feeling is not from God. Many fears are obvious. These are usually not as problematic as fears that are more subtle.

Think about the fears of doubt and indecision.

When you doubt, you are always expecting the worst. Paralyzed by the possibilities of unknown consequences, you will then be unable to make a decision. But listen to this encouraging word from the Lord: "I know the plans I have for you, plans to prosper you and not to harm you, plans to give you hope and a future" (Jer. 29:11).

God means us no harm! He has our best interests at heart, so we can approach Him with confidence. "If any of you lacks wisdom, he should ask God, who gives generously to all without finding fault, and it will be given to him. But when he asks, he must believe and not doubt" (James 1:5).

Ask the Lord for wisdom, then believe that He can and will give it to you. Once you have your answer, you are free to move, though you might want to tell the Lord to stop you if there is a chance you could make the wrong decision. Trusting Him takes the fear out of decision-making.

Superstition is another result of fear. Since fear doesn't come from God, who would be the logical one to harass you? Right. The enemy.

Take this interesting case study from the Scriptures, for example. Shortly after John the Baptist was beheaded by Herod, Jesus launched His ministry. "And King Herod heard about this, for Jesus' name had become well-known. Some were saying, 'John the Baptist has been raised from the dead, and that is why miraculous powers are at work in him.' Others said, 'He is Elijah.' And still others claimed, 'He is a prophet, like one of the prophets of long ago. But when Herod heard this, he said, 'John, the man I beheaded, has been raised from the dead' " (Mark 6:14–16).

Fear of what might happen (and probably a good dose of guilt) were at the root of Herod's mindless superstition. Yet people are still governed by fear today. That's what keeps palm readers in business in those little roadside houses with "Madam Susie Q's" name flashing in neon lights on the front. Fearful people are prime targets for any kind of scam operation that promises to answer their questions about the future in exchange for money.

If you are afraid, remember that "God has not given us a spirit of fear." He desires only your good and offers power, love, and self-discipline to help you walk into the future with boldness. Trust Him! He holds your future in His hands!

WEEK 3 — THURSDAY
A WORD TO HUSBANDS

I want to share my heart with husbands today. So if you are a husband, this message is especially for you. (If you are a wife, you might want to read it anyway. Sometimes it helps to understand what our husbands might read.)

I talk with many women as I travel around the country, and lately I've been hearing the same lament over and over: "My husband is hitting me over the head with this submission thing."

The women who confide this bit of information are usually angry, sometimes bitter, and often depressed. They are not talking about physical assault and battery. They're talking about having submission held over them as a requirement.

"If you were a good Christian, you would submit to me."

"You don't submit, so you're a lousy wife."

"As the head of this house, I don't want you to work!" (Or, "I expect you to work.")

As I talk with these wives, it is evident that, unless the husbands can see the reactions they're causing and want to change, there is little hope of turning the situation around.

In Ephesians 5, we read: "Submit to one another out of reverence for Christ. Wives, submit to your husbands as to the Lord. . . . Husbands, love your wives" (vv. 21–22, 25). Giving up one's rights for the sake of the other person is a *voluntary* decision, made in obedience to the Lord, not to the spouse. But that's what marriage is all about—two people mutually agreeing to lay down their own rights to benefit the other.

The husband's role in obedience—loving his wife—is as voluntary as her submission. Just as she can't expect to have her way by stomping her foot and demanding, "Love me . . . or else!" so it is just as foolish for the husband to expect to make his point by brute force: "Submit to me . . . or else!"

Speaking as a woman, I can tell you that love is irresistible. Remember, women are relationship-oriented, and while your goal may be to have your home in order, your wife in submission, and your children in obedience, the way to achieve that goal is through relationship.

Try an experiment for just one week. Go home, kiss your wife, and compliment her on at least one thing. Before you go to sleep, tell her you love her. Bite your tongue off before criticizing her for any reason. I guarantee that after only seven days, you'll be amazed at the results! She may be slow to believe you're on the level, but if you keep it up, you'll find she is much more flexible and pliable. Relationship is everything to her. That's why God says, "Love her." He made women and knows how they will respond.

I hope you don't mind this little word of advice from this corner today. I'll write to your wife another day and remind her that you men are goal-oriented and need order in your lives. But until then, just love her!

WEEK 3 — FRIDAY
RESTORING LOST LOVE

I'd like to ask a very personal question. Do you love your husband? Do you love your wife?

You may think that how you feel about your spouse is none of my business. But in view of the horrifying statistics that one out of every two marriages will end in divorce, I think the question is relevant.

Love is where a marriage begins. It is what makes the whole event seem like a good idea. Sometimes, somewhere along the way, love gets lost in the shuffle and many discouraged, disillusioned couples call it quits as a way out of their troubles.

19

Leaving a first love is not a new problem. In fact, it's one that Jesus Himself addresses in Revelation 2:3–5 in speaking to the church at Ephesus: "You have persevered and have endured hardships for my name, and have not grown weary. Yet I hold this against you: You have forsaken your first love. Remember the height from which you have fallen! Repent and do the things you did at first."

Here is a perfect formula for anyone who has fallen out of love with a husband or wife. The idea was shared by Dr. Richard Meier of the Minirth-Meier Clinic.

1. *Remember the height from which you have fallen.* Wedding pictures or memories you have tucked away are a reminder of the early days. The intensity of passion can't be sustained, but the sweet memories can soften your heart toward your mate. Simply recall what it was about your husband or wife that drew you to begin with. What is the very best memory you have of time spent with that person? Remember it, rehearse it, relish it . . . and while you're at it, ask God to melt your cold heart.

2. *Repent.* This simple word means a change of mind supported by a change of direction. If you find your love cooling, you can choose to change your mind and turn around. This is a conscious, rational decision that may or may not be accompanied by emotion. But there is no option for repentance in this matter. God says so!

3. *Do the things you did at first.* Jesus encouraged the Christians at Ephesus to put their remembrance and repentance to work and *do* something—something that would bring back the early days. Only you will know what that "something" is—all the sweet talk and actions that set your courtship apart from every other.

Jesus knew that the church at Ephesus had a good heart toward Him and would return to their first love if they just knew how . . . and He knows the same about you. Remember, repent and do the things you used to do. This may be the most important sermon you ever read. Your marriage is worth it!

WEEK 4 — MONDAY
SICK OF SEX

Are you sick of the way our society portrays sex?

C. S. Lewis, an intellectual who was gloriously saved as an adult, has been a wonderful resource for some of the best Christian thinking of our day. I like his comments on our society's inordinate interest in sex:

You can get a large audience together for a striptease act—that is, to watch a girl undress on the stage. Now suppose you came to a country where you could fill a theater by simply bringing a covered plate on the stage and then slowly lifting the cover so as to let everyone see, just before the lights went out, that it contained a mutton chop or a bit of bacon. Would you not think that in that country something had gone wrong with the appetite for food? And would not anyone who had grown up in a different world think there was something equally queer about the state of the sex instinct among us?[1]

Interesting images, aren't they?

William Temple has put the whole issue of sex in a more spiritual context:

It is to be recognized that sex is holy as well as wholesome. . . . It is the means by which we may cooperate with God in bringing into the world children of his own destined for eternal life. Anyone, who has once understood that, will be quite as careful as any Puritan to avoid making jokes about sex; not because it is nasty, but because it is sacred. He would no more joke about sex than he would joke about the Holy Communion—and for exactly the same reason. To joke about it is to treat with lightness something that deserves reverence.[2]

So what do we do about it, since we are entrenched in a society that twists and perverts sex?

We can start on a personal level by refusing to get caught up in loose talk about sexual subjects or by laughing at innuendos or jokes that are meant to play on words that have sexual connotations.

We can be alert to advertising that uses sex to sell a product, and refuse to buy. A good example of the effectiveness of this tactic was when Pepsi withdrew their crude, obscene commercial featuring rock singer Madonna. People who cared made a statement by refusing to buy Pepsi products.

We can seek purity before God, going before Him daily and asking Him to cleanse us of any sinful way. In this sex-saturated society, it is easy to be drawn into the mentality surrounding us. But God is faithful and, if you want to be pure, you can be.

Proverbs 30:12 tells of a hopeless generation: "There are those who are pure in their own eyes and yet are not cleansed of their filth." I honestly believe the Bible is speaking of the generation in which we are presently living, but you and I can choose not to be a part of it. We can refuse to look, listen, or speak perversely or with sexual innuendo.

By fixing our eyes on Jesus and asking Him to renew our minds, it is possible to be pure, even in this wicked and faithless generation.

WEEK 4 — TUESDAY
A PARENT'S LIMITS

If you are a parent, you are probably plagued by a raft of unanswered questions, guilt, frustration, and nameless fears. But there's only so much we can do for our children. And there comes a time in every child's life when a parent must let go . . . and let God. If we try to hang on too long, we'll only alienate the child and get in God's way.

The following poem by an unknown author puts this truth into perspective:

IT'S YOUR MOVE, DAUGHTER

I gave you life
But I cannot live it for you.
I can teach you things
But I cannot make you learn.

21

I can give you directions
But I cannot always be there to lead you.
I can allow you freedom
But I cannot account for it.
I can take you to church
But I cannot make you believe.
I can teach you right from wrong
But I can't always decide for you.
I can buy you beautiful clothes
But I cannot make you lovely inside.
I can offer you advice
But I cannot accept it for you.
I can give you love
But I cannot force it upon you.
I can teach you to be a friend
But I cannot make you one.
I can teach you to share
But I cannot make you unselfish.
I can teach you respect
But I can't force you to show honor.
I can grieve about your report card
But I cannot doubt your teachers.
I can advise you about friends
But I cannot choose them for you.
I can teach you about sex
But I cannot keep you pure.
I can tell you the facts of life
But I can't build your reputation.
I can tell you about drink
But I can't say NO for you.
I can warn you about drugs
But I can't prevent you from using them.
I can tell you about lofty goals
But I can't achieve them for you.
I can let you babysit
But I can't be responsible for your actions.
I can teach you kindness
But I can't force you to be gracious.
I can warn you about sins
But I cannot make your morals.
I can love you as a daughter
But I cannot place you in God's family.
I can pray for you
But I cannot make you walk with God.
I can teach you about Jesus
But I cannot make Him your Savior.
I can teach you to obey
But I cannot make Jesus your Lord.
I can tell you how to live
But I cannot give you eternal life.[3]

My friend, I can encourage you to release your child into God's hands, but I cannot let go for you. You and I have to come to that reality on our own.

One thing is sure: God is bigger than all of our worries and all of our concerns ... and as much as we love our children, He loves them more!

WEEK 4 — WEDNESDAY
THE BEAUTIFUL TEACUP

Have you ever been tempted to tell God you've had enough?

I recently read this little story in a book written by my friend Barbara Johnson, who is the founder of Spatula Ministries. Barbara's book title, *Fresh Elastic for Stretched-Out Moms,* speaks volumes. She knows all about pressure, having faced the tragic death of two sons and the gay lifestyle chosen by a third.

In her book, Barbara has included thoughts and anecdotes to help other moms make it through the tough times. One story she tells is entitled "The Beautiful Teacup."

A couple in England passed a china shop, which had a lovely teacup displayed in the window. They went inside to see it more closely, but suddenly the teacup spoke!

"You can't understand. I haven't always been a teacup. There was a time when I was a lump of red clay. My master took me and rolled me and patted me over and over. I screamed for him to stop, to leave me alone. But he continued to mold me, answering, 'Not yet.'

"Then I was placed on a wheel and spun around and around. It made me dizzy, spinning on and on like that. But he didn't stop when I was begging him to take me off the wheel. He continued shaping and molding and then put me in an oven! I have never felt such intense heat! I wondered if he wanted me to burn up. And I screamed and beat on the door to get out. I could see the master through the opening. And I read his lips as he said, 'Not yet.'

"Finally, the door did open. He put me up on a shelf and I began to cool. That felt better. Then suddenly, he brushed me and painted me all over. The fumes were terrible. I thought I would surely choke to death. I was gasping for air and hurting inside from the heat and choking fumes.

"Soon he put me into another oven. It wasn't like the first one, but it was twice as hot! I knew for sure that this time I would suffocate. I begged my master to stop. All the time I could see him shaking his head and saying, 'Not yet.'

"I felt there was no help. I knew I could never make it. I was ready to give up. But just then the door opened. He took me out and I could see that he was pleased with his work. He handed me a mirror and told me to look at myself. I did. And I said, 'That's not me. It couldn't be! I am so shiny and beautiful.'

"Then he said to me, 'I want you to know that I had to roll and pat you to shape you. If I had left you, then you would have dried up. I know the wheel made you dizzy and sick, but if I had stopped, you would have crumbled. I know it hurt and was hot and disagreeable in the baking oven, but if I hadn't put you there, you

23

would have cracked. I know the fumes were bad when I brushed you and then painted you all over, but you see, if I hadn't done that, you would never have hardened. And if I had not put you in the second oven, you would not have survived for very long, you would have been brittle. Now you are a finished product. You are what I had in mind when I first began with you as a lump of clay.' "4

Someday we'll be finished, conformed to the image of the Master. In the meantime, let's endure the process with patience.

WEEK 4 — THURSDAY
HUMILITY

There is an amusing story of a rabbi, a cantor, and a lowly synagogue cleaner who were preparing for the Day of Atonement. The rabbi beat his breast and intoned, "I am nothing." The cantor beat his breast and moaned, "I am nothing." The cleaner beat his breast and said, "I am nothing." And the rabbi said to the cantor, "So, look who thinks he's nothing!"

Announcing one's humility is a dead giveaway that pride is really in control!

I know a woman who demeans herself constantly, saying how unworthy she is to do this or that. But when it comes to having her way, she "humbly" goes about having it. In her own mind, I'm convinced that just because she doesn't flaunt what she does, she considers herself a humble person.

God's definition of humility is quite different. It's first of all a matter of attitude: "Your attitude should be the same as that of Christ Jesus: Who, being in very nature God, did not consider equality with God something to be grasped, but made himself nothing, taking the very nature of a servant" (Phil. 2:5–7).

Second, humility is something you learn. Jesus told us how to achieve this virtue in Matthew 11:29: "Take my yoke upon you and learn from me, for I am gentle and humble in heart, and you will find rest for your souls."

To learn humility is to learn contentment in all circumstances. Humility is not in what we own or achieve, but in maintaining a teachable attitude, a willingness to bend to the will of the Father.

Paul said, "I know what it is to be in need, and I know what it is to have plenty. I have learned the secret of being content in any and every situation, whether well fed or hungry, whether living in plenty or in want" (Phil. 4:12).

If you are in reduced circumstances, but bitter with God because life is unfair, then even though your situation may be humbling, you have not really discovered the attitude or learned the lesson of humility. If you have greater financial security than you ever imagined you would have, live in your dream house, have been promoted to the top, yet you are willing to give it all up at a moment's notice, then you probably meet God's criteria for humility.

Take time today to ask the Father to expose any prideful place in you. Ask Him to teach you His definition of humility. Then rest, content in the provisions He has made for you.

WEEK 4 — FRIDAY
BITTER ROOTS

Anger, sometimes defined as "a strong feeling of displeasure," is a powerful emotion, so much so that it has been labeled a universal sin.

It happens all the time and to all kinds of people. A perfectly pleasant conversation can be ruined when someone's displeasure surfaces. A perfectly happy relationship can be damaged under the assault of a displeased person. And a perfectly good day can be spoiled because the boss comes in with "a strong feeling of displeasure."

Anger is tricky because, unlike fear, the Scriptures say there is an appropriate time to be angry: "In your anger do not sin" (Eph. 4:26). I can become enraged over the mistreatment of a child or an animal, and if it is within my power, I will move to put a stop to the situation.

The kind of anger that is kindled by the abuse of a helpless living being is not destructive. But anger that is buried or improperly expressed has lethal power. God calls that kind of anger bitterness and warns: "See to it that no one misses the grace of God and that no bitter root grows up to cause trouble and defile many" (Heb. 12:15).

You can check yourself for bitterness in two ways:

1. *Listen to yourself.* When you speak, do you make sarcastic, cutting, or heated remarks about the person toward whom you have a "strong feeling of displeasure?" Whenever his or her name is mentioned, do you have something negative to say? As God has been showing me this truth in my own life, I have identified some anger I have to deal with. Speech is the first-line indicator of a bitterness problem.

2. *Observe your own actions.* You may not overtly attack the person with whom you are angry, but how about the many subtle ways of getting your point across? The silent treatment, for example. Silence speaks volumes and, in case you think other people don't notice the tension your "displeasure" causes, think again. You may be priding yourself on the restraint you have shown in not attacking openly, but no matter how you may try to hide it, unresolved anger shows.

Give yourself the bitterness test today. If you passed, great! If not, you have a choice to make. God says you can pull up those roots. Get rid of them and move on.

WEEK 5 — MONDAY
RUPTURED RELATIONSHIPS

If your personal devotional life—Bible reading and prayer—seems blocked, you may be reaping the results of prolonged, unresolved anger, not toward God, but toward a person or persons in your life. Maybe it's a rift in a friendship or a stalemate with a spouse, but in either case, broken human relationships affect our relationship with God.

John explains why: "Whoever hates his brother is in the darkness and walks around in the darkness; he does not know where he is going, because the darkness has blinded him" (1 John 2:11). And there is more. Jesus said: "If you are offering your gift at the altar and there remember that your brother has something against you, leave your gift there in front of the altar. First go and be reconciled to your brother; then come and offer your gift" (Matt. 5:23–24).

It seems that even our gifts to God are unacceptable if the lines of communication between ourselves and our brothers are closed down.

If you're inclined to rationalize your anger, take a look with me in a reference book in my library that is the ultimate thesaurus. In it, beside the word *anger* is listed every possible synonym—*abhor, loathe, abominate, despise, detest, not able to bear or abide, be sick of, be tired of, dislike, disfavor, disrelish.* There is not a single word in the list that fails to qualify as "a strong feeling of displeasure."

I say all this, my friend, to say that maybe your hatred is cutting you off from fellowship with God and distorting your view of life. A strong negative emotion, of which anger is one of the most powerful, can do just that. If you thought you were in some deep, dark night of the soul, chances are that the only darkness is coming from the anger that has settled into your spirit.

If that's where you find yourself, meditate on these words today: "If we claim to have fellowship with him [God] yet walk in the darkness, we lie and do not live by the truth. But if we walk in the light, as he is in the light, we have fellowship with one another, and the blood of Jesus, his Son, purifies us from all sin. . . . If we confess [agree with God about] our sins, he is faithful and just and will forgive us our sins and purify us from all unrighteousness" (1 John 1:6–7, 9).

Ask God to show you if prolonged anger has planted seeds of hatred in your heart and broken communication with Him. Then ask Him to cleanse you and restore the sweet fellowship you have known in the past.

WEEK 5 — TUESDAY
RESENTMENT—WHEN THINGS AREN'T GOING MY WAY

A friend of mine has a three-year-old granddaughter who is a total stitch. The child is so communicative, always coming up with something creative and bright. But one day her daddy denied a minor request, and all communication stopped abruptly. She ducked her head, stuck out her lower lip, and dramatically turned her back on everyone who tried to reason with her. She wanted what she wanted when she wanted it.

It's easy to overlook that kind of behavior in someone who is only three years old, knowing that she will likely mature past that stage. But the childish pout is not so cute in a forty-year-old.

The name for this manifestation of anger is resentment. According to counselor Ken Stafford, resentment is caused by "not getting what you want when you want it." When you think of it that way, resentment is really immature behavior which says, "I am hurt and angry because things have not gone my way."

Unfortunately, resentment doesn't stop with a general attitude toward life and others, but ultimately clouds one's relationship with God as well. It leaves out the fact that the Lord might want to do something in your life down the line, that He has said no now so He can say yes later. Much like my friend's granddaughter, we want what we want *now*.

There is a Scripture verse that speaks of all those—believers and unbelievers alike—who have never come under the dominion of God's authority. "The sinful mind is hostile to God. It does not submit to God's law, nor can it do so. Those controlled by the sinful nature cannot please God" (Rom. 8:7-8).

If this verse describes you, and you recognize that your resentment is really immature behavior, ask God to help you grow up.

First Peter 2:1-2 tells how: "Therefore, rid yourselves of all malice and all deceit, hypocrisy, envy, and slander of every kind. Like newborn babies, crave pure spiritual milk, so that by it you may grow up in your salvation." Resentment stunts our spiritual growth. Let's grow up!

WEEK 5 — WEDNESDAY
FORGIVE? WHY SHOULD I?

Does a specific individual come to mind when you think of the subject of anger? Someone who makes you so mad you can't see straight? Such a person is usually pretty hard to forget, and equally hard to forgive.

Proverbs 19:11 tells us the smart way to deal with irritating people and their actions: "A man's wisdom gives him patience; it is to his glory to overlook an offense." Easier said than done, though, isn't it? Still, we are advised by this wise writer to let most things slide by.

But what about the times someone's behavior toward you is so outrageous you simply can't overlook it? What then?

The key to release is forgiveness. Not only is forgiveness the wisest course of action for the Christian, but it is the one modeled by Jesus Christ Himself. When He was unjustly accused, assaulted, and crucified by unprincipled men, "he did not retaliate; when he suffered, he made no threats. Instead, he entrusted himself to [God] who judges justly" (1 Peter 2:23). In other words, He relinquished the whole matter into the Father's hands.

I like to define forgiveness as "giving up the right to punish the one who has hurt you." That's what Jesus did on the cross. And if His example of forgiveness is not enough, He spells it out in unmistakable terms: "Be kind and compassionate to one another, forgiving each other, just as in Christ God forgave you" (Eph. 4:32).

Forgiveness is a conscious decision, in no way affected by feelings. If you wait until you *feel* like forgiving, it would be similar to waiting until you felt like paying your taxes. That moment might never come!

But if you view unforgiveness as a sin against God and a self-imposed burden as well, it just makes sense to get rid of it.

What do you plan to do the next time someone offends you? There are at least three good reasons why forgiveness is the right answer: (1) because it's the wise thing to do; (2) because Jesus set the example; (3) because God has forgiven *you!*

Is there someone in your life you need to forgive right now? Every day you put it off only delays the release of all the nasty emotions that accompany anger—bitterness, resentment, malice. Joyous relief can be yours when you choose to forgive.

WEEK 5 — THURSDAY
FORGIVENESS IS FOR GIVING

Choosing to forgive is one thing. Actually forgiving is quite another. But until we make that first move toward forgiving those who have wronged us, it will remain only a nice theory, with no real power.

I want to give you some practical and biblical thoughts on how to proceed in a godly way after you have made the choice to forgive someone who has wronged you.

Perhaps you, like I, have read those passages about praying for those who have wronged us and doing good to those who hate us. It all sounds so noble and godly, but there is a big block when it comes to living out these principles. I start to pray for someone who has made my life miserable, but somehow I feel like a hypocrite. Or I think about doing something good for someone who obviously doesn't give a hoot about me, and I think, "That would be manipulative so I'll forget it!"

There is a way to get past those feelings. I believe the breakthrough comes when we make the decision to let God take responsibility for the guilty person's punishment. That leaves us free to obey the Lord and reap a blessing ourselves. Since forgiveness is a choice, not an emotion, it can happen instantaneously. Forgiveness is also a gift.

Listen to these wonderful and powerful words from Jesus: "But I tell you who hear me: Love your enemies, do good to those who hate you, bless those who curse you, pray for those who mistreat you. . . . Do to others as you would have them do to you" (Luke 6:27–28, 31).

Have you ever been in a position where you have had to ask another's forgiveness? For instance, have you gone to your husband or wife and said, "I am so sorry I spoke harshly . . ." And, did he or she reply, "Well, you are always that way. I don't know why you're asking forgiveness because you'll just turn around and do it again"?

Your mate was holding out to punish you, to assume responsibility for making you know how inconsistent or damaging your behavior was. The bridge between you stayed broken, and you felt hopeless and defeated.

These are the times when it isn't fun to forgive. But remember that forgiveness is for giving. It is a gift. Jesus encouraged us to treat people the way we want to be treated. If we make forgiveness a gift with no strings attached, we can fulfill that Scripture.

Try it. It really isn't so hard to forgive, even when the subject of your forgiveness is most undeserving. Pass on the gift that Jesus has given you. Forgiveness is for giving.

WEEK 5 — FRIDAY
JUST ONE OF THE CHILDREN

Dr. James Dobson's book, *Parenting Isn't for Cowards,* hits the nail on the head. Parenting takes strength and unity on the part of parents.

From the moment of conception, a child brings unbelievable challenges and changes into a parent's life. Unfortunately, one of the major challenges comes when parents disagree over discipline. I have heard mothers run interference with fathers when children need correction, and I have seen fathers belittle mothers when they try to administer discipline.

One woman told me, "I just hate to correct the children because my husband always contradicts what I say. Not only that, but he usually tells me what he thinks of me in front of the children!"

This kind of scene is sometimes initiated when Dad thinks of Mom as "just one of the children." There is a patronizing rather than a respectful attitude on his part which leads to a division into opposing teams, with you on one side and your husband on the other.

Since none of us has the power to change another person's actions, you will have to assume responsibility for your own and leave your husband to the discipline of the Lord. But you do have the responsibility of airing your feelings with your husband, something which is difficult for some women to do. Peace-at-any-price people would rather clam up than run the risk of starting an argument.

If you feel, however, that you are being treated like one of the children, you need to find a time to discuss the problem with your husband. Before the conversation, ask the Lord to give you the right words and tone of voice and to give your husband an open mind and hearing ears. Ask for a private audience when the two of you will be uninterrupted and when your husband is least likely to be distracted.

If he hears you out and agrees, you have achieved your goal of attaining equal partnership in the parenting process. But if he is defensive and accuses you of being overly sensitive, then continuing to press the issue will only seem like nagging. Still, there is something more you can do.

If you have been guilty of arguing and "scrapping" with the children, distance yourself from their level. Calmly let them know there will be no more arguing, and simply refuse to be caught up in the crossfire. Begin to make choices that will help you regain their respect.

If you have been guilty of running interference with Dad, sit back and let him do his job without stepping in to protect the children. They need his strength to balance their training.

And go the next mile: Confess that you have been wrong to interfere with his discipline, and ask his forgiveness. In this Christlike spirit, your husband may recognize your sincere desire to improve your teamwork.

And finally, if you are viewed as "one of the children," pray. When Jesus says, "Cast your burden on me for I care for you," He means "Hurl . . . throw that problem on me." Give Him your burden in prayer and don't take it back the next time you and your husband disagree!

WEEK 6 — MONDAY
SMOTHERED FRIENDSHIP

I recently received a letter that poses a frequent complaint women make about at least one friend in their lives: "My friend is the type of person who waits for the other person to invite her to do things. If she is not invited, then she thinks people don't like her.

"Sadly, I am getting to the point where I just don't want to be around her. If I don't sit with her in church, her feelings are hurt. I have to sneak around if I want to do something without her along. Frankly, I feel like I have a ball and chain attached to this friendship."

This writer's description is very apt. When one party in a relationship controls the other, the result is a kind of imprisonment. Unfortunately, a great deal of hurt can be inflicted before most of us catch on to the fact that something is wrong. Apparently, her friend views her as necessary to her happiness and well-being, so whenever she shows signs of acting independently, her security is threatened. She also seems to be unwilling or unable to make the first move to make friends with others.

The Scriptures say, "As iron sharpens iron, so one man sharpens another" (Prov. 27:17). In a one-sided friendship, there is no sharpening going on, only a deadly dulling.

For those who need to restore balance in your relationship, try the following suggestions:

1. Begin to loosen your friend's exclusive hold on you by planning social outings that include others, or by occasionally sitting with someone else at church.
2. Limit the amount of time you spend together. This could force your friend to seek the companionship of others.
3. Be careful to avoid bitterness. You hurt not only yourself but also those around you when you allow bitterness and unforgiveness to remain in your heart toward your friend. Deal with it moment by moment until kind thoughts become a habit.
4. Prepare for the long haul. Your friend's insecurity will not be overcome in a day.
5. Be loving and gracious even when you are accused of being just the opposite.
6. Don't withdraw your friendship completely. Allow your friend to adjust as you gradually reduce your contact with her.
7. Pray for your friend . . . even when you are most irritated. She is clinging to you because you represent security to her. She needs to know that only the Lord can supply every need. Pray that He will draw your friend into a sweet and intimate relationship with Himself that will satisfy the deepest longings of her heart.

Friendship is a wonderful gift that must be carefully tended. People who love us and desire to be our friends are all too few. Make every effort to nurture precious friendships even when your patience wears thin.

WEEK 6 — TUESDAY
CALLED TO HOLINESS

Are you comfortable with the concept of holiness? Do you consider yourself holy?

Believers are called to holiness. Though it may sound like a stained-glass word, evoking the image of soft organ music and whispered prayers, holiness simply means "to be set apart"—set apart *from* sin, set apart *to* God. Being set apart has to come from the heart. It is a choice you make because your insides are different.

When I became a Christian nineteen years ago, I was in the middle of reading the novel *Deliverance*. Before I came to know the Lord, I never had any trouble reading the foul language and the sexually explicit scenes found in so many secular novels. But after the Lord gave me true "deliverance," I just couldn't finish that book. No one told me to put it down. It was just that when I picked it up to read it, I felt dirty, out of place, as if it didn't belong in my life.

Actually, we don't have a choice about holiness. We are instructed to be holy. While the first-century Christians faced persecution, deprivation, and the possibility of being taken captive or murdered at the whim of the cruel tyrant, Nero, Peter exhorted them: "Therefore, prepare your minds for action; be self-controlled; set your hope fully on the grace to be given you when Jesus Christ is revealed. As obedient children, do not conform to the evil desires you had when you lived in ignorance. But just as he who called you is holy, so be holy in all you do; for it is written: 'Be holy, because I am holy'" (1 Peter 1:13–16).

In contemporary jargon, Peter is saying, "Watch the tendency for sloppy thinking. Don't be stressed out, but gear up for action. Look ahead hopefully to your salvation in Jesus Christ. Resist the temptation to be like the people around you who are as ignorant of the things of God as you used to be! God will not grovel with you in your sin. He has called you out—to be like Him!"

Once we have received salvation, we have new want-to's and old habits we can no longer tolerate. Even our television viewing habits are affected.

I recently watched a news report of a parade of homosexuals in New York City. The parade featured a man dressed in a loincloth made out of the American flag, and he was carrying a cross and was wearing a crown of thorns. I felt outraged that this man would dare mock the Lord Jesus and my country!

In that same parade were three homosexual pastors—two female and one male—acting as grand marshals. These people claim to speak for God. But how can a man or woman speak for God apart from being holy as He is holy?

Holiness is one of the most practical commands we have been given for living life as the children of God. We are to be like our Father!

WEEK 6 — WEDNESDAY
THE CAT AND DOG TEST

Hudson Taylor writes, "If your father and mother, your sister and brother, if the very cat and dog in the house, are not happier for your being a Christian, it is a question whether you really are."

The key to this illustration is bound up in the words *happy* and *house.* If the people in your household are not happier because Jesus Christ indwells you and controls your words and actions, if His presence is not evidenced by your kindness and grace, then more than likely He doesn't live there.

Think what that means for you as you face this day. Look at the people in your home, your colleagues at work or in your circle of friends. Are these people happier because you are a Christian, or do they feel condemned by your attitude?

The Scriptures say that when Jesus came, He was full of grace and truth. If Christ is in you, then these virtues and others will spill out of your life onto those around you.

Or do you project worry and fear? Is nagging becoming a habit? Are you irritable because no one wants to help?

Today can be a fresh new beginning.

1. Go to the Lord in prayer and confess that you know you have grieved Him by your irritability and nagging, thus robbing others of the opportunity to see Jesus in you.
2. Find a Scripture verse that suits your situation. You might begin by

examining a concordance for the word that most nearly describes your problem and then read every reference on that topic, taking notes so you won't forget. Realizing that I have a short fuse, I did a study on anger last year and was shocked to discover what a dim view the Word of God takes on this condition!

3. Ask your family and friends to help you change your negative behavior by pointing out every time you slip up and criticize, nag, complain, etc.

I want the people in my household to be happier because I am there. In order to achieve that goal, my love for Christ must be translated into unconditional love for each person who lives there . . . and so must yours.

Do the members of your household know you love the Lord? If your cat and dog could speak, how would they rate your Christian behavior?

WEEK 6 — THURSDAY
TEACHING SELF-CONTROL

I have found that it is very difficult to control anger and children at the same time. Here is a letter from a woman who knows . . .

Dear Jan,
  I am the mother of three children under six. At times it is so frustrating and I get so angry! Disciplining does not come naturally to me, and I usually end up either yelling or doing nothing at all. I just don't know what to do.

I understand completely. At one point in ancient history, I was the mother of three boys under six. I remember the sense of frustration my friend describes . . . and, yes, I even remember getting angry on a regular basis!

When my son was six, he carelessly broke the glass top on a table. The little guy felt terrible about it and went to his room in tears. I was so angry that I followed him, confronted him as he lay on his bunk crying, and told him he would have to go out and get a job to pay for the damage. You can imagine my chagrin when the little fellow said, "But, Mama, I'm only six years old!" With that, you can bet I did my share of apologizing!

If you want to bring up obedient children with a minimum of hassle, consider the following:

1. *Analyze the problem.* You are angry because you have lost control of a situation with your children. You need to reestablish your position of authority.
2. *Take the long look.* Ask yourself, "What do I want to achieve that will be the best for all of us?"
3. *Take time to get yourself under control.* If you react in anger, you have lost sight of your goal—bringing up children who can control themselves.
4. *Pray before you confront.* Ask the Lord to give you His attitude toward your children.
5. *Leave whatever you are doing.* Nothing is more important than using every opportunity to teach your children some vital truth.
6. *Be sure they understand what you expect of them, then follow*

through. I know a young boy who is disciplined constantly but never does what he's told apart from a threat. It breaks my heart to see a five-year-old, who will all too soon be a fifteen-year-old, doing whatever he wants while his parents make idle threats.

7. *Don't raise your voice.* When you escalate the volume, your child will only escalate his volume.
8. *Be consistent.* Let him know the penalty for breaking the rules, then see that you enforce them.
9. *Don't underestimate your child's ability to learn.* Several Sundays ago I had occasion to observe a toddler in church. The youngest of six children, she sat quiet and still most of the time. But when her daddy corrected her, she responded instantly. Instead of frowning and scolding, however, the daddy smiled and nodded yes, thus reinforcing her responses. That struck me as remarkable, since I recall shaking my head no when my boys were that age!

Discipline of children begins with parental self-discipline. Children mirror what they see!

WEEK 6 — FRIDAY
NOTHING IS GOING WRONG

Several weeks ago, I was hit with a disappointment that took me by surprise. I hurt and I ached, I prayed and I fussed, and although I could manage a momentary resolution, the unfairness of the situation continued to torment me.

On one of the days during this mini-crisis, I was reading one of my favorite devotional authors, Amy Carmichael. Some words she wrote grabbed my attention, and I've been holding on to them ever since:
NOTHING IS GOING WRONG HOWEVER WRONG IT SEEMS. ALL . . . ALL IS WELL.

As I have meditated on those words, I have been reminded of the precious truth of Romans 8:28: "And we know that in all things God works for the good of those who love him, who have been called according to his purpose."

Just how does that verse tell us that "nothing is going wrong however wrong it seems?" It's like this: God promises that whatever—the good, the bad, the unexplainable—whatever comes your way, He will use it for good toward you . . . toward me . . . simply because we love Him.

To be honest about it, I don't always like that promise because it removes my reason for fussing or being disappointed. If God is using the unjust and uncomfortable events of our lives to work together for good, then where do we come off complaining? What room is left for us to say, "Ah, God, this just isn't fair!"?

Has someone treated you unjustly? God says, "Don't worry. I will make it work for your good."

Have you been passed over for a promotion? God says, "Don't be anxious, I know all about it. I will use it for your growth and preparation for better things ahead."

Has someone hurt you deeply? God says, "Go ahead and cry, I know it hurts. But in the end your pain will serve a greater purpose."

Has a child disappointed you? God says, "Don't fret, dear parent, because you can depend on Me to bring reconciliation and joy to both your lives."

No matter what is clouding your sky today, hang on to this truth: NOTHING IS GOING WRONG NO MATTER HOW WRONG IT SEEMS.

If you are having trouble believing that, pray with me:

Lord, I pray today that the reality of Romans 8:28 will be engraved on the minds and hearts of every one of your children who has been hurt, shaken, or made fearful by negative circumstances. Give each person courage to believe that NOTHING IS GOING WRONG, NO MATTER HOW WRONG IT SEEMS. For Jesus' sake. Amen.

WEEK 7 — MONDAY
BEAUTY SECRET

If I were to tell you that I know of a beauty regimen guaranteed to make you irresistibly attractive, you would beat a path to my door. The truth is, I do! And it's available to you at no cost.

Simply open your Bible to the book of 1 Peter where the apostle is addressing married women. In suggesting how they could win their husbands, he writes: "Your beauty should not come from outward adornment, such as braided hair and the wearing of gold jewelry and fine clothes. Instead, it should be that of your inner self, the unfading beauty of a gentle and quiet spirit, which is of great worth in God's sight. For this is the way the holy women of the past who put their hope in God used to make themselves beautiful" (1 Peter 3:3–5).

Any woman would be intrigued with the promise of "unfading beauty," but there is a greater reason for the value of this passage. Peter says that "a gentle and quiet spirit . . . is of great worth in God's sight." Here is a beauty plan endorsed and valued by God Himself!

Since I have a strong personality, gentleness and quietness do not come naturally to me! In researching the word *gentle,* I learned that it means "kindly or amiable in manner. Mild or moderate. Not severe, violent, or loud."

Apparently, gentleness is not wimpish because David encouraged his field commanders to "be gentle" (2 Sam. 18:5) with his son Absalom even though he was in rebellion against his father and intended to overthrow him. Later on, the boy was killed, and David's heart was broken.

In the book of Matthew, Jesus is described as "gentle and mild." Although Jesus had the power to create the world, He controlled his strength for the sake of others. Gentleness is holding back your strength and your rights when it would be to another's benefit.

Gentleness can become a lifestyle . . . one that is very precious in the sight of God.

God says if you are to be pleasing to Him when you are confronted with a tense situation, you will speak with gentleness: "A gentle answer turns away wrath" (Prov. 15:1). And in Ephesians: "I urge you to live a life worthy of the calling you have received. Be completely humble and gentle; be patient, bearing with one another in love. Make every effort to keep the unity of the Spirit through the bond of peace" (Eph. 4:1–3).

What is your gentleness quotient? Have you snapped at those you love the most? Have you given a sharp answer to the one you have been praying would come to know the Lord? Has your patience worn thin with your circumstances? Have you used the strength of your personality and your verbal prowess to win a battle of words with someone in your family . . . or with a friend? God says it is worth the effort to bring your put-down power under control because it is of great value to Him.

The women of Israel must have learned well. We know that Sarah was a beautiful woman who charmed her husband well into her nineties! And she did it, not with exotic creams and fine clothes, but with her gentle and quiet spirit.

WEEK 7 — TUESDAY
"ONE EVENT IN A LIFETIME OF EVENTS"

Everywhere we turn there are sad, tragic, life-changing occurrences. To dwell on the negatives is to invite insanity. Yet, somehow, God has given us the will and ability to survive when circumstances seem too difficult to bear.

A woman I don't know personally spoke some words that have stayed with me and helped to shape my perspective on these life-altering events.

Several weeks after Lori Danz took a gun into an elementary school in the suburbs of Chicago, killed one student, and injured several others, a television news team interviewed some of the eyewitnesses. When asked about their reactions in the aftermath of this tragedy, the responses were typical: Some were experiencing nightmares; some, panic attacks; some, unexplained fears. But this wise, older woman said, "*It is one event in a lifetime of events. We must go on.*"

Paul must have been saying much the same thing when he wrote to the Corinthians: "We have this treasure in jars of clay to show that this all-surpassing power is from God and not from us. We are hard pressed on every side, but not crushed; perplexed, but not in despair; persecuted, but not abandoned; struck down, but not destroyed" (2 Cor. 4:7–8). In other words, "THIS IS ONE EVENT IN A LIFETIME OF EVENTS."

I cannot tell you how that phrase has helped me with some situations that, at the time, have seemed like the end of the world.

I think of Joni Eareckson Tada, whose life, in one split second, was irrevocably changed. As the victim of a diving accident, she has been a quadriplegic ever since. But the accident was only ONE EVENT IN A LIFETIME OF EVENTS. Despite the daily reminder of her damaged body, her life is full and productive, and she has been used to encourage people all over the world.

I think of Elisabeth Elliot, whose husband Jim was killed by the Auca Indians in South America. As tragic as it was, her husband's death was ONE EVENT IN A LIFETIME OF EVENTS, and their missionary journey was only delayed, not destroyed. Jim went to be with the Lord, and Elisabeth picked up the pieces and went on with her life, profoundly influencing countless people through her speaking and writing.

I think of my friend, Marie Chapian, whose husband left her with two little girls. Unable to drive and totally dependent on her former spouse for everything, she had to view the rejection and devastation of her broken marriage as ONE EVENT IN A LIFETIME OF EVENTS. Marie went on to earn her doctorate, to write a multitude of books, to speak all over the world, and to bring up two of the most beautiful, godly young women you would ever care to know.

What event has stopped you in your tracks? Have you lost the will to go on because you feel as though your life is over? Has some sad situation robbed you of the hope of finding joy again?

Perhaps you need to step back and take a look at the situation in light of everything else that has happened in your life. IT IS ONE EVENT IN A LIFETIME OF EVENTS.

WEEK 7 — WEDNESDAY
BEING LOVABLE

There is all the difference in the world in feeling loved and feeling lovable. Judging from my mail, this problem is not uncommon. As one woman writes:

"Dear Jan, Do you ever struggle with feeling lovable? I try to be loving toward people, but I really have a hard time thinking there is anything lovable about *me*."

Her letter brought to mind an incident from high school days. As a teenager I walked home each day with a friend. We talked as we walked, then when we both reached our homes, we talked on the phone some more. One day as we neared my house, my friend dropped a conversational bomb: "Well, I won't be walking with you any more. You're too bubbly!" End of conversation . . . forever! Taken off guard, I spent a few hours that night trying to understand what she had said. Was I really too bubbly? Did this make me unlovable? Was I worthy of being loved?

When I finally got tired of thinking about it, I decided the problem was hers. As far as I was concerned, I hadn't changed, and none of my other friends were dropping me . . . so, the problem had to lie with her. I went on with my life and she with hers, speaking when we ran into each other in the hall at school. To this day, I don't know what really happened. But, I chose not to let this person's assessment of me determine how lovable I felt.

When you feel unlovable, usually it is because someone along the way has given you the signal, and you believed it. Maybe a parent made an unfair comparison with a sibling. Or a bullying schoolmate made your life miserable. Maybe it was a teacher who had it in for you. Worse still, a mate may have delivered the death blow. Or, and this is a very real consideration, you could be your *own* worst enemy!

Check your attitude. Are you wearing an imaginary sign that says, "Don't get too close, you won't like me. I'm not lovable"? The Scriptures say that in order to have friends, we must first be friendly.

Friendliness is demonstrated in the way you speak to people. At church, when you notice a stranger in the pew next to you, do you avoid eye contact, or do you make it a point to make them feel welcome? Do you keep yourself neat and well-groomed most of the time, even when dashing to the grocery store for a last-minute item? Do you expect others to like you, or are you just waiting for everyone to discover what you have known all along—that you don't deserve their time and attention?

Have you stepped back and tried to see yourself as others see you? Are you pushy, demanding? Do you want things done your way, or are you willing to be flexible and open yourself to new methods of doing things?

And, have you analyzed yourself to determine how to make yourself more lovable? Unfortunately, when a person begins to focus on some deficiency in himself, it often becomes a self-fulfilling prophecy.

To break the cycle, read Psalm 139 each morning. Memorize verse 14: "I praise you because I am fearfully and wonderfully made; your works are wonderful, I know that full well."

And, before you leave your house for work or errands, ask God to give you someone to love today. If you begin to be self-conscious about being unlovable, recall Psalm 139 and again pray, "Lord, give me someone to love for You today."

Gradually, as you immerse yourself in God's love letter to you, you will begin to believe that it is true. He made everything . . . and everyone . . . special. His works, including you, are wonderful!

WEEK 7 — THURSDAY
JEALOUSY—THE DESTROYER

There is a rather sick motto that can be found on cups and posters in specialty stores these days: "IF YOU LOVE SOMETHING, LET IT GO. IF IT IS YOURS, IT WILL COME BACK TO YOU. IF NOT, HUNT IT DOWN AND KILL IT." Despite the morbid tone of this quotation, this is a perfect description of jealousy.

Jealousy, according to Proverbs 6:34, "arouses a husband's fury." And, in the Song of Solomon, we read: "Jealousy [is as] unyielding as the grave. It burns like blazing fire" (8:6).

Jealousy is the pain of losing what we have to someone else . . . in spite of all our efforts to keep it. Jealousy has ruined marriages, friendships, working relationships, and families. It begins as a subtle pain, an irritating concern, making us suspicious of another's every move and wary of another's motives. Jealousy makes a prisoner out of the jealous partner and his victim alike.

According to the book of Acts: "Because the patriarchs were jealous of Joseph, they sold him as a slave into Egypt" (7:9).

I really hate jealousy. I hate it when the emotion creeps up on me . . . and I hate for someone to be jealous over me. It puts up walls and creates bondage that ultimately destroys what once was free and good.

If you are struggling with jealousy in any form, here are some thoughts that I pray will help:

1. Call jealousy what it is—sin.
2. Rehearse the harmful effects of jealousy: "It makes me become what I never thought I would be."
3. Assume responsibility for your jealousy. We usually try to blame our feelings on another person's actions. "If she had not spent too much time with Harry, then I would not be jealous." Nonsense. If you are jealous, then you have allowed the emotion to set up housekeeping in your brain.
4. Determine to clean house. Every time a jealous thought comes, say, "I refuse to think that thought. It will only hurt me and cause me pain. I choose to bring every thought captive to the Lord Jesus Christ."
5. Watch out for the seeds of jealousy creeping in after you have taken

a stand against it. It is a subtle emotion you must watch out for constantly.
6. Pray that the person for whom you are jealous will know joy and peace.

Remember, if you love something, let it go. If it comes back, you are blessed. If not, God knows about it and will reward you.

WEEK 7 — FRIDAY
MORE BLESSED TO GIVE THAN RECEIVE

The early Christians loved Paul dearly. He was with them for three years—teaching, exhorting, working side by side with them. And now, it was time for him to move on. They already missed him . . . maybe they even felt a little self-pity because Paul was leaving them. He empathized with their feelings, for they reflected his own. Yet, in God's timing, he knew he must go.

Tenderly, Paul gave his friends something to help them through the loneliness, the self-pity, the feeling of abandonment. He understood their sadness, and so he gave them the key that would open doors to peace and satisfaction.

A special word described the state he desired for them—"blessed," meaning "happy, spiritually prosperous." Echoing Jesus' words, Paul said: "It is more blessed to give than to receive" (Acts 20:35).

The word Paul used to communicate his heart's desire for these early disciples is the same he gives us: "It really is more blessed [it will make you happier, make you spiritually prosperous] to give rather than to receive."

Although it is thrilling to be on the receiving end, receiving just doesn't bring the kind of lasting joy that giving does. Think about it. Once you have received something you have been wishing for, how long does it take before you are dissatisfied again? Our tendency is to want more, bigger, better, or something different.

You want love, but you soon find that your spouse doesn't measure up to the dream man you had envisioned.

You want financial security, but more money means you have to spend more to keep up with your new neighbors!

You want recognition, but how long will your promotion satisfy before you feel pressure to climb yet another rung in the corporate ladder?

I can think of so many times when I have said to myself, "I'll be happy if only I could get a new carpet (or a new car, or a new house)." But after the "new" wears off, there's always something else that promises more happiness, more security.

And how many of us have thought, "If I can just marry the man of my dreams, I know I'll be happy for the rest of my life"? Expecting someone to make you happy is always disastrous.

Jesus knew our human nature when He said, "Give . . . it will make you happier . . . it will satisfy longer."

I have noticed that when I give, the satisfaction is immediate. The more I give, the more I want to give. Giving brings a spiritual well-being that is unequaled. Best of all, the joy of giving goes on and on.

About fifteen years ago, I heard about someone who needed a little help with a dental bill. Since I had a few extra dollars at that time, I sent them to this person by way of a mutual friend, requesting only that the friend not divulge where the money had come from.

Every time I have seen this person over the years, I have been blessed. She, of course, has no idea why I take such delight in her pretty smile!

Are you willing to focus on giving and give up any expectation of receiving? If you are, Jesus said you will be happier for it. If not, maybe you will recognize the source of your unhappiness. Then you can turn it around!

WEEK 8 — MONDAY
JESUS BUYS BACK OUR MESSES

Marshall, a hairstylist friend, is a devoted Christian. Whenever he styles a woman's hair, he prays out loud before he begins. One day several years ago, just as he started to cut my hair, he prayed, "Thank you, God, that you are a Redeemer. Not only do you buy us back from the consequences of our sin, but you buy back our messes as well."

I can tell you that prayer gave me a start! I have to smile as I think of it now. Of course, I had no reason to fear. I loved the new hairstyle Marshall gave me, but more than that, he left me with a profound thought as well: We have a God who buys back our messes!

God really does buy back our messes, and He buys them back whether we have blown it or whether it is someone else who has messed up our lives.

I know a beautiful young woman who is married to the love of her life and has two handsome little boys. But her story was not always such a happy one. As a college student, she compromised her principles and became pregnant. The father of her baby ran out on her, and she was left with a baby on the way, shame, and brokenhearted parents. When she cried out for mercy, God began to buy back her mess. He drew her family together. Throughout her pregnancy, they bolstered and prayed with one another. Today, four years later, she is a young wife and mother who really *knows* the forgiving love of a God who buys back our messes.

I often remember another dear woman who was in a mess, not of her own making. As a younger person, she was stricken with a crippling illness. When she became wheelchair-bound, her husband left her and their little eight-year-old adopted daughter. For the past thirteen years, this mother and daughter have seen God's good hand provide every need as they have worked together through each day of the mess they are in. They didn't ask for it. They didn't deserve the problem. But fortunately they have a Saviour who buys back messes.

Are you in a mess today? Is it one you made yourself? Or did someone else make it for you? Are you trying to put the pieces back together on your own? If so, you are missing out on one of the benefits of your position as a child of God.

You have a Redeemer. The Scriptures tell us: "For he has rescued us from the dominion of darkness and brought us into the kingdom of the Son he loves, in whom we have redemption, the forgiveness of sins" (Col. 1:14). He further promises that "God works for the good of those who love him, who have been called according to his purpose" (Rom. 8:28).

Why not ask God to quiet your heart right now. Take a moment to thank Him for not deserting you when your life is in a mess. He is the Redeemer, the Holy One of Israel, who specializes in buying back our messes!

WEEK 8 — TUESDAY
"CALL BACK TO ME"

Since I've just hit my mid-forties, I'm old enough now to look back on some tough experiences and see the value in them.

I now have enough perspective to value the desperation I felt when my husband of only two years left for Viet Nam as a helicopter pilot. Our little son was just six months old, and I thought I would die when I kissed my husband goodbye. Since I was not yet a Christian, I trudged through the year he was away in a constant state of depression, with only one hope, that my husband would come home. Now that I know the Lord as my personal Savior, I have learned that there is purpose in all the experiences of life, and that we do not have to walk through them alone.

Paul also knew the importance of life experiences as a platform for sharing with others what we have learned. He wrote to the Corinthians: "Praise be to the God and Father of our Lord Jesus Christ, the Father of compassion and the God of all comfort, who comforts us in all our troubles, so that we can comfort those in any trouble with the comfort we ourselves have received from God" (2 Cor. 1:3–4).

What ordeal have you survived, with God's help, that you can share with a fellow sojourner? What trial has He walked you through that gives you the testimony: "Hey, my friend, He was here and He was sufficient for all my needs!" As believers, we are obligated to comfort others with the comfort God has given us.

If you have gone a little way
  ahead of me, call back—
'Twill cheer my heart and help my feet
  along the stony track;
And if, per chance, Faith's light is dim
  because the oil is low,
Your call will guide my lagging course
  as wearily I go.

Call back and tell me that He
  went with you in the storm;
Call back, and say He kept you
  when the forest's roots were torn;
That when the heavens thunder
  and the earthquake shook the hill,
He bore you up and held you
  where the very air was still.

Oh, friend, call back and tell me
  for I cannot see your face;
They say it glows with triumph
  and your feet bound in the race;
But there are mists between us
  and my spirit eyes are dim,
And I cannot see the glory,
  though I long for word of Him.

But if you'll say He heard you
  when your prayer was but a cry,

*And if you'll say He saw you
   through the night's sub-darkened sky—
If you have gone a little way ahead,
   oh friend, call back—
Twill cheer my heart and help my feet
   along the stony track.[1]*

Who needs your comfort today? Who is crying, "Call back to me . . . please call back and tell me I'll be okay"?

WEEK 8 — WEDNESDAY
GRACE—GETTING WHAT I DON'T DESERVE

Grace is a word that has always held a fascination for me. I guess that's because I need it so badly, for grace is unmerited favor. It is getting the good I don't deserve from God, who can give or withhold anything He wishes.

There is something very practical about God's grace. In Titus, Paul says, "For the grace of God that brings salvation has appeared to all men. It teaches us to say 'No' to ungodliness and worldly passions, and to live self-controlled, upright and godly lives in this present age" (2:11–12).

Grace brings salvation, then shows us how to live out our salvation. Grace teaches us to say no to ungodliness and yes to godliness. While the law does motivate obedience, acting as a schoolmaster to bring us to Christ, the incredible grace of God is an even greater motivator.

When I was a young girl, two Sunday school teachers had a profound influence on me. I distinctly remember one who always presented truth, but in such a tone of voice that I wasn't moved to do what was right. In fact, because she meted out approval according to my good behavior, I sometimes wanted to do just the opposite! Another teacher consistently extended unmerited favor to me, always treating me with kindness I did not deserve. Consequently, I developed a passionate desire to please her and to say no to the things that might make her unhappy.

Grace is like that! It brings out the best in people, not the worst. True grace that pours from the heart of the crucified Saviour will generate a desire to say no to ungodliness and worldly passions, and to say yes to self-controlled, upright, and godly living.

The desire to say no to all that would hurt the heart of Jesus should be a natural response to grace. And yet, when I stubbornly refuse to show love for others who do not measure up to my expectations, my self-imposed rules, I know He is grieved.

He makes it easy for us. Grace is the radiance of the first-love that Christ extended toward us. We love because He first loved us (1 John 4:19).

Is yours a life of grace? Are the people around you inspired to godliness because you offer grace? When you make a decision about right or wrong, is it made on the basis of loopholes in God's law, or do you take a long look into the face of Him who loves and keeps on loving no matter how disappointing your actions might have been?

Take time today to read Luke 7:40–50. It could change your life!

41

WEEK 8 — THURSDAY
BORED WITH THE WORD

"I hate to admit it," a listener writes, " but sometimes I get bored reading the Bible. Some days it doesn't seem to be saying anything to me. Can you help?"

This is a painfully honest admission for any of us to make. It seems so unspiritual. Whatever happened to the idea that, when one becomes a Christian, the Word of God comes so alive that you can't put it down?

Still, practically every Christian has dry days. And rather than caving in to guilt and condemnation, there is something we can do.

E. Stanley Jones has made a statement that makes sense to me. "Come to God's Word expectantly," he writes. "Come ready to surrender to the truths revealed. Come to it even when nothing apparently comes from your coming."

How often do we fail to come to God's Word expectantly? To be very honest about it, there are times when I read it just because I think I should; I'm not really expecting anything at all. Those are very often dry times.

On other occasions the Lord meets me at the point of my need in spite of my reluctance. He has said, "The word of God is living and active. Sharper than any double-edged sword, it penetrates even to dividing soul and spirit, joints and marrow; it judges the thoughts and attitudes of the heart" (Heb. 4:12). So, if I get into His Word, I am dealing with something that is "living and active," and if I stay with it long enough, something is bound to happen!

If you are experiencing too many dry times, consider how you might be approaching your time in God's Word.

1. *Come to the Word honestly.* Tell Him that you are tired, distracted, bored, and that you just can't get past the words on the page. Promise Him that you will fulfill your part in reading the Word, if He will help you by pointing out something you need to hear, something He has just for you. Then follow through . . . and read. (The Psalms are a wonderful place to retreat to on such days, especially if you stumble over dates, names of kings, and who-begat-whos!)

2. *Come to the Word with a desire to obey.* Boredom when reading the Bible is often the result of a closed mind. Because we're afraid we might be convicted, we shut off our minds to what God is saying.

3. *Come to the Word prayerfully.* "Open my eyes that I may see wonderful things in your law" (Ps. 119:18). Pray with the psalmist that you may be able to see "wonderful things." Communion with God is surely worth whatever it takes to overcome boredom and restlessness.

4. *Come to the Word persistently.* In the end, persistence is really what it is all about. "Keep coming even when nothing apparently comes from your coming." Because God honors faithfulness, you will be blessed for giving Him the time He needs to speak to you through His Word.

WEEK 8 — FRIDAY
"I AM THERE WITH YOU"

There is nothing that hurts quite so much as loneliness. If you are lonely today, I want you to know I care and I want to encourage you. More than that, the Lord cares. While you and I are separated by distance, He is right there with you.

Listen with your heart to His thoughts for you from Marie Chapian's excellent book, *His Thoughts Toward Me.*

You see yourself as a small sparrow alone on a housetop;
your heart quakes.
   I hear your groaning in the late hours,
     your eyes dull;
      your soul despairs.
       But I am with you.

If you are lauded
   as the star of a million parades,
     or if you are alone
      as a frightened bird on a rooftop,
       I am there.

If your name commands the reverence of nations
   and your laurels march before you,
     of if you huddle
      chilled, friendless and poor against a wall,
       I am there.

If you sleep in the beds of kings
   and ride the wings of skillful wisdom in all things,
     or if you shiver alone
      with pain and muddled thoughts,
       I am there.

If joyful laughter floods your house
   and the smells of bubbling pots of food
     and bulging ovens pour happily from your windows
      or if you sit hunched, cross-legged and alone,
       spooning dinner from a can,
        I am there.

If you leap like a deer
   across gymnasium floors,
     muscles taut and body lithe—
      or if you amble slowly, heavily
       from sitting place to sitting place,
        I am there.

If you love to conquer impossible worlds,
   wielding the powerful sword of the Spirit
     and the mighty banner of faith that I give to you,
      or if you cower in fear of failure
       or rebuke,
        I am there.
       I am there so you may turn to me.
      I stick to you, like your own skin.
The mountains of the earth will shake and crumble,
Yet My tender love for you is never shaken—
   not a shiver,

not a breath,
not the barest vibration or change.
Because I am there with you.
(Ps. 139:9–10; Prov. 18:24)[2]

WEEK 9 — MONDAY
LOVE—PROOF POSITIVE

Every time I go through a major airport, I see people who are trying to let me know that they stand for something. They have formed an opinion about everything from nuclear war, to AIDS, to abortion . . . and they are gutsy enough to try to flag me down, tell me what they think, and ask me to give them my support. I am rarely moved by such an appeal, but I can tell you I'm impressed with the dedication of the people who will spend their time trying to convince others that they have the truth.

How do you rate in your efforts to convince others of the truth of Jesus Christ? Is your claim to fame your church attendance?

Do you tithe?

Do you have a fish sticker on your car?

Or, do you honk since you love Jesus?

Those things are all okay, but the Scriptures tell us how to spot the Lord's people: "All men will know that you are my disciples if you love one another" (John 13:35).

That's convicting, isn't it? Let's take a look at how this love looks and acts.

1. *Love is not choosy*; it's all-inclusive. Matthew 5:44 says we are even to "love [our] enemies." Love means "seeking another person's highest good." So, condoning sin, putting a stamp of approval on your enemy's wrong action is not love, but seeking his or her highest good is!
2. *Love tells the truth.* Flattering someone to make them feel good is not honest, it is deception. Disciples should be able to count on one another to be truthful, but gentle. Ephesians 4:15 reminds us to "speak the truth in love." In the Greek, that comes out "truthing it in love." Have you been "truthing it in love," or have you been fudging on the truth with your Christian brothers and sisters?
3. *Love is active.* "Dear children, let us not love with words or tongue but with actions and in truth" (1 John 3:18).

It is so easy to say, "I love you," and in most cases, those are powerful, healing words. The Scriptures warn us not to stop with lip service, but to show our love by our actions, our gifts, and our service. Instead of saying, "Call me if there is anything I can do," love says, "I'm fixing dinner for your family tomorrow night. What time may I deliver it?" There is all the difference in the world between half-hearted offers and the robust delivery of a tangible gift.

This type of action caused the townspeople during the time of the early church to comment, "Oh how they love one another!" These believers loved in tangible ways—offering a place to sleep, food to eat, and money to buy supplies.

In our affluent society, we may forget sometimes that love can be spelled h-e-l-p. We need to look for subtle ways to lend a hand—sitting with an elderly parent or a handicapped child, running errands for the homebound, making repairs around the house for a widow.

So how are folks going to know that you are a disciple? How are they going to know that I am? Can they tell from our impressive and convicting words?

That's great, but words don't prove a thing.

There is only one proof positive: Others will know you and I are disciples by our love . . . our practical, non-choosy, truth-telling, action-oriented love.

WEEK 9 — TUESDAY
WAIT MEANS STAYING PUT

I'm at an interesting stage of life. There are so many ideas and experiences that I'm chomping at the bit to use, but almost a year ago, the Lord gave me a verse of Scripture. It was almost as if He were saying, "Jan, this one's for you." I read, "Wait for the LORD; be strong and take heart and wait for the LORD" (Ps. 27:14).

Now, I've looked and looked, but I can't find a single English word that defines the word *wait* as anything but "wait." I even checked out my new little electronic thesaurus, thinking surely it would have a different meaning. But no! You know what *wait* means—stay, abide, linger, remain, tarry, stick around. If you hear anything but "wait" in those words, I'd like to know.

The reason I'm in such a stir over this word *wait* is because I see so many folks, including myself, who want to jump into the first opportunity that comes along, whether it is in line with the calling God has on our lives or not. I speak from experience when I tell you that I'd personally rather go through a half dozen possible doors than to wait. The only problem is when you launch out in a direction God did not intend, you usually have a bill to pay or a mess to clean up. My last little adventure through one of those doors cost me $300, but I can tell you I got $3000 worth of experience. God doesn't waste our detours, but there is usually a price to pay for the ride!

For those of you who are having trouble following this biblical admonition, let me give you some thoughts that might save you a detour or two, some time, and maybe even a few dollars.

As you wait, remember:

1. There is a God . . . and you are not He!
2. God is trustworthy and all-knowing. He even knows your zip code.
3. No matter how much your circumstances hurt, He loves you and is already at work in your behalf.

When I read in the Scriptures what God promises to those who wait, I decided to test them for myself. He said He would be with me through the fires and waters (Isa. 43:2). He said He would be with me in the valleys (Ps. 23:4). He said His peace would guard my heart (Phil. 4:6–8). His promises have all been true!

Oh, my sweet friend, if the Lord has told you to wait, then He also is saying to you, "If you will do it, you won't be ashamed. You will be exalted. You won't have to think about vengeance, because I will take care of it for you."

Are you waiting for God to move in the life of a loved one and are tempted to meddle because He isn't working quickly enough to suit you? Don't rush it. He will move in His time.

Are you waiting for God to bring an end to your present circumstances and fretting because the end is not in sight? Don't try to second-guess Him. Just wait patiently.

Are you waiting for God to change your attitude, but are about ready to give up on yourself? Keep praying and faithfully presenting your concerns to Him.

If you are feeling stressed out today, maybe you need to take a seat and wait. Listen for the still, small voice to tell you the next move to make.

WEEK 9 — WEDNESDAY
TRUE FRIENDS

I have just written a book called *Please Don't Say You Need Me*. Its topic is codependency, the addiction that occurs when one person begins to believe that a mate, a child, a friend, a counselor, a boyfriend or girlfriend, is necessary to life. When this happens, watch out for trouble—jealousy, mistrust, anger, possessiveness, and a whole raft of others problems.

Codependency can slip up on anyone. Even if all of your past relationships have been mature and stable, you may be in a dependency situation. It often happens to a strong person who feels protective of a weaker one. The first thing you know, you are playing God in the life of someone who desperately needs to look to Him for protection, strength, and value.

Loyal friends are there in the tough times, but when we substitute human friendship for the companionship and provision of God, we fall into sin.

If you think you might be in a dependent relationship, check your situation against this list:

- Frequent jealousy
- Possessiveness
- Exclusivity
- Irrational anger
- Depression when the friend withdraws slightly
- Unwillingness to make plans without involvement of the friend
- Inappropriate physical affection

If you recognize any of these danger signals, take immediate action before it is too late to prevent damage.

True friendship is built on mutuality, respect, trust and love. If your relationship with a friend is characterized by angry exchanges, possessiveness, and jealous outbursts, it can hardly be called a friendship. True friends, such as David and Jonathan, strengthen one another's trust in God.

WEEK 9 — THURSDAY
MEETING EMOTIONAL NEEDS

A common complaint from women is summed up in this brief letter:

Dear Jan,
    My husband says I want more than he can give emotionally. I want to talk to him about everything, but he doesn't want to hear

it. I love him, but I need and want more emotional involvement. Any suggestions?

You are not alone, my friend. Many couples have difficulty in this area. At the risk of sounding negative, I will have to say that, unless your husband had a very good role model as a young man growing up, he may never be able to satisfy your need for in-depth communication. Still, there are some practical steps you can take.

1. Determine that you will not seek fulfillment in illegitimate ways. Looking to another man for emotional support can set up the climate for an affair.
2. If you have tried all the marriage books and courses, and nothing seems to work, think about a "heart bypass." You may literally have to bypass your heart—die to any expectations you have for your husband to meet your emotional needs.
   - Don't blame your husband for what he can't give.
   - Continue to be a wife in whom he can safely trust to protect his privacy and reputation.
   - Look for friends *of the same sex* who can make you feel loved, supported, and probably most of all, understood.
   - Find fulfillment in activities apart from him if you can do it without depriving him of what he needs from you. I talked with an older woman in this situation who said, "When I realized I did not have to place all my expectations for emotional support on my husband, it made all the difference in the world. I was left free to love him . . . with no strings attached!"
3. Resist bitterness.
   - Learn to accept your husband the way he is. God created him, and the chances of your changing him are slim.
   - Remove the pressure of meeting your emotional needs from him. No one person can fully meet another's needs, especially a man who has never come to grips with his own emotions.
   - Take responsibility for your own emotional support. You will feel stronger and better about yourself if you will assume responsibility for your own feelings.

If you are able to accomplish these things, both of you will be happier for the effort. And you may even find that God has rewarded your faithfulness by remodeling your husband!

WEEK 9 — FRIDAY
LIFE IS A SERIES OF CHOICES

The rhetoric of our society is laced with one-liners that are packed with more punch than whole paragraphs. Phrases like these say a lot:
"Just say no."
"Winner takes all."
"He's a brick shy of a load." Or, the now famous . . .
"Read my lips."
There's another power-packed statement that I believe encompasses just about everything a person needs to know about life. It covers getting along

with people, making career choices and cross-country moves, deciding whom you will marry and how many children you should have. It even includes where you will spend eternity—in heaven or hell!

"LIFE IS A SERIES OF CHOICES."

Let me run that by you again . . .

"LIFE IS A SERIES OF CHOICES."

Consider how your choices have affected your life as well as the lives of those you love. What if you had chosen to marry someone else? How different your life might be! What if you had chosen another career? Where would you be today? What if you had remained pure before marriage? What would be the state of your marriage now?

"What if's" are the natural by-products of our choices. But then so are the actual circumstances in which we live day in and day out. They are very much a part of our choices. No guesswork there!

Not only that, but God says our choices are important to Him. He puts His feelings on the line: "But if serving the Lord seems undesirable to you, then choose for yourselves this day whom you will serve" (Josh. 24:15).

What choices are you facing today?

- Is gossip the chief pastime of the crowd you run with? You don't have to participate. Choose another crowd!
- Will you be with people who think off-color jokes are funny? Choose to be somewhere else!
- Is there someone you'll see today who uses the Lord's name in vain? Choose to bless the Lord verbally.

Life is a series of choices, not only in the big things that change our lives forever, but also in routine, everyday matters. In this moment of time, which will you choose today?

WEEK 10 — MONDAY
GOD IS ABLE

Buried deep within the record of all the great heroes of the faith, there is a powerful verse. Referring to Abraham when he went up the mountain to offer his son Isaac as a sacrifice to God, the verse reads: "He considered that God is able to raise men even from the dead" (Heb. 11:19 NASB).

Have you considered that "God is able"? If He is able to raise men from the dead, then . . .

- He is able to transform your loved one's life, even though he is rebellious and stubborn.
- He is able to mend your broken heart, even when you feel you'll never be whole again.
- He is able to raise up a ministry for you, even though you think there's no way God could use you.

One of the reasons we may hesitate to release those who are dearest to us, or that part of ourselves that is most tender, is our shaky confidence that "God is able." He doesn't come prying things, problems, hurts, and people we love out of our tightly clenched fists. But He does take what we give Him and do what needs to be done when we are willing to let go.

I recently heard a testimony from a widow who had turned her back on

God. "My life was a mess," she said. "With two abortions behind me, I was on my way to have a third when someone reached out to me, took me in, and introduced me to Jesus Christ as my Lord and Savior." Today, six years later, this woman runs a counseling center for crisis pregnancies.

God is able.

And what about Feodor, an old man from Russia? Feodor's family here in the States had prayed for him for years when they received a call one night that he was in the Chicago airport, having suddenly been allowed to leave Russia. The family flew to Chicago and brought him home, where he spent the three weeks granted by his visa. During that time, they told him of Jesus, quoting a personalized version of John 3:16: "For God so loved Feodor that he gave his only begotten Son, that if Feodor believes in him, Feodor shall not perish but have everlasting life."

With tears streaming down his face, the old man confessed his new-found faith. "I believe."

In a few days, Feodor returned to Russia, and his family never saw him again. He died a few months later after writing to tell them the good news of his salvation in Christ. Though their hearts were broken when they received news of Feodor's death, they are confident that someday they will see him in heaven, bowing at the feet of his God who was able to bring a little old man out of Russia to hear the simple message of salvation through Jesus!

God is able . . . in your life today. No matter what you need from Him, or how impossible it seems, He is able!

WEEK 10 — TUESDAY
SUFFICIENT OR SATISFIED?

When I was a little girl, I had an old relative who used to say, "Have you 'et' sufficiently?" I always thought that was so funny! In fact, now I find myself imitating her when someone asks if I've had enough to eat. I'll say, "I believe I've 'et' sufficiently." Of course, in my mind, I may think I haven't 'et" 'till I'm satisfied, but it is sufficient!

There can be a vast difference between having sufficient and being satisfied. Often the difference is between what we need and what we think we need. My goal is usually to be satisfied because being sufficient may just barely cover the bare spots, and I like to have plenty of whatever I have. Are you that way? I hope so, because if not, I could really be embarrassed sharing my weaknesses.

I recently read this quote from Elisabeth Elliot in the Ligonier Ministries' magazine. Think about it as you read . . .

Is God's love sufficient?
It is sufficient. It's not all I want, it's not all I think I need, but it is enough. But there's no sense in imagining that God's love takes the place of every kind of earthly comfort. If the air conditioning goes off, the love of God is not going to air condition us.

I lived in a house in Ecuador with no walls, and I didn't particularly like that. I'm a person of great reserve and privacy, and I like solitude. I had Indians in my house all the time hanging over my shoulder, going through my stuff.

"What's this? What's that? Where did you get it? What's it made of? Why don't you give it to me, you've got two of these?" I had two changes of clothes. One on and one that I had just washed. I would just get tired of having company all the time. But I can look back and remember what the Lord asked the disciples, "When I sent you forth, lacked ye anything?" And they said, "Nothing." God's love is sufficient. We can't expect Him to satisfy everything we think we need. It is in heaven where we will be truly satisfied.[1]

When I read Elisabeth's words, I thought, "Oh, my—I think I need to focus on how sufficient God is, especially when I get irritable or uncomfortable with my lot." Often we act so spoiled even when we have enough. I wonder how that affects God's heart. My friend, if this problem afflicts you as much as it does me, then we probably need to stop and pray together right now.

Lord, forgive us for wanting more and more when you have told us that you will be our satisfaction and our sufficiency. Sometimes we look at the good gifts you give us and can't find it in ourselves to be satisfied with what you provide. May we have sense enough to stop right now and realize what you have given. Give us, Lord, eyes to see all that we have in you, this very moment . . . and may we be satisfied with the gift of your sufficiency. In Jesus' name. Amen.

WEEK 10 — WEDNESDAY
THE ACCUSER

Have you ever struggled with "feeling forgiven"? If so, then you can relate to the person who wrote these words:

"I am a Christian, and several years ago I committed a sin for which I am very sorry. I have confessed it to God. I have repented. I wouldn't dream of doing it again and there is no way I can make restitution for it. So, to my knowledge, I've done all I can do. But, still I feel guilty and as though God hasn't really forgiven me."

I understand what this individual is saying. She is a courageous and sensitive person to openly admit her feelings. This situation is not without hope. I truly believe there is an answer.

Revelation 12:10 says, ". . . for the accuser of our brothers, who accuses them before our God day and night, has been hurled down."

This Scripture gives us a clue to the fact that we have an accuser who works overtime pointing out our sins to God. Think about this scene with me.

It's the throne room of God. Jesus is seated at the right hand of the Father. Satan intrudes to scream, "Now look what your child is doing! And you think she's so good!"

With eyes that pierce through eternity, the Lord Jesus raises His nail-pierced hand and Satan is silenced as the eternal reminder of His defeat is raised for the hosts of heaven to see.

Then he, this tormentor-accuser, turns his fire-burning arrows at the target of your mind. He can't shake God, so he goes to work on you. That is when you feel guilty, unforgiven. He brings thoughts about your sin and whispers questions such as, "How could you?" and even says, "You don't really believe God forgives you . . ."

These are the times the Bible says, "Raise your shield of faith . . . raise your determination to take God at His Word . . ." when He says through the apostle Paul:

What, then, shall we say to these things? If God is for us, who is against us?

He who did not spare His own Son, but delivered Him up for us all, how will He not also with Him freely give us all things? Who will bring a charge against God's elect? God is the one who justifies;

who is the one who condemns? Christ Jesus is He who died, yes, rather who was raised, who is at the right hand of God, who also intercedes for us.

Who shall separate us from the love of Christ? Shall tribulation, or distress, or persecution, or famine, or nakedness, or peril, or sword?

Just as it is written,

"For Thy sake we are being put to death all day long; We were considered as sheep to be slaughtered."

But in all these things we overwhelmingly conquer through Him who loved us.

For I am convinced that neither death, nor life, nor angels, nor principalities, nor things present, nor things to come, nor powers, nor height, nor depth, nor any other created thing, shall be able to separate us from the love of God, which is in Christ Jesus our Lord. (Rom. 8:31–39 NASB)

My friend, the fact God has forgiven you is settled. The difficulty is in your feelings. But feelings can be changed when we choose to believe the Truth.

Believe. Talk to yourself and remind Satan by giving him God's Word.

WEEK 10 — THURSDAY
DIFFERENCES THAT MAKE A DIFFERENCE

I was at lunch the other day and a family came in and sat at the next table. I watched them eat and thought, "Oh, dear Father, these people look like the walking dead." Mother, father, and son . . . all sat and ate in silence. They had dull eyes and, from all I could tell, they had dull lives. I don't know if they are Christians or not, although I imagine if I had asked, they would have said, "Yes."

I breathed a prayer for the Lord to please deliver me from living death. I said, "Lord, may I never lose my zest for life. As long as I have You, I have no excuse to walk around as if I am dead waiting to be buried."

As I left the restaurant and breathed the fresh air, I began to think about the difference that makes a difference.

It makes a difference when you know who you are and where you've come from. I had a camp director when I was a kid who would call an assembly before we ever went on a trip on the camp bus. She was an older woman with a very commanding presence. She would say, "Schweeties, remember who you are, where you're from, and what you represent." She would then roll her eyes and we would know that, because we were from Camp Crestridge, we had best be on our best behavior wherever we went, because if we were not we would have to deal with her when we got back.

Paul knew the value of remembering who you are and where you are from. He told the Corinthians that they needed to remember when he wrote:

Do not be deceived; neither fornicators, nor idolaters, nor adulterers, nor effeminate, nor homosexuals, nor thieves, nor the covetous, nor drunkards, nor revilers, nor swindlers, shall inherit the kingdom of God. AND SUCH WERE SOME OF YOU; but you were washed, but you were sanctified, but you were justified in the name of the Lord Jesus Christ, and in the Spirit of our God. (1 Cor. 6:9–11 NASB)

Just think about it, if you remember where you have come from and then compare it to what God has done in your life, it has to make a difference. Nineteen years ago I was afraid of death and so I was looking for a way I could deal with my fear. Edgar Cayce and his philosophy of reincarnation seemed like a good idea to me. So I read everything I could on that topic . . . thinking, "Wow. This is exciting!" But God, in His sovereignty, reached down and touched my life and a verse literally jumped off the page. "There is a way which seems right to a man, but in the end it leads to death" (Prov. 16:25). My friend, that's Truth, and when you realize that God has intervened in your life, called you to Himself, and put you on the right track, it has to make a difference!

Then, when you find out that God calls you a chosen race, a royal priesthood, a holy nation, a people for His own possession, that you might proclaim the excellencies of Him who has called you out of darkness into His marvelous light . . . it should make all the difference in the world (1 Pet. 2:9).

If you and I would ever grasp this, we would look better, smell better, smile better, and treat folks better than anyone else they meet today. That's the way it should be!

Think about it. Do you want to make a difference in your world? Do you want to be among the walking dead who die at twenty and are buried at eighty-five? I don't. I want to make a difference! It doesn't take me long to remember where I came from . . . I can go back to that time of frustration in a minute, and you probably can too. But God doesn't do that. He doesn't even remember the mud He scraped off of us. He spotlights our beauty. You are part of a chosen race with one job . . . and that is to show how excellent our God is . . . how merciful, how kind, how joyful.

Will you think about that today? Will you remember who you are, where you're from, and what you represent? It could make a difference in someone's life . . . and it definitely will make a difference in yours!

WEEK 10 — FRIDAY
BITTERNESS

Bitterness is a topic none of us likes to look at, but there's a short little reminder in Hebrews 12:15 that could rearrange the way you think today. Listen to it carefully as I read:

See to it that no one comes short of the grace of God; that no root of bitterness springing up causes trouble, and by it many be defiled. (NASB)

Did you catch how important digging up roots of bitterness is? The verse is so short, sometimes we can roll right over it and miss what God is saying about that word that can break you in a minute, bitterness.

When you taste something bitter, you will go to all lengths to get rid of it. You'll rush for a glass of juice to wash away the taste. Why? Because no one likes the taste of bitterness. It's nasty. And we don't have any trouble identifying it when we taste it. How about when you see it? Can you describe bitterness?

Let me give you a description:

How about hardness, coldness, indifference, cutting people off, not speaking. That's bitterness and if you think it's pretty, you need to look again. If we ever saw how nasty it really is, we would spare no effort to get rid of it. And, today is as good a day as any to get started . . .

Is there anyone you feel bitter toward? Is there anyone you're not speaking to? Is there anyone you are avoiding like the plague because you are bitter? Then, you need to face how ugly that looks and do something about it now.

God says His Word is like a mirror. We can come to it, see the ugliness and walk away, or we can stay long enough to see what to do about it and then get busy (James 1:23–25).

Well, God says you get rid of bitterness by pulling out the root. I think God calls it a root so we can really get the picture. The root has to go.

Last spring a friend and I were standing in my front yard talking. I was absentmindedly picking at my dandelions. I broke them off at the ground. She watched for a while and said, "That's killing me to see you just break them off. If you want to get rid of them, you have to go for the roots." Then she went to work and got rid of them with a vengeance.

That's what you have to do with bitterness . . . just breaking it off at the ground doesn't take the root away. Just deciding to smile and be under control doesn't remove the bitterness.

If you really are serious, go to God and tell Him you have tried and failed to deal with your bitterness and you need help. Every time a cold, hard thought comes to your mind toward that other person, take it to God. "Lord, here I am again. That thought is bothering me, but I want to dig up the root, so I give it to you."

Then go to the Word. I think this is one of the best Scriptures we can read to put it all in perspective:

By this the love of God was manifested in us, that God has sent His only begotten Son into the world so that we might live through Him.

In this is love, not that we loved God, but that He loved us and sent His Son to be the propitiation for our sins.

Beloved, if God so loved us, we also ought to love one another. (1 John 4:9–11 NASB)

And then, when you have done serious business with the Lord, if the person is alive and knows you have a problem, go to him and ask forgiveness. When you call your sin "sin," it's amazing how ugly it looks and just how dissatisfied you'll be to let it stay.

Is bitterness bothering you today? Why not get busy on that root right now?

WEEK 11 — MONDAY
KEEPING AN OPEN HAND

Let's talk today about your treasure. I don't mean your IRA's, CD's or even your checkbook. I mean the person, place, or thing you don't feel you could live without.

You know where it is, it's where your heart is. It's where your thoughts are. It's what gets your attention quicker than anything else.

Jesus says in Matthew 6:21, "For where your treasure is, there your heart will be also."

We tell a lot about ourselves by the way we try to protect our treasure. If you can't hold it with an open hand, you are saying one thing, "God, I'm not sure I can trust you. This treasure of mine is too valuable for me to hold my hand open and see what you will do with it."

Is your treasure your husband, your wife, your boyfriend, your girlfriend?

Are you willing to dare to open your hand and say, "Lord, he or she is yours. I trust you to let me keep her or lose her. I trust you to guard him in all of his ways and I refuse to worry or be anxious."

How did you do on that test? Pretty good? Well, let's get a little closer.

Moms and Dads, are you willing to open your hand and say, "Lord, whatever it takes to make my son or my daughter into the person you want them to be, I will not interfere." These are easy words, huh? I understand, because they are not so easy to say when the pressure mounts and it looks like your child is going the other way. It is tough not to panic. It's even tougher not to step in and rescue. My friend, that's where your faith becomes real.

Listen to these words from Hannah Whitall Smith in her book, *God Is Enough*:

> If we trust for ourselves, we must trust for our loved ones also, especially for our children. God is more their Father than their earthly fathers are, and if they are dear to us they are far dearer to Him. We cannot, therefore, do anything better for them than to trust them in God's care, or do hardly anything worse for them than to try to keep them in our own care.
>
> I knew a Christian mother who trusted peacefully for her own salvation but was racked with anxiety about her sons, who seemed entirely indifferent to all religious subjects. One evening she heard about putting those we love into the fortress of God by faith and leaving them there. Like a flash of heavenly light, she saw the inconsistency of hiding herself in God's fortress and leaving her beloved sons outside. At once her faith took them into the fortress with her, and she abandoned them to the care of God.
>
> She did this so fully that all her anxiety vanished and perfect peace dawned on her soul. She told me she felt somehow that her sons were God's sons now and no longer hers. He loved them far better than she could and would care for them far more wisely and effectually. She held herself in readiness to do for them whatever the Lord might suggest, but she felt that He was the One

who would know what was best, and she was content to leave the matter in His hands.[1]

Well, how about you? This has been a good reminder for me . . . I hope it has for you!

WEEK 11 — TUESDAY
IMPATIENCE

How patient are you? Do you tap your foot and start to boil when things don't move quickly enough for you? Have you had to deal with impatience lately? I have. I want things to happen when I want them to. Waiting just seems unacceptable. I want things to happen when I pray for them, too. I used to get really upset with people who could not just take God at His Word and wait and be patient. But, at this stage of my life, I'm ready to see some answers to some questions I've asked and some prayers I've prayed. And right now, God seems really quiet. It's hard to know if and when God is going to respond to your request. As a parent, that has really bothered me. Sometimes I think, "I want my children to learn to pray, but how will I explain God's 'No' or His 'Later'?"

I thought of this one night in a snow several years ago. It had come very suddenly and my three sons and I were at the grocery store. When we came home, we were confronted by a very steep hill. Several people had tried to navigate it, and there were some men standing around saying, "Lady, you can't make it up that hill." Well, I had a trunk full of groceries, a car full of boys, and I don't like to be told, "You can't." So, they might as well have waved a red flag in front of me! I looked around and noticed that only one side of the hill was icy. Everyone had tried to go up on the right side. The left side was snowy and soft. No one was coming down. I said, "Boys, let's ask the Lord to get us up that hill. He can give us the traction we need." I prayed out loud and silently thought, "Lord, if we don't make it, you'll have to tell me what to say."

Well, we went straight up, no problems, not a hitch. I had to smile as the men standing around saying "Don't try it," stood back and watched. And I thanked the Lord as we neared the top to remind the boys that God had enabled us to have the traction we needed.

But sometimes we have to deal with the "no's" and, even harder, the "laters."

There is a dual nature to the way God deals with us. On one hand He says, "I care about everything about you. I even know the number of hairs on your head." But, He also says, "I am working something in you that is very special . . . I am doing an eternal work that goes far beyond your food, your clothing and your hair. I am making you into an accurate reflection of my son." So, sometimes the "wait's" and the "no's" just have to be.

If you're feeling impatient today, let me encourage you with these Scriptures:

> We also exult in our tribulations, knowing that tribulation brings about perseverance [or patience]; and perseverance, proven character; and proven character, hope. (Rom. 5:3–4 NASB)

Patience is worth more than it would seem.

Consider it all joy, my brethren, when you encounter various trials, knowing that the testing of your faith produces endurance. And let endurance [patience] have its perfect result, that you may be perfect and complete [mature], lacking in nothing. (James 1:2–4 NASB)

In both of these passages there is a goal . . . the maturity and endurance that marks the character of a man or woman of God.

One thing is sure, if you just look at what's going on in your life today, you may get impatient. But, from God's perspective, there is an eternal view. And He loves you enough not to let you miss it by giving in to your, "I want it right now."

So, I guess the best word we can hang on to today is this: Be patient. There's more to this "wait" than meets the eye.

WEEK 11 — WEDNESDAY
JEHOVAH JIREH

Several summers ago I was teaching a group of teenagers about the different names of God. I was explaining how God reveals Himself through His names. He tells something about His character with each name that He tells us about in Scripture.

I was explaining the name, Jehovah Jireh, the God who Provides. I told them how God had tested Abraham by asking him to take Isaac, his only son, to Mount Moriah to be killed. They were very quiet as I explained that Abraham set out very early in the morning to obey the Lord and how Isaac went up the mountain with him and asked his father where the sacrifice was. Then, as I explained that God provided a ram, just at the moment Abraham was raising the knife to slay Isaac, there was a hush. I told them that Abraham was so grateful that he called the name of the place "The Lord Will Provide." The name of God that means "The Lord provides," . . . is Jehovah Jireh.

At that moment, a young girl raised her hand and said, "I know Jehovah Jireh." All the other teenagers turned to look at her and I held my breath, not sure what she would say. "My parents divorced and my mom and I live together. We have had a real hard time with money and it's embarrassing to say, but one time we didn't have any toilet tissue. So we prayed and told the Lord about our need. That night we were driving home and I said, 'Mom, what's that over there on the side of the road?' As she slowed down, we both saw it. It was a gigantic package of toilet paper! You know, one of those great big packages! I jumped out and picked it up and we thanked God for the answer to our prayer. So, I know Jehovah Jireh."

All of the teens were quiet, because they had heard firsthand from one of their own who knew Jehovah Jireh.

What does that name of God mean in your life? Does the fact that He was a provider for Abraham and that one of His names means "The Lord will provide" have anything to do with you today?

What do you need? Do you need a calm and quiet spirit? He says you can have it.

Do you need wisdom? He says it's yours!

Do you need love, joy, and peace? It's there for you.

56

Do you need someone to bear your burden? He says He is waiting to carry it for you.

Do you need to know that He is with you during the hard times? He says when you walk through the waters, He won't let you drown . . . when the fires leap around you, He won't let you be burned.

Do you need forgiveness? He is there with it before you even know you need it.

When you realize you have a need, Jehovah Jireh is already there to give it to you.

The theme song for my daily radio program, "Jan's Journal," is a song called "When He is Everything." The words, which were written by my friend, Debra Martin, are:

> When He is everything,
> Then I have everything I need.
> When He is everything,
> Not just a name in a book I read.
> But I mean everything,
> Yes, everything I need. . .
> When He is everything,
> Then I have everything I need.

When the Lord becomes everything to you, as He was to Abraham and Isaac, then He is the Provider for everything.

What do you need that He has not provided? What do you expect that He has not given? Why not go back to Him and ask Him to show you if you are waiting for a need to be filled or for a wish to come true. They are two different things.

When you truly have a need, you can be sure Jehovah Jireh will provide.

WEEK 11 — THURSDAY
LISTENING

Have you ever thought what it requires to really listen to another person?

Webster says, "Listening is giving close attention in order to hear." Obviously, hearing and listening are two different things.

How many times have you heard your child talking but you failed to pay close enough attention to really listen?

When my youngest son was five, he was playing outside in a muddy field. I was on the phone talking with a friend when he came in. I heard him coming in, calling me, but before he could get his message out, I called to him and told him to sit down in the entrance hall until I finished talking so I could help him take off his boots. He answered back, "O.K." and I went on with my conversation for about ten more minutes. At that point, I heard this little voice say, "Momma, does it matter if I'm bleeding?" Of course, I immediately hung up the phone and ran to the entrance hall! There sat my precious little boy, with a gash in his chin that would require five stitches. Blood covered his jacket and he was sitting there waiting. I felt terrible. He intended to tell me about it right away, but I had answered before I heard what he was saying. I had not taken time to listen.

57

The Scriptures say, "He who gives an answer before he hears, it is folly and shame to him" (Prov. 18:13 NASB).

I believe that Scripture is referring to the person who does not know how to listen. A lot of folly and and a lot of shame has come from jumping in with a solution before you ever hear the question.

If you are going to be with other people today, here are some thoughts that will help you learn to pay attention when you listen:

1. *Pay attention to what is really being said.* On more than one occasion I have asked an irritable waitress or store clerk if she has had a bad day. I try to ask with compassion and, more often than not, the answer is, "You bet I have." I then try to let that person know I understand and I would like to make their day a little easier. It's amazing how that breaks down barriers.

2. *Pay attention to the circumstances.* If my children are tired, it is no time to talk about discipline. They won't hear me and, if I am concentrating on the issues of discipline, I won't really hear them. Play "heads up" with the circumstances.

3. *Don't put words in the other person's mouth.* Have you ever had a discussion with the desire to be heard, and the other person said, "I know what you're going to say. You always say that." You can believe that discussion is over.

By putting words in another's mouth, you are saying, "I don't want to listen." This kind of tramping on one another's feelings most frequently happens in families. Husbands and wives, parents and children have been together so long, there is a great temptation to refuse to listen. That's a way to play "get back." It can be a real form of punishment.

Are you guilty? If so, why not bite off the end of your tongue before you tell anyone, "I know what you're going to say."

If you are a person who has a lot of things going at home, at work, and at church, and you are involved with many people, you may have trained yourself to hear just enough to be dangerous. You hear certain comments, but you don't really pay attention. Training yourself to listen means forcing yourself to concentrate on one track . . . to the person who is with you at that moment.

Think about the people who have had the most positive impact in your life since you were a little child. I would imagine that the person who looked you in the eye and paid attention to what you were saying is the one who is long remembered.

How about you, my friend? Have you gotten sort of frazzled lately? Are you only half there when someone is talking with you? Do you walk away from a conversation with someone you love and have to think about what was really said?

Maybe today would be a good day to begin listening, really listening! Pay close attention. It will be worth it!

WEEK 11 — FRIDAY
FOR TIMES OF DISCOURAGEMENT

Have you had a rough week? Sometimes Fridays can take a little extra courage to get through. Oh, I know the weekend is coming, but if you are conscientious, there's a lot that can be on top of you on Friday.

Do you have a relationship that has been strained?

How about circumstances that have challenged you?

Or maybe you have been battling some physical problem all week and it's not getting any better.

And, frankly, you are just down!

I thought it would be good to give you some thoughts from God's Word to encourage you wherever you are in your life today . . .

God says:

1. *Be determined to endure.* "Do not throw away your confidence, which has a great reward. For you have need of endurance, so that when you have done the will of God, you may receive what was promised" (Heb. 10:35–36 NASB). This is a favorite verse of mine. God says to hang in there and you will receive what He has promised for you.

   "And let us not lose heart in doing good, for in due time we shall reap if we do not grow weary" (Gal. 6:9 NASB). This is one of those easy-to-say but hard-to-do verses. Sometimes "doing good" can be tough when no one seems to appreciate it. But, just remember . . . God sees, and someday you will reap.

   God works best in the lives of those who are determined.

2. *Wait on the Lord.* "I would have despaired unless I had believed that I would see the goodness of the Lord in the land of the living. Wait for the Lord; Be strong, and let your heart take courage; Yes, wait for the Lord" (Ps. 27:13–14 NASB). Don't rush in to relieve or to fix a situation. Stand back and wait on the Lord to show you what to do.

3. *Recognize His hand.* There is nothing that happens that has not been filtered through God's fingers of love. And, never forget. There is a purpose. "In this you greatly rejoice, even though now for a little while, if necessary, you have been distressed by various trials, that the proof of your faith, being more precious than gold which is perishable, even though tested by fire, may be found to result in praise and glory and honor at the revelation of Jesus Christ" (1 Pet. 1:6–7 NASB).

There are no accidents. Every time you are in a trial, there is one goal . . . to prove your faith . . . to show you that you have a faith that shines like gold. When you are feeling pressured and can't see anything good going on, it can be tough to remember that your faith is being proved.

Father, we're like little children . . . and sometimes, by the time Friday rolls around, we are tired and cranky and don't know what to do with ourselves. I know someone praying with me right now needs a gentle touch of encouragement today. So, I pray you will ever so tenderly give the touch that is needed. Thank you, Lord, for letting us know that you understand our frailty and you love us in spite of it. In Jesus' name. Amen.

WEEK 12 — MONDAY
GOOD ADVICE

Amy Carmichael was a missionary to India for over fifty years. She went there to rescue little girls from prostitution in the Hindu temples and she encountered unbelievable opposition as she marched right into Satan's domain to reclaim these precious little babies, toddlers and pre-teens who were offered to the temple priests by their parents.

She founded the Donahver Fellowship which is still in existence today, although Amy Carmichael has gone on to be with the Lord.

When young people volunteered to join her on the front lines of her mission field in India, they had no idea about the difficulties they would encounter. So, she tried to prepare them with these words, and they are great words for you today, no matter what you are facing: "Guard against depression. Bear evenly with all that is uneven. Never be shocked out of loving."

Think about it. When things go wrong, what is the hardest emotion to overcome? Depression. Everything looks gray and cloudy. Everything looks as if it will never work out. You feel hopeless. I imagine Amy had encountered many raw recruits who became depressed when they lost a child back to the temple or when they had prayed and prayed and God seemed to be silent. So, she knew the first obstacle to overcome was depression.

The next—"Bear evenly with all that is uneven." It is always a jolt to realize that not everyone is pleasant or fair even among Christians. There are many uneven events that occur. It's just the nature of life in this fallen world. We can choose to respond evenly or we can throw a fit and let everyone know how awful this is. Amy knew on the mission field emotions would run high and feelings would be strung tight. To keep the peace that would honor the Lord, she cautioned, "Bear evenly with all that is uneven." Don't let someone else plan the agenda of your emotions.

Then the last point was the clincher. "Never be shocked out of loving." No matter how determined we are that we will be loving under all circumstances, often it happens that the shock of someone's betrayal or their injustice or their insensitive actions might cause us to be blown out of the saddle when it comes to loving. Amy knew the worst thing that could happen at the Donahver Fellowship was to have the love disrupted. In all of her writings, she stressed . . . "Keep on loving." It is love that binds people together. It is love that motivates service. It is love that makes other people tolerable when they are being difficult.

> *Father, we are broken by sin and incapable in our own strength to avoid these pitfalls of depression, being uneven and unloving. But, you have given us all we need to rise above the damage in our lives. Give us the power and courage we need to face this day in your strength. Amen.*

WEEK 12 — TUESDAY
WORDS

If you are like me, you never bought into the lie that, "Sticks and stones may break my bones, but words can never hurt me." I never believed that even when I was a little girl. I was hurt a lot more by words than I was ever hurt by sticks or stones. As I have gotten older, I now realize the truth: "There are more hearts broken by words than bones broken by sticks and stones."

James says, "We all stumble in many ways. If anyone does not stumble in what he says, he is a perfect man, able to bridle the whole body as well" (3:2 NASB).

You know, I can't help what people say to me, nor can you. And, according to the Scripture, it's not the easiest thing in the world to control what we say to other people. But we can surely choose to say what is appropriate and kind and, as we grow, surely we will get better at it.

Here are some thoughts I am trying to keep in mind when I open my mouth. Maybe you'd like to join me in the exercise:

1. *Your words set the atmosphere.* I have a sign at home that says, "If Mama ain't happy, ain't nobody happy." That's so true. I have set the atmosphere for my whole family at times when I didn't realize I was doing it. I recently fussed about some mud that had been tracked in the house. And although it was not such a big deal to me, just a minor irritation, I could tell by the looks on everyone's faces, I had really been heavy handed about a little mud. My words had ruined the atmosphere.

2. *Your words are remembered longer than your actions.* My parents have always done a lot for me. They have been good to me and have been generous with me. But, over the years, I remember their words of encouragement and assurance far more than anything they ever gave me.

   How will the people you love remember you? What kind of words are stuck in their minds? No gift, no money, no trip will ever make up for unkind words.

3. *Your words show what is inside of you.* James says, "Out of the same mouth come praise and cursing. My brothers, this should not be" (James 3:10). What happens when you are bumped? What comes out of you when you are inconvenienced? What do you say when someone makes a mistake at your expense? Whatever comes out has already been in your mind. It is no mistake.

When you are shocked at your own words and you really want to change, from my experience, there is but one way you can begin to get control of your tongue. Psalm 19:14 is a prayer that says, "May the words of my mouth and the meditation of my heart be pleasing in your sight, O LORD, my Rock and my Redeemer." If the meditations of your heart, the things you think about, are acceptable to God, then you can believe that your words will be, too. Whatever is in your cup will come out when you are tipped!

Well, my friend, this is heavy-duty. It makes me so accountable. And, now that you have read it, you are accountable too. Won't it be wonderful when we mature to the point when we can control our tongues? And, although it may be one of the hardest things you will ever do, why not begin today by asking God to control the meditations of your heart. Oh that you and I might have thoughts and words that are acceptable in God's sight.

WEEK 12 — WEDNESDAY
A BRUISED REED

There is a wonderful Scripture about Jesus that says, "A bruised reed he will not break, and a smoldering wick he will not snuff out" (Matt. 12:20). I am always fascinated by that because it tells me something about Jesus that is so

61

dear to me. He understands my weakness and He is not going to push me beyond my point of endurance.

What I love about that whole concept is that Jesus knows and understands when you just can't do what you ordinarily would . . . because you are just about to snap or to go out.

I was involved in a little scenario several years ago that has been a wonderful reminder to me over the years that I don't always know what people need to do and it is not my job to push them.

A friend and I were walking by a lake in Pennsylvania. It was spring time and the ducks were quacking and swimming with great fervor. We stood and watched for a moment, and then my friend, who is very athletic, a great swimmer, and loves action, saw a duck sitting on the bank. Confident that this duck just needed some encouragement to join the others, she pushed him in. She had noticed he had an unusual growth on his head, but didn't think anything of it. As he hit the water and started to swim, the biggest duck in the pond came toward him, jumped on him and held him under, trying to drown him!

We were horrified, especially my friend who had thrown him in! She pulled her shoes off, grabbed my hand and said, "Hold on to me," as she waded out to where the ducks were. They were just close enough to shore that she could grab them. So, she got hold of the big duck who was assaulting the little one and threw him with all her might. She failed to remember that I was right behind her on the bank and that I was standing higher than she was, so when she threw him back over her head, he got *me* . . . feathers, wet feet, and all! It took a moment for the scene to become clear. The smaller duck was okay. He made his way to shore and resumed his place on the bank, none the worse for his forced swim.

Later, as we talked about the incident, we agreed that it was a lot like life. Sometimes we expect people to jump in and do what they just can't do. They may be a smoking flax that is just about to go out and some well-meaning friend might say, "This is what you need to do." Or, they may be a bruised reed, dangling by one strand. And someone might suggest some vigorous emotional activity they just aren't ready to tackle. You know, we can be hard on one another. We can expect and demand more than a person can possibly give. But Jesus just isn't that way. He knows our weakness and He doesn't force us into situations that will blow out our candles . . . or break our stems.

I don't know what may be close to snapping in your world today. Maybe no one can see it. Maybe you are the only one who knows how desperately close to breaking you are.

I just want to encourage you, my friend. There is One who is there to hold you, to comfort you, to love you . . . to protect you. Turn to Him and tell Him you feel as though your candle is about to go out . . . your last strand of rope is about to break.

He knows and He understands and He will help you.

WEEK 12 — THURSDAY
FIVE VOTES OF CONFIDENCE

Today is a new day. Have you ever thought about the wonderful promise we have in those words? It's as if we are handed a clean sheet of paper to write something new.

Max Lucado, a favorite author of mine, has given these five votes of confidence for a new day. He writes:

"Today is a new day. Hence,
1. I refuse to be shackled by yesterday's failures.
2. What I don't know will no longer be an intimidation; it will be an opportunity.
3. I will not allow people to define my mood, method, image, or mission.
4. I will pursue a mission greater than myself by making at least one person happy he saw me.
5. I will have no time for self-pity, gossip, or negativism . . . from myself or others."[1]

Let's look at those one by one. Why not stop for a moment and think about what you face today. You have a wonderful opportunity to make today a very special moment in time.

1. *Refuse to be shackled by yesterday's failures.* If you are facing today with a black cloud left over from some mistake you made yesterday, you are missing out on the promise of a new day. God says in Lamentations, "[My] compassions never fail. They are new every morning" (3:22–23). There is forgiveness . . . there is understanding . . . there is going on. I think we often hold onto yesterday's failures because, in some perverted way, we believe we have to punish ourselves for failure. Just don't forget that Jesus has already paid the price for your failure. If you keep beating yourself you are really saying that the blood of Christ just wasn't sufficient for you.

2. *Don't let ignorance intimidate you . . . consider it an opportunity.* I hate to be in a situation and feel that I should know something, and yet I don't. You know how it feels . . . like the guy who drinks out of the finger bowl at an elegant restaurant and then finds out later the bowl was there to wash his fingers. Slinking into a hole will never make you grow. If you have been ignorant about something and you feel the sting, don't quit. Consider it a chance to grow. Listen. Ask questions. Go to the Lord and ask Him to teach you what you need to know.

3. *Don't let others define your mood, method, image, or mission.* Today is a golden opportunity to assume responsibility for your own feelings and actions. As you go to the office, take care of little ones at home, or work to help an aged parent, remember . . . your mood is controlled by you, not someone else. No one makes you sad, glad, or mad. You have power over that. You are a person of value who has been given all you need for life and godliness according to second Peter. So, since that is the case, you can walk in strength and make your own decisions today.

4. *Look outside of yourself for one person whose life you can enrich.* Maybe it will be someone you meet at the store or someone you have to call from the church. Set out to invest your life in theirs for a moment. Have one aim—to make their life brighter. We live in a hurting, sin-sick world. Everywhere you turn there is sadness. You can be the one to make a difference to someone's pain today.

5. *Have no time for self-pity, gossip, or negativism from yourself or*

anyone else. Whenever you have self-pity, you are in a state of "me." And anytime you are the center of your concern, you are virtually worthless in being able to help others. You become a prime candidate for gossip and negativism because misery loves company.

I know this is a tall order for your day. But I promise, if you determine that you will have a changed attitude today, you can make a difference in your world.

WEEK 12 — FRIDAY
FAITHFULNESS

I have just one question to ask today, and it's a toughy. How faithful are you? I don't mean it in the way we usually talk about faithfulness, although faithfulness to our marriage vows is certainly part of it. I mean, how faithful are you in the little things? How many times have you been asked to do something, and yet, you forgot, or put it off, or just didn't do it?

I've been reading through Proverbs lately and, I've found that God has a lot to say about faithfulness. If being faithful is a battle for you, you better pull your toes back as we look at these Scriptures, because you just might get stepped on.

Many a man claims to have unfailing love, but a faithful man who can find? (Prov. 20:6)

Apparently faithfulness is a virtue hard to come by, and yet, many of us claim to have it. Let's look at the ways of faithfulness that are important to the Lord.

A truthful witness does not deceive, but a false witness pours out lies. (Prov. 14:5)

A gossip betrays a confidence, but a trustworthy man keeps a secret. (Prov. 11:13)

God says "faithfulness" will show up in your truthfulness and in your ability to keep your mouth shut when it comes to sharing something that is a secret. How do you rate in this area? I think this is one of the most stretching areas we encounter. It is tough not to tell a secret. Having a secret makes you feel good . . . in the know . . . important. But a life that is marked by faithfulness is marked by keeping secrets.

Have you told a secret, and later regretted it? Have you tried to go back to explain and stood there with egg on your face because you have no explanation for telling a secret other than, "I just decided to tell it"?

I've known people who have said, "Oh, they just got it out of me." But a secret is a secret, and it is one of the biggest marks of faithfulness. If you, like I, have been unfaithful in this area, there is only one way to become faithful. Confess it and determine in your heart that, by God's grace, from this moment forward, you will be faithful in keeping secrets.

Faithfulness is a quality that allows others to have confidence in you. Listen to this verse:

Like a bad tooth or a lame foot is reliance on the unfaithful in times of trouble. (Prov. 25:19)

God is making it very clear that it's a pain to trust a person who is unfaithful, especially when the going gets tough.

I find that in the things I really like to do, I am as faithful as the day is long. I am unwavering. But, when it comes to the duties or obligations that are uncomfortable or boring, I usually find that my faithfulness can waver and I can come up with every excuse in the book as to why I just won't be able to do it.

But, you know what? I want to be *thought* of as a person who is faithful in every area. I have always believed that God meant what He said in Luke 16:10: "Whoever can be trusted with very little can also be trusted with much." That means if you or I are going to be considered a faithful people, we will have to take the little things seriously.

- Do you have library books you need to return?
- Do you have someone you said you would call?
- Did you sign up to sing in the choir, but you have gotten out of the habit of going?
- Did you promise to take care of a button on a shirt for someone in your family?

Oh my, I think I'm glad our time together is about over! I think my toes are bleeding. How about yours? If faithfulness is so important, I think we had better take it seriously.

WEEK 13 — MONDAY
SATISFIED

Have you ever looked at someone who has a lot of material wealth and thought, "You know, if I could buy whatever I want, I think I would be satisfied." Yet, have you ever seen a person who has it all that was really happy?

God says, "He who is full loathes honey, but to the hungry even what is bitter tastes sweet." That comes from the book of wisdom, Proverbs 27:7.

And, it really is wisdom. Think about your life today. Is there one thing that you have longed for, worked for, hoped for, dreamed for that has made you really satisfied longer than a few months or perhaps years?

I remember when my husband and I were first married. We were on a very tight budget. Charlie was still in college, and our funds were limited. We spent $15 a week for groceries and never went out to eat. But one day, our first pet, a little parakeet named Zeke, breathed his last breath and fell to the bottom of the cage. I was crushed. I cried until Charlie came home from class. He tried to comfort me and then said, "Let's go bury Zeke and then I'll buy you a hamburger." (Now remember, we never went out to eat, so this was a treat.) We went out and buried the little bird. Then we went to the local hamburger place and bought hamburgers. Although I was sad, having a hamburger was a special moment.

Today, a hamburger is easy to come by. There is nothing special about it, and the last thing it could ever do would be to make me feel loved and special in a painful time.

Now, I require far more. Then, the simple delight of having something so scarce was a very special treat.

Often, as we grow older and our lives become more complex, we forget the joys of the honeycomb God speaks of in Proverbs. We forget the joys of simple things. When is the last time you made a "moment" out of a simple thing?

I'd like to give you a few ideas that will bring you back to a time of simple pleasures and moments that will satisfy.

1. Take a walk at night with someone special and talk about the stars. Talk about the people who looked up and saw those same stars long ago.
   - Abraham, the night before he went out into a land he didn't know . . .
   - Moses, the night before he crossed the Red Sea . . .
   - Joseph, the night He left to take his wife, Mary, and baby Jesus into Egypt . . .
   - Jesus, as He went up into a quiet place . . .
2. Fix a simple meal of beans and cornbread and ask someone you want to get to know to share it with you in front of your fireplace. Drop the pretense. Forget the best china and silver. Make it a simple moment.
3. Take a rose to the home of a friend who is having a hard time. Leave it in her car or on her front steps, with a note that says, "Just because I love you."
4. Clip cartoons that remind you of something you have shared and send them to someone you love. I like to clip diet cartoons for my friends who are always with me on the eternal search for the skinny kingdom.

Ask God to give you a heart that responds to the simple things in life. If you catch yourself needing more and more and spending more and more and you just don't find anything that really tastes good to you, then you need to stop and pray this wonderful prayer found in Proverbs 30:7–9:

> Two things I ask of you, O Lord;
> do not refuse me before I die:
> Keep falsehood and lies far from me;
> give me neither poverty nor riches,
> but give me only my daily bread.
> Otherwise I may have too much and disown you
> and say, "Who is the Lord?"
> Or I may become poor and steal,
> and so dishonor the name of my God.

WEEK 13 — TUESDAY
SAVING ANOTHER

When is the last time you tried to save someone? I don't mean by grabbing them out of a river or by pulling them from a burning car, but by really trying to apply enough pressure in another's life so that he would see that Jesus Christ is the only way to God?

Think about it. Do you have a wife, or husband, mother, child, or friend who has never made a move toward your Lord?
- Have you talked and prayed, gotten others to pray, put their names on prayer lists, talked some more, and yet, they just won't be saved?

- Have you heard preachers say, "There is blood on your hands"?
- Have you heard others say, "Someday they will scream from Hell, 'Why didn't you tell me?'"
- Have you hurt with guilt and been panicked as you have tried to bring that precious one to salvation?

Well, if you have, then no doubt you have failed and no doubt you don't feel good about it.

There's a great verse in Psalm 49 that puts the whole thing in perspective. "No man can redeem the life of another or give to God a ransom for him—the ransom for a life is costly, no payment is ever enough" (vv. 7–8).

All your blood, sweat, and tears will do nothing to bring about the redemption of the soul of one you love. That is God's job. Your job is to love and to pray.

God gives us a mandate in Ephesians that is powerful. He says, "Let all bitterness and wrath and anger and clamor and slander be put away from you along with all malice. And be kind to one another, tender-hearted, forgiving each other, just as God in Christ also has forgiven you. Therefore be imitators of God, as beloved children; and walk in love, just as Christ also loved you, and gave Himself up for us, an offering and a sacrifice to God as a fragrant aroma" (4:31–5:2 NASB).

There is no amount of coercion or manipulation or threatening that can save the soul of one you love. You are to love in truth and pray in power.

That is what Barbara Johnson, the author of *Where Does a Mother Go to Resign*, had to do. She was the mother of four boys. The eldest, a sweet Christian, was killed in Viet Nam, the next, another precious Christian, was killed in an automobile accident . . . and then her dear third son wandered away into the homosexual lifestyle. Barbara wept, pled, retreated, and fought her own battle to survive. Her son got worse. In fact, he walked away from the family, not to be heard from for eleven years. Barbara prayed faithfully for her beloved, lost son while she continued to reach out and minister to women who found themselves in the same situation she was in. Finally, in the eleventh year, her son came home. He denounced his lifestyle, turned his life completely to the Lord, and today ministers with his mother to families torn apart by homosexuality.

Barbara loved her son dearly, but she, like you, had no power to save.

If you are wrestling with an unsaved loved one today, why not lay down the fight and give it to the Lord. He says "The battle is mine." Take on the challenge of loving and praying and leave the results to God.

I think it would be good if we prayed together right now. This situation is so hard.

Father, in our hearts, we long to be able to make our loved ones come to you. And yet, we know that it is your Spirit who draws all those who will come. Thank you for taking the responsibility off of our shoulders. Give us willing hearts, ready to release those who are dearest to us into your care. I pray in Jesus' name. Amen.

WEEK 13 — WEDNESDAY
YOU MAKE ME SO . . .

When is the last time you said to someone close to you, "You make me so mad"? Was it today? Yesterday? Have you said it often? You know, for some of us "You make me so mad" is just a natural part of our vocabulary.

Maybe you're wondering, "What's so wrong with that? He does make me so mad. He leaves his dirty clothes all over the floor, never admits when he is wrong, and won't get up to wipe the kid's nose. You bet he makes me mad!"

Well, I understand that you *think* he makes you mad. He may be insensitive, lazy, and even difficult. But, he *doesn't* make you mad. If you are mad, you are choosing to be mad.

So, again you are probably wondering, what difference does it make, it doesn't change the situation! That's true, but if you recognize that "You make me " puts all the power into his hands and leaves you powerless, you might be more interested in listening to what I have to say.

God knew, because of this fallen world, we would have pain in our relationships. Friends would disagree. Parents and children would not see eye-to-eye and husbands and wives would get on one another's nerves. He also knew that blaming the other person for the way we feel and for what we do would be characteristic of our behavior.

I mean, look at Adam. "This woman that you gave me . . . caused me to eat of the fruit of the tree." And look at us today . . . "This husband that you gave me makes me so mad." Or this wife . . . or this friend.

In Ephesians 4:26, God acknowledges the fact that at times we will be angry. He says, "Be angry . . ." He doesn't say, "So-and-so will make you angry." He says, "Be angry and sin not." There is a time to express feelings of frustration, hurt, and anger, but it is to be done with a view toward letting the sun go down on a clear slate. If you hang on to the fact that someone else makes you angry, then there is no way you can do anything about it. If they make you angry, then they can do that to you over and over again. But if you choose to be responsible for your anger, then you can learn to act appropriately, in line with God and His word.

Let's say your child cut up in the grocery store. You take him out in the parking lot and say, "You make me so mad every time you act that way." You have just let that little child know that he knows exactly where you keep your goat and he can get it any time he cuts up. If you would say instead, "I am angry with your behavior and we are going to deal with it right now. This is what you did that was unacceptable. This is what I am going to do about it. Once I have done it, then I will not continue to bring it up." It is over. You are in control of your emotions and of the situation.

God says we are to be transformed by the renewing of our minds through the Word. That means we are responsible to allow God's Word to change the way we think. Nowhere in all of Scripture will you find God saying anything except you are responsible for your own behavior. So, it simply is not true that anyone makes you angry. They may do things and you may choose to be angry about them. That keeps the responsibility where it belongs, in your corner.

I know this is tough. When I get irritable and speak harshly, I don't want to think that I am responsible for that. I prefer to think that someone else has caused me to have a righteous indignation to their behavior. But, in truth, I am irritable because I do not choose to control my emotions.

Well, my friend, let me meddle in your life just a little . . .
* Who do you blame for your bad moods?
* Whom have you given the power to hit your hot button? Are you courageous enough to take that power back today?

Are you trusting enough to ask God to show you that you are responsible for your own reactions? Are you honest enough to admit to yourself that no one makes you anything? Whatever you are, you have chosen to be!

WEEK 13 — THURSDAY
GOD CAN REPAIR YOU

It seems that "giving up" on ourselves is one of the best things we do. When I first became a Christian over nineteen years ago, I became so discouraged every time I made a mistake or sinned. If I lost my temper, I would ache for days. If I became critical, I would believe there was no hope for me to become a godly woman. I felt all I did was try and fail.

Then one day I read two special Scriptures. I certainly didn't know where to find it by myself, but I had a big Bible open on a table in the living room and it was opened to the Psalms. (I guess I thought that would help me be spiritual.) As I read, I thought, "Do you really mean that?" Listen to these words: "Thy vows are binding upon me, O God; I will render thank offerings to Thee. For Thou hast delivered my soul from death, [surely you can keep] my feet from stumbling, so that I may walk before God in the light of the living" (Ps. 56:12–13 NASB).

God showed me once and for all that His vows were on me and that He was committed to finish what He had begun in my life . . . and not only that, He would make beauty out of the broken parts of me. If He had saved me, surely He could keep me from falling. Understanding that literally changed my perspective.

There's a sweet story told by Corrie ten Boom that illustrates this same principle in another way. Corrie told it this way:

In Russia, many people lived in a certain apartment house. The basement of the house was filled with the junk of all the families. Amongst the junk was a beautiful harp, which nobody had been able to fix. One snowy night, a tramp asked if he could sleep in the building. The people cleared a space for him in the corner of the basement and he was happy to stay there.

In a little while, the people heard beautiful music coming from the basement. The owner of the harp rushed downstairs and found the tramp playing it.

"But how could you repair it? We couldn't," he said.

The tramp smiled and replied, "I made this harp years ago and when you make something, you can repair it."

Then Corrie goes on to say, "Lord, you made me. What a joy that You are willing and able to repair me."

Well, my friend, I just want to encourage you if you feel rather broken and unfixable today. Maybe you have tried to fix yourself or you have let someone who doesn't know you as well as your heavenly Father tell you what you should do to be fixed and you're frustrated because you're not getting any better. Why don't you quit looking in all the wrong places and take your struggles and brokenness to the Lord. His vows are upon you. He has saved you from death, He promises to keep your foot from slipping, and not only that, He can fix whatever might be broken in you.

Why don't we just commit it to Him right now . . .

Father, thank you for letting us know that before we were even conceived, you knew the number of hairs on our heads and what we would look like. I come into your presence with a friend who needs to feel your healing touch in the broken areas of her life today. I pray you will cut through her defenses and good ideas and mend her brokenness as only You can. For Jesus' sake. Amen.

WEEK 13 — FRIDAY
WHEN YOU WANT TO RUN

Have you ever had the urge to run away? Do you ever think, "I could go to another city and start all over and maybe find some happiness"?

I think we have all had rash moments when we have wanted to just throw in the towel and leave it all behind. Very few of us do, but whenever we feel that way, it is usually because things just aren't going well. There are problems and hurts we can't make go away, so in desperation, we contemplate escape. None of that sounds very spiritual, but maybe you can identify anyway. That's why I believe the Lord made sure these words of David were recorded in Psalm 55. God knows how we feel when our hearts are wounded. No man ever described a wounded heart like David. Listen to what he wrote: "Oh, that I had wings like a dove! I would fly away and be at rest. Behold I would wander far away, I would lodge in the wilderness. I would hasten to my place of refuge from the stormy wind and tempest" (vv. 6–8 NASB).

I think it's interesting that David mentions a place of refuge. So many times we want to run away to find refuge. You know what I mean. When we cry out, "I've got to get out of here," or "I can't take this anymore, I've got to get away!" Yet, in Scripture we read where our refuge really is.

Psalm 91:1–4 says, "He who dwells in the shelter of the Most High will abide in the shadow of the Almighty. I will say to the LORD, 'My refuge and my fortress, my God in whom I trust!' . . . He will cover you with His pinions, and under His wings you may seek refuge; His faithfulness is a shield and bulwark" (NASB).

God says, "When you want to run away, run to me. When you don't think you can stand it anymore, cast it all on Me."

Think about it, my friend. If you want to run away today, you are seeking a way of escape. Isn't it something to realize that, if you are a believer, the way of escape is in your heart. You don't have to run away. The very One Who is your refuge and your fortress is in you.

And in that same Psalm where David cried out with a broken heart, Psalm 55, he writes: "Cast your burden upon the LORD, and He will sustain you; He will never allow the righteous to be shaken" (v. 22 NASB).

Do you feel shaky because your whole world feels like it's caving in? Does your heart hurt so badly you think you will die if you don't get relief? Well there is an answer that will allow you to face this day in quietness and confidence. God says, "Cast that burden on me and I will sustain you."

It will feel as if you have put all your might into carrying a load too heavy for you. And when you drop it into the Lord's hands, your muscles get weak and you feel as if you will fall. God says at that very moment of release when you have peeled your fingers back and relaxed your muscles . . . at that very moment when you are as weak as water . . . He will sustain you and hold you up. You will not be shaken!

My friend, maybe you are in the midst of getting together a few things so you can get out of there and leave your situation behind. Why not take a moment, be still and know that the answer to all of your conflict lies within your very heart. Why not stop right now and let that burden of your broken heart drop into His hands and feel His sustaining strength surge through you as you give it all up to Him.

WEEK 14 — MONDAY
MY LAST DAY

Sometimes when I am reading through the newspaper, I read the obituaries and I often wonder, "Did this person know he was living his last day yesterday?" I'm sure some were so ill that they knew their time was short but others, no doubt, were taken by surprise when they woke up in the arms of Jesus.

I wonder if they had known the hours were ticking away, if they would have lived life differently. How about you . . . if you knew that today were your last day on earth, what would you do, where would you go, who would you see?

I think if this were my last day, I would want to spend it with the people I love the most. I would would want to assure and reassure them that nothing they ever have done or ever could do would sever my love for them. No problem or disagreement would be worth holding on to. I would just want to enjoy giving them enough love to sustain them after I was gone.

How about you . . . how would you want to spend today if this were your last day on earth?

What was the last thing our Lord Jesus did before his hands were bound and he was led to his death? Read Luke 22:50–51:

And one of them struck the servant of the high priest, cutting off his right ear. But Jesus answered, "No more of this!" And he touched the man's ear and healed him.

As Amy Carmichael notes in her book, *Edges of His Ways*: "The last thing the Lord Jesus did before His hands were bound was to heal."[1]

Have you ever asked yourself, "If I knew this were the last thing I should do, what would I do?" I have never found the answer to that question. There are so very, very many things that we would want to do for those whom we love that I do not think we are likely to be able to find the chief one of all these. So the best thing is just to go on simply doing each thing as it comes as well as we can.

Our Lord Jesus spent much time in healing sick people, and, in the natural course of events, it happened that the last thing He did with His kind hands was to heal a bad cut. (I wonder how they could have the heart to bind His hands after that.) In this, as in everything, He left us an example that we should follow in His steps. Do the thing that this next minute—this next hour—brings you to do faithfully, lovingly, and patiently; and then the last thing you do, before power to do is taken away from you, (if that should be) will be only the continuation of all that went before.

My friend, today, for starters, before you leave home, tell everyone who

71

lives there you love them. Never leave in a quarrelsome, hateful way. If they have already scattered, make a point to give them a call and simply say, "I love you." Or, leave a note . . . or do something to express your love.

We have *today* to leave a legacy of kindness and goodness. With all that our Lord endured during His last hours on earth, He took the time to touch the life of a simple servant who was in pain. It was natural to the way He lived.

What is natural in your life? Do you have the time today to act in kindness? Or, perhaps the question should be, "Do you have the time not to?"

WEEK 14 — TUESDAY
TESTING

I recently decided to take a postgraduate course. I thought I could go back to school and increase my knowledge and maybe even come up with a graduate degree that would give me some extra credentials. Well, I took lots of notes and studied hard, but when it came to test time I realized that I was not being tested in order to succeed, but instead, the tests were designed to make me fail. Now, that may seem a bit paranoid, but I've taken enough tests to know how they look when the goal is success for the student. This particular test was full of trick questions and was formatted in a difficult-to-follow sequence. Needless to say, I did not ace this course. In fact, I finally withdrew, feeling a little like a forty-four-year-old failure. But, as often happens, I learned a lesson.

When all was said and done, I thought, "I'm really grateful that when God puts me through a test, He always wants me to succeed." His goal is never for me or you to fail. All the way through Scripture that has been consistent with His character.

Consider these words from Deuteronomy 8:

> Remember how the LORD your God led you all the way in the desert these forty years, to humble you and to test you in order to know what was in your heart, whether or not you would keep his commands. He humbled you, causing you to hunger and then feeding you with manna, which neither you nor your fathers had known, to teach you that man does not live on bread alone but on every word that comes from the mouth of the LORD. (vv. 2–3)

How many times have you been in a test in which you found that you were in need? You had a real need for God to supply something. You felt stripped of all comfort and you were devoid of all resources. Then, the very God who allowed you to be tested by need, was the one who gave you the supply.

I love that part where the Scriptures say, "He humbled you, causing you to hunger and then feeding you with manna . . . to teach you that man does not live by bread alone."

In my own life, when my need has been the greatest, my understanding of God has always deepened.

A couple of years ago I went through a little trial when I developed an optic neuritis. Basically, that is an inflammation of the optic nerve that is quite painful and often does a lot of damage. After several weeks of pain and blindness in that eye, my vision began to return slowly . . . and then it stopped healing. I can remember the day I realized that my vision was permanently impaired. I was in need. My perception was distorted and I had difficulty doing some of the things I usually did. Then the Lord fed me with manna. In time, He showed me that one eye would compensate for the other. And, He tenderly reminded me that I was going through this problem to see what was in my heart . . . to see if the faith I so freely proclaimed on the good days was still there on the bad days.

Whatever you are going through today, maybe you just need a gentle reminder that, although God has made you hungry, He also assumes responsibility for feeding you manna. In the dark moments of our lives when we know no human source will do, God is there to provide.

WEEK 14 — WEDNESDAY
THE BROKEN PLATE

There is a wonderful song we have all heard in our Christian experience that says a lot to you and to me today. It is simple:

I have decided to follow Jesus,
I have decided to follow Jesus,
I have decided to follow Jesus
No turning back, no turning back.

That phrase, "no turning back," always captures my heart. Because, like you, I have days when I want to turn back.

Sometimes I want to retreat to the safety of being average and to the comfort zone of just looking after me and mine. Do you relate to that? Do you ever want to just "turn back" . . . oh, not from relationship to the Father through Jesus, but from those hard things He challenges you to do.

Max Lucado describes such an encounter in human terms:

It was midnight in Dalton, Georgia, as I stood in a dimly lit phone booth making a call to my folks. My first summer job away from home wasn't panning out as it was supposed to. The work was hard. My two best friends had quit and gone back to Texas, and I was bunking in the Salvation Army until I could find an apartment.

For a big, tough nineteen year old, I sure felt small. The voices of my mom and dad never sounded so sweet. And although I tried to hide it, my loneliness was obvious. I had promised my parents that if they'd let me go, I'd stick it out for the whole summer. But now those three months looked like eternity.

As I explained my plight, I could tell my mom wanted me to come home. But just as she said, "Why don't you come . . ." my dad, who was on the extension, interrupted her. "We'd love for you to come back, but we've already broken your plate." (That was West Texas talk for "We love you, Max, but it's time to grow up.")

It takes a wise father to know when to push his son out of the nest. It's painful, but it has to be done. I'll always be thankful that my dad gave me wings and then made me use them.[2]

Well, there are a lot of applications we can make to Max's story. Maybe its time to tell one of your children that his plate has been broken. Or more than that, maybe it's time to realize what God is saying to you right now. Those gentle nudges you are experiencing may be the hand of God giving you a little shove so you will try the wings He has given you.

In Deuteronomy 32:11, God describes an eagle as she deals with her young and compares it to Himself: "Like an eagle that stirs up its nest and hovers over its young, that spread its wings to catch them and carries them on its pinions."

When a young eagle is ready to be taught to fly, the mother removes all the soft feathers from the nest, leaving only the prickly, thorny branches from which she has made it. Then she stirs up the nest, making a great fuss and literally pushing the little eaglets out to fly. As they squawl and flutter while they plummet to the ground, she flies underneath them and catches them on her strong wings. She calms them, reassures them, and then puts them through the ordeal again and again, until finally they can fly.

Well . . . you may feel as if you are plummeting through space today, not sure there is anyone there to catch you. Or, you may feel as if your plate has been broken and you're going to have to stand tall in a situation where you really feel small.

I just want to encourage you to hang on. Your God, who knows every whisper of your heart, is hovering over you, beneath you, and around you. You may feel frightened and maybe even a little panicked. But, my friend, our God will not let you fall. Keep that thought in front of you as you feel the wind in your face and see the fast approaching rocks below.

In a moment, if you will listen . . . you will hear the flapping of great wings.

WEEK 14 — THURSDAY
KINDNESS

Kindness is a word that reflects the very best in our Christian values. The Greeks explain kindness as "the disposition of mind which thinks as much of its neighbor as it does of itself." Kindness is as concerned with the feelings of other people as it is with its own feelings. Kindness takes an outward look more often than it takes an inward look.

I think that you and I would do well to stop and take a moment to consider how kind we are. What have you been thinking about today? Have your thoughts been about what will face you or have you been thinking about how you might bless the lives of those you encounter? I know . . . I know . . . that's one of those super spiritual questions we don't even bother to really answer.

But let's dig a little deeper. Let's get a little more honest. Is there something in your life you dwell on a great deal? Do you think a lot about what has happened to you? Do you spend a lot of time analyzing what has happened and why? Is a lot of your prayer time, talk time, reading time taken up with your problem? If so, then let me ask you, "How kind are you?"

I really believe that is a fair question because if you are absorbed in your own life and your own problems, then no matter how nice you are, you really are not kind to other people. You can be sweet, but not helpful. I have met many very nice people who are so absorbed in themselves and their difficult backgrounds that they are unable to be kind.

Kindness is active interest in others, not just a passing hello. Kindness is going out of your way to come alongside or to lend a hand to someone who needs you. If you are absorbed with yourself, you will never see that others are in need too.

There is a very special woman who lives in California. I would call her kind. Her name is Carolyn Koons. She was on a mission trip to Mexico where she discovered a little five-year-old boy who was in jail for killing his infant brother. The truth later came out that the child's mother had done the killing and had accused her own son. Carolyn is single, so she arranged for a couple back in the States to adopt this little boy. Once she finally managed to get him out of prison, the couple was unable to adopt him, so Carolyn took him home and adopted him herself. He has now graduated from a Christian college and is doing well. He freely gives credit for who he is to his adopted mother, who extended him kindness.

But that isn't all of the story. Carolyn Koons had every reason to be a total basket case. Her father tried to kill her on several occasions because he discovered she was not his child. When she was a teenager he abandoned her beside the road when the family moved. She remembers the pre-teen birthday when it was customary for the child celebrating to receive a bicycle. Her brothers had each received shiny, new bikes on their birthdays. But on her birthday, her father gave her a broken, rusty, dilapidated bike. Her young heart was broken. Rejection was the sum total of her existence. She was rebellious and difficult until she accepted Christ as the Lord and Savior of her life. At that point, she slowly began to change. And today, her life is filled with kindness. She actively reaches out to other people. In fact, she had raised her young Mexican son and written a book about that experience before she ever mentioned the problems in her own background.

Well, how are you doing with your kindness today? Are you actively looking for ways to serve others, or are you actively contemplating how you might find service for your needs? If Jesus Christ is in your life, then you have every reason to be able to reach out to others. The Scriptures say in 2 Corinthians 5:17, "If anyone is in Christ, he is a new creation; the old has gone, the new has come!" I honestly believe that the new things that have come give us eyes to see the needs of others and freedom from the old things that keep us focused on ourselves.

WEEK 14 — FRIDAY
DEEP WATERS

I was looking through some quotes the other day and I came across this one that touched something in my heart.

God brings men into deep waters, not to drown them but to cleanse them.

I like that. And I hope it says something to you, especially if you feel the waters rising around you.

Often when we feel the lapping of the waves around our knees, then our waists, and finally our necks, we believe the inevitable result will be drowning.

75

But when we feel that way, we forget who controls the waves. We forget the eternal purposes of God are often beyond our comprehension.

Luke 8:22–25 records a story I can relate to . . . and I believe you can, too.

> Now it came about on one of those days, that [Jesus] and His disciples got into a boat, and He said to them, "Let us go over to the other side of the lake." And they launched out. But as they were sailing along He fell asleep; and a fierce gale of wind descended upon the lake, and they began to be swamped and to be in danger. And they came to Him and woke Him up, saying, "Master, master, we are perishing!" And being aroused, He rebuked the wind and the surging waves, and they stopped, and it became calm. And he said to them, "Where is your faith?" (NASB)

When the waters of problems begin to swirl, I don't know about you, but I want to see a lighthouse and land. I sometimes have a hard time seeing "the promise of things hoped for, the evidence of things not seen." And yet, when it comes to the Lord, He delights to see us take Him at His Word when the water is the deepest. And there is a reason for that . . . He is doing a cleansing work through the rising waters. Did you get that? He is doing a *cleansing work* through the rising waters.

Think about the impurities you have asked the Lord to remove from your life. Have you said, "Lord, I really need to be more patient"? Or have you said, "Lord, I really need to control my tongue"? Or, have you said, "Lord, my temper is just too strong . . . I need you to help me." Then you can be sure He will use the rising waters to cleanse you.

If you need more patience, it is the nature of God to allow waters of tribulation to wash that out of you. You will find that you are confronted with situations that keep bringing your impatience to the surface so it can be washed away.

I can remember when I had three little boys underfoot that patience sometimes ran thin. When they fought with each other or wouldn't sit still, I found that I had very little patience for their antics. But as I weathered those experiences and have been cleansed of some of my impatience, I find I can exhibit the very quality I wanted all along . . . I can be patient. If the Lord had not allowed me to go through the rising waters of dealing with these three little boys, I doubt I would be as patient as I am today.

My friend, if you feel the waves of difficulty and impending trial lapping at your feet, I want to encourage you to remember a couple of very important facts:

1. *There is more going on than you can see.* You are looking at the water and God is looking at you. He sees the water as only an agent of change to be used to make you more into His own image. While you study the waves inch by inch, He is studying you. God promises in Isaiah 43:2, "When you pass through the waters, I will be with you; and when you pass through the rivers, they will not sweep over you."
2. *When you ask the Lord to work in your life, He will do just that.* He will work to fashion you with pressure, difficulty, and the lapping of waves, if need be. His goal is to bring you to the end result . . . not to make you comfortable in the process.

A good thought to remember is, "God brings men into deep waters, not to drown them but to cleanse them." You're not drowning . . . you are being cleansed. So hold on . . . and don't give up!

WEEK 15 — MONDAY
BLAME

Well, my friend, I think it would be good for us to meddle in our thought-lives today. I am discovering a truth that is one of those "hard sayings" that I don't like but I know is important. And that is: "I have no one to blame for the way I feel or the way I act." Let me say that again: "I have no one to blame for the way I feel or the way I act." I am responsible. And so are you.

Now, let's talk about how this translates into your life today . . . and mine, too. We will both face some sort of disappointment. Someone will not live up to our expectations. When that happens, we will probably feel hurt, anger, or irritation. And our first reaction might be to say, "So-and-so made me feel sad, or mad." But the truth is "So-and-so" may have been as wrong as wrong can be, but the way you responded to what she did is totally your responsibility.

Let's talk about neighbors and children and how they cause problems sometimes. Nothing can cause two mothers to get at odds any quicker than a problem between their children. And the minute blame begins to be assigned to another child, you are avoiding the responsibility that you and your child should assume.

When I was about ten years old, I built a Christmas tree fort out of old Christmas trees that people had thrown away. I worked all day on it, and about four o'clock a little girl whom I had never liked came to see what I was doing. Since I wasn't too pleased with her being there, I didn't welcome her. In fact, I told her to go away. She wouldn't leave and actually tried to enter my fort without permission. I tried to stop her by pushing her shoulder . . . but I missed and hit her nose. She was a fragile little thing and I have always been built like an Amazon. So needless to say, she had to go and bleed . . . and run home and tell her mother. I knew they would be at my doorstep before long, so I went in and explained to my parents what had happened.

They immediately talked with me about my responsibility . . . never mind that this little girl had made my life miserable for a long time. I had acted irresponsibly, and if she had been the meanest kid in six counties, I was responsible for my actions. So off we went to her doorstep, so I could assume responsibility.

I'll never forget. She came to the door looking like the walking wounded and although I really wanted to punch her again for looking like such a martyr, I apologized and assumed responsibility for my actions. Mind you, she smiled knowingly and never apologized for harassing me, but I had done what was right and felt better.

Her actions were wrong, but I had given her an excuse to justify her behavior by being wrong myself.

Who do you have in your life who knows exactly where you park your goat every night and makes a real point to get it whenever possible?

Who do you allow to have power over your emotions? Who has access to your "hot buttons"?

Friend, you are responsible for your attitudes and behavior. Whenever

77

you choose to carelessly spout off or react, you have just absolved the other person of his responsibility. We give other people permission to control our emotions and to set the agenda for our moods when we are irresponsible with our behavior. If a spouse, friend, mate, or child can point to your poor behavior as an excuse for his own wrongdoing, then responsibility on both sides has been thrown out the door.

You can't do anything about another's carelessness . . . but you can assume responsibility for the way *you* behave.

Why not begin thinking about how responsible your attitude and behavior is today? When you really begin to take a look at these things, you'll be amazed at the changes that will come into your relationships . . . and you will begin to feel better about the way you behave.

WEEK 15 — TUESDAY
LETTING THE LIGHT OUT

There is an old song that says, "Let the sun shine in, face it with a grin . . . smilers never lose and frowners never win . . ." And it is true that we must have light in our lives to face whatever comes. But, have you ever thought about the light you already have in your life and the way you allow it to shine out?

In the Living Bible, Mark 4:21 quotes Jesus as saying, "When someone lights a lamp, does he put a box over it to shut out the light? Of course not! The light couldn't be seen or used. A lamp is placed on a stand to shine and be useful."

If Jesus is in you, then you have a light that needs to shine . . . in your home, at work and among your friends. But all too often we allow boxes to block the light.

Let's talk about the boxes in your life today. What do you have covering the light of Christ? What is standing between the light that is in you and the people who share your world?

How about the box of disobedience? That's a "biggy." Are you letting your resistance to obeying God block out the light of Christ in your life?

What has God expressly told you to do that you are holding out on?

Has He asked you to go make things right with someone?

Is there a friend or family member you know needs to hear from you, but you keep putting it off?

Do you need to make restitution of a broken or borrowed item? God has brought it to your mind . . . over and over . . . yet you just keep putting it off?

It is hard to shine when you are refusing to obey. If you want your light to really shine, then you need to choose to do what God has said to do, or else you might as well wear a box over your light . . . because it is not shining through.

Or, maybe you try to be obedient but the box of ego is in your way. I have decided that the word ego needs to be spelled "sin." A person whose ego has to be stroked continually is a person whose light is under the box of self.

Whether ego is found in a male or a female, the same root problem blocks the light of Christ's Spirit. Do you have to be stroked by your mate or your friends to feel important? Do you need for your children or co-workers to admire you to feel good about you? Then you probably have an ego box blocking the light of Christ to their lives that they desperately need to see. I'm not so out of touch that I don't think we all need people in our lives who think we are special, but I do believe that the notion of making a person feel good about himself by stroking his ego plays to the self in each of us. If I allow my ego to control my response to another person, then every time I let it get out of control, there is no way she can see the light of Christ shine through.

How about the box of resentment? Do you resent anyone in your life? You know, I have experienced that feeling and nothing makes me feel worse . . . nothing blocks the light within me from coming out any more than resentment. I know I am resentful when the mention of another person's name makes me feel cold and indifferent. I know I am resentful when I can't think of anything good about that person. I know I am resentful when I just don't want to pray for that person's success and well-being.

How on earth is the light of Christ going to shine through that kind of block?

Jesus has chosen to confine Himself to the bodies of believers. He has chosen to shine through us to a hard and darkened world. If you and I block the light with boxes of disobedience, ego, and resentment . . . the people we want to view the light of Christ the clearest will only have a dim view of Him.

Why not go before the Lord and ask Him to show you what blocks the sun in your life. . . .

WEEK 15 — WEDNESDAY
RUN ON, MY FRIEND

Running can become very tedious if there is a long way to run and there are no cheering crowds along the road. In the past year, I have been acutely aware of the tedium of running the race. I know I've been called to run it. I know I've been equipped to run it. And yet, there have been days when all I could see was hot pavement and steep inclines with no relief in sight. Maybe you can relate. Maybe today is that kind of day for you.

I've kept on running on those days because there have been a few who have made it their business to yell out from the sidelines, "Run on . . . don't quit . . . I need for you to keep running so I can follow."

In the Scriptures, we read, "Therefore, since we are surrounded by such a great cloud of witnesses, let us throw off everything that hinders and the sin that so easily entangles, and let us run with perseverance the race marked out for us" (Heb. 12:1).

The scene is a common one. It is a race. The runners are straining every fiber of their being to run. The crowds are cheering them on. And if you are like me, you can picture yourself in both positions. I have been out there running and know that if someone had not yelled, "Keep on running, Jan!" I might have sat down and missed out on my race. And I've also stood on the sidelines and watched someone I love strain to run and I've wanted to call out the right words, but sometimes I've not succeeded.

Learning to encourage is an art that we in the body of Christ need to pursue with the zeal we pursue the souls of men and women. We need to be able to come alongside to extend that hand, to shout, "Keep on keeping on!" . . . to say in a hundred ways, "I believe in you." It is a gift we desperately need to give each other.

There are some truths I've learned about encouragement I would like to share with you. And I would ask you to apply them as you sit in the stands and

79

watch those running who need you to yell, "I believe in you. Keep on!" The winners out in front aren't the only ones who need your cheers. The runner at the back, the runner who has fallen, the runner whose lungs scream with exhaustion need you to call out as well. Ask God to give you eyes to see the one who needs you to call, "Run on, my friend!"

1. *When you encourage, always be sincere.* Flowery words blow away like the breeze and the one who needs them will be able to tell whether they were really sincere.
2. *Use the Word of God whenever possible.* There is a gracious power in the Word that pierces through a person's mentality to his very being. Use Scripture to remind your runner how very precious he is to God. Ask the Lord to give you wisdom in your choice of Scripture because someone who is weary doesn't need a lot of strong conviction at that moment. The Lord will deal with other areas in his life in due time. Your job is to encourage.
3. *Pray for your runner.* Let him know that he matters enough for you to faithfully take him before the Lord in prayer. Just a simple, "I prayed for you yesterday," from someone you didn't dream was praying is a wonderful surprise and a priceless gift.
4. *Do unexpected things that say, "I'm cheering you on."* A note, a flower, an appropriate card, a small gift are all ways to say, "You are special enough to me for me to take the time to encourage you."
5. *Let your encouragement be there for a lifetime.* Periodically continuing to call out, "Hey, I'm for you! I see your potential. I see your growth in the Lord," can meet a person's need even when you don't have any knowledge that this is what they need to hear.

Maybe you're thinking, "That's great! I need to do that, but frankly, right now I wish someone would call out to me. I'm weary and the uphill climb is about to get me." Well, dear runner, here is a Scripture someone put in my hand and encouraged me and now I want to put in yours. "The Lord longs to be gracious to you; he rises to show you compassion" (Isa. 30:18). "Let us fix our eyes on Jesus . . . so that you will not grow weary and lose heart" (Heb. 12:2–3). There is a race marked out for you. Run on!

WEEK 15 — THURSDAY
RUNNING BEFORE THE LORD

I was reading Paul's familiar words in Philippians 4:12 and for the first time, a sentence in that verse jumped out and grabbed my attention. Listen to what he says, "I know how to get along with humble means, and I also know how to live in prosperity; in any and every circumstance I have learned the secret of being filled and going hungry, both of having abundance and suffering need" (NASB).

I have always focused on the fact that Paul knew the secret of making it through the tough, lean times. But, the words "I also know how to live in prosperity" are powerful, especially for those of us who live in America. Often we let our guilt for having so much blind us to the idea that it takes just as much of God's grace to live with "things" and "luxury" as it does to live without and to experience want.

When you have ready access to resources the greatest temptation you will face is to run ahead of the Lord. I know. I have done it and every time it has cost me dearly.

No matter what you are planning to do today, make sure that you are doing it at the urging of the Lord, not just because you have the money, the organization, or the people to do it.

Listen to these words of an old saint of God, Amy Carmichael:

> *Thou hast enough to pay thy fare?*
> *Well, be it so;*
> *But thou shouldst know, does thy God send thee there,*
> *Is that it all? To pay thy fare?*
> *There's many a coin flung lightly down*
> *Brings back a load of care.*
> *It may cost what thou knowest not*
> *To bring thee home from there.*[1]

Those are powerful words: "It may cost what thou knowest not to bring thee home from there."

Are you paying the price today for launching out into something God never intended for you to get into? Did you jump in because the money was available? Or was just the right person there at the right time . . . and now you are paying the price you never intended to pay.

You know we can't go back and fix situations where we have run ahead of the Lord because it all seemed so right . . . although, in our hearts there were reservations. But we can learn a lesson and be wiser with the next decision we have to make.

Here are some thoughts for you if you are teetering on the brink of jumping into something that looks like it just can't fail.

1. What is your deep heart motive . . . known only to you and to God?
2. Have you received clear direction from the Word, from prayer, from wise counselors?
3. Are you rushing to move because you fear the opportunity slipping away? If God is in it, and He wants it to be, will it get away?
4. Have you counted the cost? You know the only time you have to be concerned about the cost is when you have the resources to pay the price, but often we forget to check the hidden charges . . . things we would ordinarily check if our resources were not so unlimited.
5. As the last point to consider, has it crossed your mind that, "It may cost what thou knowest not to bring thee home from there"?

WEEK 15 — FRIDAY
LIVING IN HARMONY

There is a little Psalm in the Scriptures that always fascinates me, yet it is so short that I don't think the impact of it really comes through fully.

How good and pleasant it is when brothers live together in unity! It is like precious oil poured on the head, running down on the beard, running down on Aaron's beard, down upon the collar of his robes. It as if the dew of Hermon were falling on Mount Zion.

For there the Lord bestows his blessing, even life forevermore.
(Ps. 133)

The dictionary defines *harmony* as "a sympathetic relationship." It means I am sympathetic to your views and you are to mine, although we may hold different views and may handle ourselves very differently.

In this Psalm, harmony is described as precious as the fragrant anointing oil that was poured over Aaron's head, ran down onto his beard, and onto the collar of his robe. In the Old Testament, that anointing oil was used by Moses to anoint Aaron as the first high priest of Israel and to dedicate all the priests into God's service. Harmony, like this oil that poured all over Aaron, shows that we are dedicated to serve the Lord wholeheartedly.

Now, that is a very bold statement, but think about what Jesus said in John 13:35, "By this all men will know that you are my disciples, if you love one another."

Harmony that can only come when you love enough to be sympathetic to the other person's viewpoint is the mark that is as precious and fragrant and noticeable as the oil running down Aaron's hair and beard and clothes.

What would a visitor to your church encounter if he sat and listened quietly?

Or, let's get even more personal. What if he could listen in to your conversation as you drove home in the car?

Would he hear about the petty things that were irritating to you?

Would he hear your opinion of the pastor and staff and the way they conducted themselves?

Or would he hear you complain about the church not meeting the needs of people who are sick or who are experiencing difficulty?

I learned something a long time ago. When I begin to see an area that is deficient, the burden is mine to do something about—not mine to put on someone else who probably is already overworked.

Living together in harmony means that I have to be sympathetic to another's limitations and feelings. My expectations are just that . . . they are mine . . . not to be put on someone else in the body of Christ so they can gain my approval.

I need to ask you a question, as I have had to ask myself. What are you doing to promote harmony in the body of Christ? What words of soothing encouragement have you spoken in the last week? Are there issues you have tried to understand instead of confronting?

My friend, harmony doesn't just happen. Harmony takes concentration and a deep determination to compliment and extend mercy to your brother.

Today, as you talk with fellow-believers in Christ, remember the precious oil that ran down the beard of Aaron . . . and gently covered his whole body. Be determined that the words you say will be sympathetic, caring words that show the world harmony among believers.

WEEK 16 — MONDAY
DO NOT PROVOKE YOUR CHILDREN

Have you ever provoked your child?

Have you ever seen the anger flash in his eyes when you have said something you thought was perfectly innocent?

Well, I have, and because of that, I am working to communicate with my children. I have found that first I have to listen to the information I am receiving back from them. And then, I need to follow some basic rules that build respect.

Remember:

1. *Be genuinely interested in what your child is doing.*
2. *Be willing to talk when they are in a talking mood.* I have stayed up many nights with my son, the night owl, when I was so sleepy I thought I would drop. But I have learned that conversations with your children are too easy to miss if you have to have them when it's convenient for you.
3. *Value their opinions.* Don't be too quick to jump on their ideas that seem naive or radical. If they take an opposing political view, then hear them out. The best way to stop conversation is to belittle what they say.
4. *Joke with them.* I was walking across the parking lot with one of my sons, who was showing me a stain on his shirt. I said, "Well, honey, I guess I'll just have to shout it out." Then I reached over, grabbed his shirt, and shouted at it! He shook his head but had a broad smile on his face. Kids love the unpredictable as long as it's not embarrassing. (I never would have done that in front of his friends.)
5. *Be generous with "I love you."* They may think it's not cool right now for you to say it to them and they may rather die than say it back. But one thing is for sure . . . in days to come when they are sitting around talking about their parents, they won't be able to chime in with the one who complains, "My mom never said she loved me."
6. *Attack problems, never attack the person.* Always keep your correction centered on the situation and not on the character or personality of the child. Let's say you find cigarettes in his room and it's against the rules of the house to smoke. Talk with him about the violation of the rules, your disappointment, and your belief that he is too fine a person to continue to deceive you. Be firm but respectful.
7. *Be friendly to their friends.* Make your child's friends feel welcome. If you sense a problem with one of them, talk to your child about the problem but not about the personality of the friend.
8. *Say good-night.* End each day peacefully and make your last words sweet. Even if you have had a difficult day, be big enough to go to your child, no matter how old, tell him you love him, and say good-night.

The next time you see anger flash in your child's eyes, remember: You can build respect . . . if you will work to respect him.

WEEK 16 — TUESDAY
YOU MADE ME

I was reading the comics the other day and came across one of my favorite comic strips. It's "The Born Loser." There is a little girl with long dark curls who waltzes across the frames of this strip from time to time and her name is Hurricane. I think she reminds me of myself as a little girl, so her antics, which are often mischievous, give me a chuckle.

On this particular day, she was being dragged to the principal's office by her very stern teacher who was telling her, "You told a falsehood, Hurricane, and you're going to the principal's office!" Then we saw her being confronted by the principal with a very prim Miss Nurk behind her. He said, "Why did you lie, young lady?" "Miss Nurk made me!" "Made you?" Then Hurricane replied, "If she hadn't asked me the question, I wouldn't have fibbed."

Have you ever thought, "If she hadn't asked me about the situation, then I never would have spread that gossip. She asked, so what was I to do?"

It is so hard to confront the sin in our own lives because we can see so many contributing factors. There are many sins we could talk about, but I want to focus on one. It's one that I really believe is key, and that is the sin of rationalizing.

It is often so subtle that you do not recognize it, but it often shows itself like this. When you are confronted on anything from, "Did you leave the back door open?" to "Did you spread that rumor?" your first response is to defend yourself. It is natural. It comes to your mind quickly. But it will always block growth.

When you are defensive, you become like the three monkeys who hear no evil, see no evil, and speak no evil. The problem is you don't see, hear, or speak about your own sin. So, how on earth will you ever examine a problem you fail to acknowledge?

What has been said to you more than once? What recurring complaint have you heard from your family and friends? Have you been told you are bossy? Have you been told you are irritable? Have you been told . . . well, I'll let you fill in the blank. You get the point. Any time several people love you enough to risk confronting you and you excuse it because you just don't want to look at it, then you are defensive.

When you read through the New Testament, you will find defensiveness in its most virile form in the lives of the Pharisees and the government rulers. When John the Baptist confronted Herod, the ruler did not have the sense to listen and examine his lifestyle. He became defensive and violent instead. When Jesus confronted the Pharisees, they gnashed their teeth and turned in fury on Him, never stopping to look at their own sin.

When the Lord allows other people to point out a problem area in your life, have you thought He might be trying to get your attention for your own good? Could they possibly be His agent of change? Oh my friend, stop and listen to yourself today. If you are defensive, then you are like a walled fortress, impervious to penetration by the very truths that could transform your life if you would let them.

WEEK 16 — WEDNESDAY
UNREST IN THE NEST

Have you been feeling as if every time you get one situation under control, here comes something else to keep you stirred up? Have you felt as if you are being pushed out of a situation you thought was just right for you? If you have been going through this kind of upheaval, you are probably experiencing "Unrest in the Nest Syndrome."

Let me give you a little story that illustrates what I mean:

A farmer's attention was drawn to a bird that was busily engaged in building a nest. Unfortunately, the spot it had chosen was a heap of dead branches recently pruned from some trees. Realizing that this was a dangerous place for hatching a brood of songsters, the farmer destroyed the work of the industrious bird. The next day, the persistent mother-to-be tried again, and for a second time the farmer thwarted her efforts. On the third day the bird finally constructed her nest on a limb near the man's kitchen door. This time he gave an approving smile and let it remain. The unsafe pile of branches from which he had twice driven her was burned long before the bird's eggs were hatched. (Author unknown)

Our idea of a safe place and God's idea of a safe place can be two different things.

Are you in a job that seems just perfect for you, and yet, you know that the nest there is being stirred up? Maybe a new boss has come on board and your comfort zone is being squeezed to the point you feel you must leave. Could it be that God is stirring up your nest? Is it possible that He has something far beyond your imagination, just beyond your sight, that will better suit you? Can you think that maybe He is protecting you from some unknown occurrence you would never dream possible?

Are you a young person who is having doubts about the person you were just sure you should marry? Perhaps God is stirring up your nest, to protect you, to keep you from getting burned by a fire you don't even know is there. I would encourage you to heed the restlessness and questions you have. I have met more sad people than I care to remember who have said, "You know, I knew before we were ever married that I didn't love him, but it was just too much to think of calling it off." Better to deal with your sense of restlessness now than later.

Are you being uprooted from your home because of your husband's job transfer? Do you feel as if your nest is being dumped out on the ground just when you were feeling comfortable? Could it be that God knows something you don't, and for the protection and provision for your family, He is turning your nest upside down?

It is hard when God seems to uproot the nests we have tried so hard to build. It can be excruciatingly painful to see something you have poured your heart and soul into slip away from you, but there are times God must create unrest in your nest to protect you, to allow you to grow, to make you the person you are intended to be. Remember that His view of things allows Him to see the beginning from the end, the peaks and the valleys, and He knows what is best for you. He is simply saying, "Trust me."

If you feel as if all you do is flutter in mid-air with wings that are weak and wounded, and as if all your efforts are for naught, remember these words of the Psalmist:

I am still confident of this: I will see the goodness of the LORD in the land of the living. Wait for the LORD; be strong and take heart and wait for the LORD. (Ps. 27:13–14)

Our God is honor bound to make even the tearing up of our nests, the unraveling of our hopes and dreams, the canceling of our plans and appointments, to work together for our good. Remember that today as you struggle with a nest that feels shaky beneath your feet.

THINGS THAT HAVE TO GO

The apostle Paul always had a way of putting his finger on the things that really count. He may have written in long sentences, but you can't miss his plain-spoken, direct admonitions to believers.

In the 4th chapter of Ephesians, verses 31–32, he lists some things that have to go if you are a Christian. There is no "when it is convenient" or "from time to time" in his words. He simply makes a list of things that have to go.

First, there is bitterness. According to William Barclay, the Greeks defined this word as "long-standing resentment or as the spirit which refuses to be reconciled."[1] It is the nursing or brooding over insults and injuries that have been hurled our way by others. Paul knew the more we think about these things, the more deep-seated they will become. A good prayer to pray when you are plagued by this kind of problem is "Lord, teach me to forget!"

Another good practice is to say to yourself, "This is only an insult if I let it be. This is only an injury if I let it damage me." We, as believers, have the power within us to look beyond the pain of the moment to the promise of all things being made right. That is why we have the advantage of not having to play get back for the things that hurt us . . . or not having to hang on to hurts to make sure no one forgets. God says, "Give it to me. I will judge righteously."

Second, there are outbreaks of passion and long-lived anger. The Greeks had two words for anger. The first was *thumos* which is like a flame that flares and then goes out. The other is *orge*, an anger which has become a habit and is deep-rooted. Both are damaging. Paul says that whether you have a quick temper—you blow up and then everything is okay—or if you are a person who hangs on to your anger for a long time, they both have to go. There just aren't any loopholes for the comfort zones of our personalities.

I am more the quick *thumos* type of person. If I flare up in anger, I am over it just as quickly. And sometimes I can feel a little smug with my friends and family who take a little longer to come around. But Paul says both are sin.

The third trait that has to go is loud talking and insulting language. Loud talking or shouting does nothing to accomplish a point. If you have a point to make, don't ruin it by raising your voice. You have just lost your audience. And insulting language is unforgivable. Insults usually spring forth from anger and end in name-calling that puts another person down. What kind of argument can ever be won that way? James says it is impossible for sweet and bitter water to come from the same well. And so, it goes against all that is right for sweet and bitter words to come out of the same mouth.

When I read that passage in Ephesians and I see that Paul says, "Let *all* bitterness, anger, loud talking and insulting language be put away from you," I am shamed for the ways I have excused myself.

How about you? How many times have you shown a little temper and then excused yourself because "He made me. He was yelling at me"? Or when have you said, "But you don't know what she did. I don't think you would let her get by with it either." I know. I understand. I have the same emotions you have, but the Scripture does say *all*. And so putting away "all" must be possible.

In the wisdom of God, He knew that once we let a little anger, a little loud talking, a tiny insult into our behavior, then we are in trouble. And not only that, He says that if we are people set apart for God's purposes and plans, are we really different from the people who don't have the power of Christ within them?

Think about it as you go about your work today. Are there some things you need to just put away? Are there some habits you have rationalized, and yet, deep down inside, you know you shouldn't be allowing yourself the luxury of such actions? Then why not read Ephesians 4:25–32 and ask God to give you a heart to be serious about His Word?

WEEK 16 — FRIDAY
ANGER

I recently flew home from a speaking engagement and, since I am a confirmed people-watcher, I immediately noticed a young woman a few seats in front of mine. She was tense, she looked hostile, and on our two-hour flight, she consumed two cocktails in swift succession. She gave every indication of being angry by the way she held herself. And I could not help but wonder what she was angry about. Who had hurt her? Who had thwarted her? What did she want that she could not get?

Anger is something none of us can hide. It is like fire. It has to be dealt with or eventually it will flare up and be seen by people we don't even know are looking.

You may be thinking "I am not an angry person . . . I have never raised my voice to anyone." Well, that is not always the mark of anger.

Have you wanted something for a long time, but you have been thwarted every way you turn? And every time it comes up you seethe inside? Then you are habitually angry.

Do you take things so personally that you are upset with yourself a good deal of the time? Then you are angry.

Are you depressed because of hurt or disappointment? Then, believe it or not, you are angry. Depression that is non-medical is anger turned inward.

Anger can be defined as "habitual revenge." When you are angry, you are constantly planning revenge on yourself or someone else. And by the way, it is not just the affliction of the outspoken, vocal person. Anger can boil inside a quiet, sweet-tempered person for years and then flare at the strangest times.

Consider some of the following Scriptures on anger. God is very specific about how He feels about it.

A quick-tempered man does foolish things. (Prov. 14:17)

Better a patient man than a warrior, a man who controls his temper than one who takes a city. (Prov. 16:32)

A hot-tempered man stirs up dissension, but a patient man calms a quarrel. (Prov. 15:18)

And then there is this very convicting statement in Proverbs 19:11: "A man's wisdom gives him patience; it is to his glory to overlook an offense." Well, what kind of shape is your temper in today? Did you have a wild morning? Have you already blown your cool? Well, there is nothing you can do about the past, but repent, confess your wrong, and then decide you will get God's perspective on anger.

In Psalm 4:3–4 He gives us insight into what He wants from us . . . His children . . . His covenant people: "Know that the LORD has set apart the godly for himself; the LORD will hear when I call to him. In your anger do not sin; when you are on your beds, search your hearts and be silent."

If it is the glory of a man to overlook an offense, then it is important to prepare ahead of time to deal with it. While you are still in your bed tomorrow morning, ask the Lord to give you the grace to overlook an offense that might come your way during the day. And if there is a particular person you can count on to offend you, then ask Him for a special grace to overlook whatever is said or done. Anger, hot tempers, and hostility have never worked the righteousness of God (James 1:20).

WEEK 17 — MONDAY
INFERIORITY COMPLEX

In many ways, we all feel inferior to other people. I'm sure you can think of someone smarter, better looking, more spiritual, or wealthier than you are. And when you think of that person, you feel intimidated because you feel inferior. That happens to all of us from time to time. But if you are a person who constantly lives in that mode of thinking that you are inferior to just about everyone, then I would encourage you today.

You might think, "Oh, I don't feel inferior, I just don't like who I am." If so, you probably respond in some of the following ways:

1. *Copy cat.* Hiding behind sameness in dress or behavior, looking like one of "the crowd."
2. *Compensation.* Performing perfectly in an area where you can excel.
3. *Withdrawal.* Retreating from people in shyness.
4. *Obstinance.* Drving people away with your tough, crude behavior.
5. *Jokester.* Joking to hide your pain.

Why not take a moment to compare your thoughts to God's thoughts? "We do not dare to classify or compare ourselves with some who commend themselves. When they measure themselves by themselves and compare themselves with themselves, they are not wise" (2 Cor. 10:12).

"So then, men ought to regard us as servants of Christ and as those entrusted with the secret things of God. Now it is required that those who have been given a trust must prove faithful. I care very little if I am judged by you or by any human court; indeed, I do not even judge myself. My conscience is clear, but that does not make me innocent. It is the Lord who judges me" (1 Cor. 4:1–4).

"For you created my inmost being; you knit me together in my mother's womb. I praise you because I am fearfully and wonderfully made; your works are wonderful, I know that full well. My frame was not hidden from you when I was made in the secret place. When I was woven together in the depths of the earth, your eyes saw my unformed body. All the days ordained for me were written in your book before one of them came to be. How precious to me are your thoughts, O God! How vast is the sum of them! Were I to count them, they would outnumber the grains of sand. When I awake, I am still with you" (Ps. 139:13–18).

"To keep me from becoming conceited because of these surpassingly great revelations, there was given me a thorn in my flesh, a messenger of Satan, to torment me. Three times I pleaded with the Lord to take it away from me. But he said to me, 'My grace is sufficient for you, for my power is made perfect in weakness.' Therefore I will boast all the more gladly about my weaknesses, so that Christ's power may rest on me" (2 Cor. 12:7–9).

"Therefore I will boast all the more gladly about my weaknesses, so that Christ's power may rest on me. That is why, for Christ's sake, I delight in weaknesses, in insults, in hardships, in persecutions, in difficulties. For when I am weak, then I am strong" (2 Cor. 12:9–10).

When you know and understand the Lord's great love and grand plans for you, then you will begin to see inferiority not as a complex, but as sin. Why not think about your "thinking" today?

WEEK 17 — TUESDAY
BROKEN HEARTS

Max Reich tells of passing a repair shop with a sign in the window, reading: "We mend everything except broken hearts."

Brother Reich retraced his steps and entered the store. When a beautiful young Jewess came forward to serve him, he said, "I saw your sign, and want to ask what you do with people who have broken hearts."

"Oh!" she said. "We send them to the hospital."

"You are a Jewess, are you not? Did you ever read Isaiah 57:15: 'For thus saith the high and lofty One that inhabiteth eternity, whose name is Holy; I dwell in the high and holy place, with him also that is of a contrite and humble spirit, to revive the spirit of the humble and to revive the heart of the contrite ones'?

"Much later in the course of history," Mr. Reich continued, "there was One who read Isaiah 61:1 in his hometown synagogue at Nazareth: 'He hath sent me to bind up the brokenhearted.' "[1]

Broken hearts are never quick to mend. The heart is such a tender part of us that when it succumbs, the healing takes awhile. But one of the sweetest promises Jesus gives us is that He came for the purpose of binding up broken hearts.

I can remember a time when I thought my heart would literally break. In fact, I felt that Psalm 73 was addressed to me personally: "When my heart was grieved and my spirit embittered, I was senseless and ignorant; I was a brute beast before you" (vv. 21–22).

One day during this period, I was reading in Isaiah when I came across the words that Mr. Reich shared with that dear Jewish woman: "He has sent me to bind up the brokenhearted." If Jesus came only to deliver us from hell, it would be enough. But there is more. As someone has said, "God mends the broken heart when you give Him all the pieces."

Why not give Him the broken pieces of your heart today? Begin by casting all your cares on Him. If you are burdened and your heart is broken, He says, "Tell Me about it, cast it on Me . . . and I promise that even this hurt and pain will be used for good in your life."

My friend, if some tragedy or trauma has shattered your heart, Jesus Christ can make it whole again.

WEEK 17 — WEDNESDAY
HOW WARS BEGIN

The story is told of a young boy who asked, "Dad, how do wars begin?"

"Well, take the First World War," began the father. "That one got started when Germany invaded Belgium."

Immediately, his wife contradicted him. "Tell the boy the truth. It began because somebody was murdered."

The husband drew himself up with an air of superiority and snapped back, "Are you answering the question, or am I?"

Turning her back on him in a huff, the wife walked out of the room and slammed the door as hard as she could.

When the dishes stopped rattling in the cupboard, an uneasy silence followed, broken by the son: "Daddy, you don't have to tell me how wars begin; I know how!"

Quarrels and arguments are rooted in one source. In James 4:1–2, James writes: "What causes fights and quarrels among you? Don't they come from your desires that battle within you? You want something but don't get it. You kill and covet, but you cannot have what you want. You quarrel and fight."

Like the boy in the story, even a child can recognize the source of quarrels. It is a very basic problem: We want what we want—whether it is to be right, to be acknowledged for something we have done, or to have something that belongs to someone else.

Some of us are ready to pick a fight at the drop of hat. Others are more deliberate, letting tensions build until a small irritation erupts into a full-fledged quarrel.

When I feel myself getting dangerously near the boiling point, I have learned to ask myself, "Why are you ready to explode?" Since the Scriptures say that there is only one reason, I know that my anger is likely due to something I want that I'm not getting. Actually verbalizing this truth helps me avoid a confrontation.

My friend, as you tackle life today with other fallen creatures just like yourself, who want what they want, determine that you will remind yourself of the source of quarrels before you say anything that has the potential to kindle anger in another person. Knowing the source is the first step toward ending an argument before it begins. Then ask God to give you the grace to respond in love and forgiveness.

WEEK 17 — THURSDAY
I MUST TELL JESUS

Few of us are isolated from the fear that when the phone rings in the middle of the night, it will bring the tragic news of loss.

As a teenager, I can remember hearing the phone ring in the middle of the night. In those days, people usually had only one telephone centrally located in the house. Ours was in the hallway between the bedrooms, so when it rang, I was instantly awake and could hear my father answer.

"What's the word?" He sighed quietly. "We'll call back in a little while." I listened as he went back into the bedroom and told my mother, "Glen's dead." The shock to her was enormous. As the oldest child, she had been a surrogate mother to Glen after their mother died giving birth to him. Now, Glen was dead, killed in an automobile accident while still in his early twenties.

Tragic news has a way of leaving one speechless, numb, and full of questions. Where do you go when the news you have heard alters your whole life forever? Where do you turn in the dark hours of the night when the pain is most intense?

In Matthew 14, there is an example of just such an event. When John the Baptist was executed by order of Herod the king, John's disciples and friends "came and took his body and buried it. Then they went and told Jesus" (v. 12). At the moment of their deepest need, *they told Jesus*.

H. G. Bosch tells of an incident that occurred when he was a young boy. "A dear neighbor who lived two doors down the street experienced a great sorrow. She often played and sang at her piano, but after the tragedy struck in her life, the first song with which she would open her 'daily concert' was the lovely hymn, 'I Must Tell Jesus.' "

What better place to go than straight to Jesus when life hurts too much for words? I cannot know what pain or tragedy may knock at your door today, but I can tell you that there is One who waits for you to call on Him for help and assurance.

WEEK 17 — FRIDAY
DISCOURAGEMENT

Well, here we are at Friday again. For some of you, the thought of the weekend ahead is exhilarating. For others, it is discouraging. While others rest and recreate, you are facing situations that seem never ending. If that is where you are today, then I want to encourage you with some words from the Scriptures.

Hebrews 10:35—36 says: "Do not throw away your confidence; it will be richly rewarded. You need to persevere so that when you have done the will of God, you will receive what he has promised."

Discouragement often causes our confidence in all we know to be true of the Lord to waver. Yet, He tells us not to throw away our confidence by quitting, giving up, or thinking a situation is hopeless.

Here are some thoughts that might go with you today:

1. Be determined to endure. God works best in the lives of those who are determined to press on no matter what. Survivors are survivors for a reason. Against all odds, they never gave up.
2. Wait on the Lord. Don't rush in to relieve or fix the problem. Sometimes when you are discouraged, you will give in to something that you know is not right, but just to get some relief, you will go against your better judgment. Wait on the Lord, my friend . . . His timing is perfect.
3. Recognize His hand in your situation. There are no accidents. If you are under pressure today it is because God is about the work of making gold out of you. He is allowing you to be in a furnace for one reason . . . to purify you. Just as the goldsmith puts the gold into the furnace seven times, never leaving it, always watching to make sure the gold is not destroyed, but the dross is scraped off, then you can know that He is doing the same thing for you. He promises when you

91

walk through the fires you will not be burned, and when you go through the waters, you will not drown.

4. Your thinking will determine whether you see yourself as downtrodden or in a school of preparation. Paul said it best in 2 Corinthians 4:8–9, "We are hard pressed on every side, but not crushed; perplexed, but not in despair; persecuted, but not abandoned; struck down, but not destroyed."

5. Often when you need to be pouring out your heart to God you will shy away because you are discouraged . . . and He hasn't done anything about it so far . . . so why should He come to your aid now? But in Philippians 4, He says, "Be anxious [stop being worried, upset, all in a stew] about nothing, but bring it to me and I will do what is best for you in the long run. I will cause it all to work together for good" (vv. 6–7).

My friend, if you are discouraged this morning, I want to assure you on the authority of God's Word that if you are God's child, you are the apple of His eye and you are engraved on the palms of His hands. He knows where you are. He knows how you feel and He will rise to show you compassion.

Don't give up and look inward. Begin to rehearse all of the ways He has been there in your life and thank Him for your past victories.

WEEK 18 — MONDAY
STRONG SHOES

One of the pieces of mail I look forward to receiving each month is from Spatula Ministries, founded by Barbara Johnson. I've told you about Barbara. She ministers to people whose children have chosen a homosexual lifestyle, leaving parents who need a spatula to peel them off the ceiling!

In a recent newsletter, she writes:

If God sends us on stony paths, He provides strong shoes. I like that picture because it supports the principle that God will not give us more than we can bear. Never mind that the rocks beneath our feet are jagged and sharp, He will simply give us the proper gear.

If the pain you face with your child is great, He will equip you to bear it and to go the distance.

God is at work in our children, though we can't always see what He is doing. I spoke with a man this week who, along with his father, had recently given his life to Christ and been baptized. When the mother of this grown son and wife of this older dad was asked if she were surprised, she said, "Oh my, no! It's just an answer to thirty years of prayer."

Never give up. God may be silent but He is not still.

If we worry, we tie God's hands. Somehow we have bought into the belief that if we will just worry about something long enough, then everything will come out right. The truth is that God has commanded us to stop worrying and get busy praying if we expect to see changes.

If you are worried about your child today, then turn that worry into prayer. Speak his or her name to the Father. He loves that child more than you ever could and has the power to bring about the transformation for which you are praying.

We have a great God who will do within us what we cannot do for ourselves. Often in the face of horror stories about children in rebellion, our God's greatness seems to dwindle. But consider the alternatives. You can continue to assume responsibility for your child, fretting over every detail of his or her life, and interfering in the work God wants to do. Or you can take that child with you into the throne room of God and leave him at the feet of the One who died for every rebellious thing that child ever did!

WEEK 18 — TUESDAY
HOW DO YOU KNOW?

God honors right choices. The question is, How can we be sure the decisions we make are right?

In His Word, He has given us a pattern for making wise and correct choices: "Who is wise and understanding among you? Let him show it by his good life, by deeds done in the humility that comes from wisdom. But if you harbor bitter envy and selfish ambition in your hearts, do not boast about it or deny the truth. Such 'wisdom' does not come down from heaven but is earthly, unspiritual, of the devil. For where you have envy and selfish ambition, there you find disorder and every evil practice.

"But the wisdom that comes from heaven is first of all pure; then peace-loving, considerate, submissive, full of mercy and good fruit, impartial and sincere" (James 3:13–17).

Any time you are led to believe that a decision you are making is right, and yet, it has come about as a result of bitter jealousy or selfish ambition, then you may be sure your decision is wrong.

As a teenager working at a Christian camp, I desperately wanted the position of drama director. The current director was plenty competent, but I happened to know that she smoked, which was against the camp rules. Now I had a choice to make—I could expose her sin, making me look good in the eyes of camp officials and almost certainly earning me the coveted position, or I could keep quiet and miss out on my golden opportunity.

I was not a Christian, so I was most concerned with *me* and *my* wants. It was easy to tell the truth and feel good about it. It has been difficult over the years to remember that I cost another person her job.

To gauge the rightness of a decision, check it out with God's standard for wise decision-making as spelled out in verse 17. A godly decision bears the distinctive mark of God. It is *pure,* with no way of mistaking it for something tainted by the world, the flesh, and the devil. A right decision is always *peaceable, gentle, and does not defy reason or the counsel of God.* Anything approved by Him will be *full of mercy,* for He would never sanction vengeance. Most of all, God says a wise decision will *not be hypocritical,* but sincere. You will never have to wear a mask of pretense.

I don't know how many sleepless nights you have spent lately, wrestling with a decision. But after you have meditated on this passage from James, ask the Lord to help you weigh your options in view of His design. Sweet dreams!

WEEK 18 — WEDNESDAY
TURN YOUR EYES UPON JESUS

Yesterday was one of those days when everything started off wrong and steadily declined! After oversleeping due to a faulty alarm clock, our mad dash to get ready for work and school was interrupted by a telephone call from a difficult person. And by the time I had delivered my son, late, to school, I was thoroughly depressed and consumed with negative thinking.

As the morning limped along, I was suddenly aware that not once had my thoughts turned to God. So I sat down with my Bible and began to read:

> I cried out to God for help;
> I cried out to God to hear me.
> When I was in distress, I sought the Lord;
> at night I stretched out untiring hands
> and my soul refused to be comforted.
>
> I remembered you, O God, and I groaned;
> I mused, and my spirit grew faint . . .
>
> Then I thought, "To this I will appeal:
> the years of the right hand of the Most High."
> I will remember the deeds of the Lord;
> yes, I will remember your miracles of long ago.
> I will meditate on all your works
> and consider all your mighty deeds.
>
> Your ways, O God, are holy.
> What god is so great as our God?
>
> You are the God who performs miracles;
> you display your power among the peoples.
> (Ps. 77:1–3, 10–14)

I wish I could say that my burdens lifted immediately and I arose with a song in my heart. It didn't happen quite that way, but I did come away with a different focus. No longer did I waste time stewing over the difficulties, but rather, I thought about how faithful our God is and how He works untiringly on my behalf, even when my focus has turned inward.

Another thing I brought away with me that morning was a reminder of the battle to defeat and depress God's children. If we won't yield to fleshly temptations—drugs, alcohol, pornography, infidelity—Satan simply makes a more subtle approach, self-pity! When we focus on our own inadequacies and sins, we are easy prey for the devourer and ripe for depression, cynicism, doubts, and unbelief. If the enemy can draw our attention to ourselves, he has won.

But if we concentrate on Jesus, remembering past victories, Satan will get the idea and give up. The Lord reminded me of something He had done a few years ago. We needed to sell a house by December 31 or lose a great deal of money. We prayed, gave the need to Him, and on December 30 He provided a buyer. Ever since then, when there seems to be no way to have a specific need taken care of, I remember God came through in the final hour. He said He would supply all of my needs, and over and over, He has.

My friend, if you are prone to look inward, I suggest you pick up your Bible and begin reading in the Psalms, or in Ephesians, or Colossians. Resist the temptation to take your eyes off the great love and majesty of God. Remember all He has already done for you and be encouraged. Satan will have to slink away, foiled again!

WEEK 18 — THURSDAY
RUN FOR YOUR LIFE!

I recently spoke with a woman who is a composite of so many who are innocent victims of lust. Her husband came home one day and announced that he didn't love her anymore and was planning to move out of the house. There was another woman in the picture, but he refused to identify her, only that it was "someone who needs me to take care of her."

In disgust, I thought to myself, *How blind can a man be? This whole thing is a set-up to appeal to his ego and destroy his home!*

No doubt, the man fell into the situation innocently enough, but he should have turned away the instant he recognized the first hint of danger. The Bible gives a clear warning in 2 Timothy 2:22: "Flee the evil desires of youth." There is a reason we are to flee. Our flesh is so powerful and so persuasive that we can find ourselves, as this husband did, involved in a compromising situation before our minds catch up!

There is something about the nature of illicit relationships that draws us like a magnet. It is a pull to the former lifestyle which once held such fascination and such promise. But when we become believers in Jesus Christ, we are under new management.

Sometime after the conversion of Augustine, the story is told of an encounter he had with the woman who had been his evil genius for many months, having dragged him deeper and deeper into the slavery of sin until he was freed from its bonds by the regenerating power of the cross. When he attempted to pass her with only a formal nod, she stopped him with a challenge: "Augustine, do you not know me any more? See, it is I." Looking at her a moment and knowing that she no longer held him in her spell, Augustine replied, "But it is not I."

You can avoid tragedy and heartbreak in your life if you will count yourself as dead to any illicit relationship that has held you captive. The moment you begin to entertain the idea that you can afford to be around the person and can control the situation in your own strength, you are on the way to becoming ensnared again.

One of the most dangerous impediments to our Christian walk is our unhealthy regard for the ability we have to say no. To see ourselves as totally incapable of doing what is right apart from slavish recognition of the Lordship of Christ is the only way we will be on guard against the relationships that could destroy us.

If you, as a believer, are toying with the idea of entering into an illicit relationship, you are commanded to flee! As you count yourself dead to the pull of the flesh, the Lord God of the universe will supply the strength to overcome. Don't allow yourself to become one of His kingdom's tragic statistics.

WEEK 18 — FRIDAY
IT'S NOT FUNNY

When the AIDS epidemic first broke out, I heard an older preacher make a joke about the fact that he had aids, referring to his hearing aids. Chuckling, he quickly added, "My wife told me I shouldn't joke like that!"

His wife isn't the only one who feels that way. In Ephesians 5:4, God says that there must be no "obscenity, foolish talk or coarse joking, which are out of place, but rather thanksgiving."

Unfortunately, even in Christian circles, some who are above the proverbial dirty joke, apparently think nothing of jokes about sin or the sad consequences of sin.

Barclay gives us this insight into what is being said in Ephesians. Paul says that these shameful sins are "not even to be talked about. . . . They are not to become a subject for foolish talking and graceless jesting. The Persians had a rule by which it was not even allowed to speak such things as it was not allowed to do. To talk about a thing, to jest about a thing, to make it a frequent subject of conversation is to introduce it into the mind."[1]

To discuss, joke about, or watch something that God has labeled as sin is to engrave it indelibly on your mind. It is like entering a paragraph into a computer that has no delete button. Once entered, it cannot be erased.

I once was present at a dinner attended by a mixed group of believers and non-believers. One particularly loud and vulgar woman began to tell a joke. Those sitting nearby were her captive audience. Although that incident occurred many years ago, I can still remember the joke, and I hate the image it left in my mind.

Paul gives an alternative to the silly talk and coarse joking that is not fitting for believers. He says we are to give thanks instead. The great lion of God seems to be saying, "Why focus on silly, empty chatter? Why not talk about the good things I have done, and by so doing, increase your faith? Those are the things that will edify your life."

My friend, we can prepare ourselves to face situations in which people engage in the coarse talk that wounds God's heart. At that point, it is not for us to condemn or to try to change minds. Rather, we can refrain from laughing at lewd jokes or telling them ourselves. Further, we can program our minds to tune out when such jokes are being told by "giving thanks to God" in our speech and conduct.

WEEK 19 — MONDAY
A MEMO FOR CHRISTIAN EMPLOYEES

In Ephesians, Paul leaves a memo which gives us insight into his work ethic for believers. Here he addresses his readers as "slaves," which was an appropriate term, for many who had experienced freedom in Christ remained as slaves in their jobs. Today, this passage is equally applicable to Christian employees.

Slaves, obey your earthly masters with respect and fear, and with sincerity of heart, just as you would obey Christ. Obey them not only to win their favor when their eye is on you, but like slaves of Christ, doing the will of God from your heart. Serve wholeheartedly, as if you were serving the Lord, not men, because you know that the Lord will reward everyone for whatever good he does, whether he is slave or free. (Eph. 6:5-9)

What is the Lord saying to you in your workplace—at home or in the office?

1. *Treat your employer as you would treat Christ.* The great message of the Bible is to live out the Christian life *where God has placed you.* Christianity does not offer escape from circumstances; it offers conquest of circumstances.

   Wherever you serve today, God knows what you're up against. He knows how unreasonable and irritable your boss or co-workers can be. He has placed you in a strategic position with a big job to do—to show the most unreasonable person in your workplace how a child of God reacts to stress.

2. *Set your standards of productivity and quality higher than the world's standards and perform your work as if God were your supervisor.* Will you be typing a letter today? Putting together a report? Repairing a car? Changing a baby's diapers? Preparing a legal brief? Teaching a room full of disinterested kids with spring fever? Would you earn God's approval if he were inspecting your work?

William Barclay makes an interesting statement I believe is true: "The problem that the world has always faced, and that the world is facing acutely today, is not basically an economic problem at all; it is a religious problem. We will never make men good workmen by increasing pay, or bettering conditions or heightening rewards. It is quite true that it is a Christian duty to see to these things; but they in themselves will never produce good work. Still less will we produce good work by intensifying threats and increasing oversight and multiplying punishments and penalties. The only secret of good workmanship is that it be done for God. It is only when a man is taking all his work and showing it to God that work can be good."[1]

As you go to your place of business today, consider who it is you are really working for. Whom are you trying to please? As you walk in the door, give your day, your work, your attitude, and everything you do to God. He has promoted you to this position to show the world how His children operate when no one is looking.

WEEK 19 — TUESDAY
STAND FIRM

What would you do if you had the ocean in front of you and an enemy army bearing down behind? You would be in the same position as the Israelites after the Exodus from Egypt—between a rock and a hard place!

The alternatives are few and deadly at such a time. If you go toward the sea, you'll drown. If you turn around and fight, you'll be outnumbered and killed. If you stand still and close your eyes, maybe it won't hurt so much when you are crushed and pushed into the sea.

When the Israelites heard the sound of horses and chariots racing across the desert in their direction, they turned to Moses, their leader, who told them: "Do not be afraid. Stand firm and you will see the deliverance the Lord will bring you today. The Egyptians you see today you will never see again. The Lord will fight for you; you need only to be still" (Ex. 14:13–14).

"Be still." What a simple solution, yet how very hard to do. When the odds are against us, and we are caught in a vise, our first inclination is not to be still, but to do something! Still, there are times when any kind of action is suicidal, or at the very least, could result in producing a greater problem than the one we started with. At those times, will we trust God, or not?

That's what God means when He says, "Be still and know that I am God." As we accept His offer of deliverance, focusing on His strength and power and might, our fears subside and we can stand firm in the knowledge and assurance that He is fighting our battles for us. What relief to know that He acts in our behalf, facing down and overcoming the formidable enemies that threaten us.

Sometimes there is nothing we can do but trust. When the news from the war zone is grim, when the diagnosis is terminal illness, when the divorce decree is final, there is only one thing to do—"stand firm and . . . see the deliverance the Lord will bring."

If you are stalled between the enemy's army and the Red Sea, remember these words of George Mueller, a great man of faith: "The beginning of anxiety is the end of faith, and the beginning of true faith is the end of anxiety."

WEEK 19 — WEDNESDAY
THE GIANT-KILLER

When that wonderful, articulate black pastor, E. V. Hill, had been married only a short time, he came home one evening to a beautifully appointed candlelight dinner. Puzzled, he asked his bride the reason for the occasion. She kissed him and said, "I thought we should celebrate being married for three months." Content with his wife's explanation, Dr. Hill went into the bathroom to wash his hands. But when he turned on the switch and there was no light, he knew something was wrong.

His wife, Babe, told him that the electric company had turned off their electricity for failure to pay their bill. Hoping to spare her new husband the humiliation, she had not complained or criticized, but had quietly set about to make a celebration out of adversity.

Years later he would say, "I've had victories in my life, but that candlelight dinner was a victory that held me in the days ahead"—even when he had to bury his beloved Babe. The small events had made the big events bearable.

That's how God works in all our lives. As He proves Himself faithful in the small things, we build a treasury of faith from which to draw when confronting the big, frightening, heartbreaking moments.

Do you remember how it was with David? The young shepherd boy did not begin his giant-killing career with Goliath. He first built a huge reservoir of skill and faith while tending his father's sheep.

"When a lion or a bear came and carried off a sheep from the flock, I went after it, struck it and rescued the sheep from its mouth. When it turned on me, I seized it by its hair, struck it and killed it. Your servant has killed both the lion and the bear; this uncircumcised Philistine will be like one of them, because he has defied the armies of the living God. The Lord who delivered me from the paw of the lion and the paw of the bear will deliver me from the hand of this Philistine" (1 Sam. 17:34–37).

My friend, if you are one of God's children, you have experienced some victories—times when you have been delivered, held firm, or taken through disaster. Those times are intended to prepare us for the greater trials that loom like giants on the horizon. When we do, the memory of the small victories will give us courage to overcome.

WEEK 19 — THURSDAY
A SPECK OF SAWDUST

When I was about twelve years old, my parents pulled up in front of a grocery store and sent me in to buy some cayenne pepper. The clerk I questioned didn't seem to know where the pepper was located, so I came back out and reported the problem to my parents.

In disbelief, my dad went into the store, asked someone for the pepper, and found it right away. Since I was scolded for failing to follow instructions, you can imagine my frustration! With the evidence stacked against me, there was no way to prove my innocence, and I was hurt that my parents didn't believe me. This was especially true because they rarely doubted me.

Whenever I am tempted to pass judgment, based on circumstances, I am reminded of that incident.

This passage from Matthew warns us to beware of jumping to conclusions: "Do not judge, or you too will be judged. For in the same way you judge others, you will be judged, and with the measure you use, it will be measured to you.

"Why do you look at the speck of sawdust in your brother's eye and pay no attention to the plank in your own eye? How can you say to your brother, 'Let me take the speck out of your eye,' when all the time there is a plank in your own eye? You hypocrite, first take the plank out of your own eye, and then you will see clearly to remove the speck from your brother's eye" (7:1–5).

God tells us not to be quick to judge because we cannot know all the circumstances surrounding an incident, nor do we know a person's heart. Just as I would have appreciated my parents giving me the benefit of the doubt in the cayenne pepper episode, I must give others the benefit of the doubt when I don't know all the details.

This passage also suggests that we'd better check in the mirror before forming an opinion about someone else's attitudes or actions. Do I judge others for being unfriendly, yet fail to speak or act in a friendly, concerned manner myself? Do I judge others for not honoring the Lord, yet dishonor Him by judging?

God doesn't mince words. One of His most scathing indictments—"hypocrites"—is reserved for people who live by this kind of double standard. What nerve to think we don't have to tend to our own wrongs, yet feel free to judge the world for theirs!

Think about it. Maybe you and I need to take a long look at ourselves and remove our "plank" before we take a short look and judge another's "speck of sawdust."

WEEK 19 — FRIDAY
HIDDEN SINS

Does it disturb you when negative attitudes and thoughts hide behind your most godly smile? You know what I mean—those feelings that lie just beneath the surface and pop out when you least expect them to. Not only that, but they are apt to be discovered when you most want to make a good impression!

This poem expresses the dilemma of hidden sins:

> Lord, it's not the dirt and clutter in plain sight
>   that nag at me.
> It's that hidden dirt, you know, behind the refrigerator,
>   in the closets, under the beds.
> Dirt that no one sees or knows about but me.
>
> It's the same way with my life, God.
> It's those hidden sins that I can't keep up with . . .
>   those petty little grievances, the grudges, the
>   resentments,
>   the unspoken, harsh feelings, the superior attitudes.
> Thoughts and feelings that no one else knows about but
>   me
>   . . . and You, God.
>
> Help me Father, to clean my heart as I should my home;
> Take away all dust and cobwebs of pride, ill feelings
>   and prejudice.
> The dirt behind my refrigerator will never hurt anyone.
> The dirt in my heart will.
>
> (Author unknown)

Is it time for a spiritual housecleaning? Is there dirt in your mind? Bitterness and resentment in your heart? Have you stubbornly held on to musty beliefs when God is waiting to shine the searchlight of His truth into all the cobwebby corners of your life?

David knew the devastation of secret sins. He cries out: "Forgive my hidden faults. Keep your servant also from willful sins; may they not rule over me" (Ps. 19:12–13). Then, when confronted by the prophet Nathan after his adulterous union with Bathsheba, he prays: "Have mercy on me, O God, according to your unfailing love; according to your great compassion blot out my transgressions. Wash away all my iniquity and cleanse me from my sin. For I know my transgressions, and my sin is always before me. Against you, you only, have I sinned and done what is evil in your sight. . . . Create in me a pure heart, O God, and renew a steadfast spirit within me. Do not cast me from your presence or take your Holy Spirit from me" (Ps. 51:1–4, 10–11).

If you are harboring a secret sin, a hidden attitude, don't wait until God sends a Nathan to convict you. Seek Him and ask Him to reveal all the areas that hinder your worship. He can create a pure heart and restore the joy of your salvation.

WEEK 20 — MONDAY
DO YOU WANT TO GET WELL?

The story of the man at the pool of Bethesda is either a testimony to patience . . . or to lack of faith!

The disabled—the lame, the blind, the ill—gathered here to wait for the moving of the waters. After each such stirring by an angel of the Lord, "the first one into the pool . . . would be healed of his disease." But this poor man had no one to help him into the water, and so he had waited for a very long time, hoping that God would intervene.

John tells us how long he waited: "One who was there had been an invalid *for thirty-eight years*. When Jesus saw him lying there and learned that he had been in this condition for a long time, he asked him, 'Do you want to get well?' " (John 5:5–6).

Therein is the question you and I must face as we struggle with the things that bind us, that hold us back, that keep us from moving on. It is easy to believe we *want* to get well, to be free of our anger, or bitterness, or bad temper, or addiction to pills, or gossip, or a myriad of other sicknesses that are produced by sin. But when it really comes down to the actual question which demands action, "Do you want to get well?" that is quite another story.

Jesus responded to the lame man's evasive answer with a direct command: "Get up! Pick up your mat and walk."

If you are ever going to be free of the infirmity that holds you at the pool, hoping and waiting and trying and failing, then you will have to do what you never thought possible: Get up . . . shut down any possibility of turning back . . . and move on.

One of the major reasons you are still trapped is that you have not taken the first step. You have not chosen to say, "Yes, I will move on." The invalid at the pool said he couldn't move because he had no friends to help him, and because others were faster than he.

But if you really want to change, to be whole, then you have to make a choice to move on and take your bed with you, making no provision to return to your old habits.

What comes to mind today when you think of something that you have been struggling with for a long time? Could it be that Jesus has already told you how to break free? That you are to leave comfortable old habits and move on? Have you run out of excuses for failing to follow Him? Are you halting between getting on with your life or staying in the place where you have been lame and ineffective?

Today is the day. Jesus of Nazareth is calling: "Get up! Fold up your bed . . . and walk."

WEEK 20 — TUESDAY
HOLIER THAN THOU

Holiness is to be set apart, separated for God. But separation is not a popular idea in our society. One who tries to be separate from others on the

101

basis of holiness risks being branded "holier than thou." While no one desires this label, committed Christians who are serious about their walk with the Lord cannot avoid it.

There are some, however, who stage their holiness as a melodrama. These individuals may say, "Oh, I don't do that" or "I really couldn't go there. That's a place where sinners go." In fact, there are even some churches who practice a form of separation so severe that their children are forbidden to attend any church function outside their own denomination.

In a perverted way, we have managed to turn the holiness of God from a sweet response to His call on our life into a list of man-made rules that leave us in bondage. Holiness is never bondage, always freedom.

True holiness is Godlikeness. Recognizing that we have missed the mark of God's character, true holiness shows up in the very practical act of confessing one's unkind or sarcastic comments moments after they have been uttered. The more one develops "holy" living, the more quickly confession and restitution for wrongs take place—no matter whether or not it is deserved. The issue is not the other person's sin, but the righteousness of your own heart.

A friend who spent years as the victim of unkind, unloving parents, determined to try to resolve the long-standing problem between them. She had never confronted them with the matter, choosing to pretend everything was all right, but when she found that her younger brother and sister were also being adversely affected, she realized the time had come.

While on the plane en route to her parents' home, my friend read through the four pages of notes cataloging their sins against her. She also picked up a little book she had brought along, *The Calvary Road,* and read a chapter entitled "Revival in the Home." So moved was she by what she had read that she tore up her notes.

Following the suggestions given in the book, she went to her parents, confessing her own shortcomings as a daughter, and asking them to tell her how she had failed them. They obliged, spelling out all her failures in detail. After asking their forgiveness, my friend returned home completely depleted, but relieved that she had followed the leading of the Holy Spirit.

It was only the beginning! My friend later reported that a sister-in-law had received Christ as a result of her visit, her brother has reached out to her in love, her nephews are asking questions about Jesus, and even her parents are making an attempt to try to heal the breach!

Holiness is not static. It is a dynamic oneness with the living Lord that allows His power to be revealed in unexpected ways and in unexpected places!

WEEK 20 — WEDNESDAY
NEVER ALONE

A couple of years ago, I went to a picnic where I was the only person present who did not know a single soul. All about me, old friends seemed to be delighted to be together. And while I am usually a sociable being who enjoys making conversation, I was appalled to find myself gradually withdrawing, becoming less talkative, and pulling into my shell.

I have also experienced this kind of isolation in a doctor's waiting room, crowded with fellow sufferers who seem to prefer to be locked into their own world of pain and misery rather than to communicate with those around them.

No matter how many people surround us, we are all afflicted with a common malady—loneliness. It is the feeling of being cut off, a sense of isolation in the midst of people, or being destitute of sympathetic or friendly companionship.

If you are feeling lonely today, let me remind you that God is present . . . everywhere.

Jeremiah expresses it in poetic imagery:

"Am I only a God nearby," declares the Lord, "and not a God far away? Can anyone hide in secret places so that I cannot see him?" declares the Lord. "Do not I fill heaven and earth?" (23:23–24).

And David exults in God's omnipresence:

Where can I go from your Spirit?
Where can I flee from your presence?
If I go up to the heavens, you are there;
If I make my bed in the depths, you are there.
If I rise on the wings of the dawn,
    if I settle on the far side of the sea,
even there your hand will guide me,
    your right hand will hold me fast.

(Ps. 139:7–10)

If you are ill or facing a painful procedure, God is there. If you are adjusting to a new job or a new neighborhood and you feel frightened, God is there. If you are having difficulty with someone you love, and can't even tell your closest friend, God is there.

And if He is there, then you are forever in the presence of the One who calls you "beloved," "the apple of my eye," and promises, "I will never leave you nor forsake you."

Meditate on this truth today, and if you begin to feel lonely and threatened, take a moment to breathe a prayer: "Lord, I thank you that I am not alone because You have promised never to leave me. You are here."

WEEK 20 — THURSDAY
LET THE LORD LOVE YOU

The story is told of an elderly Scottish woman who was asked what she did all day long. "Well," she replied, "I get my hymnbook and sing. Then I get the Bible and let the Lord speak to me. When I get tired of reading and cannot sing anymore, I just sit still and let the Lord love me."

How long has it been since you sat still and let the Lord love you? Maybe that concept is a little foreign to you. We Christians who live in the fast lane resist sitting still and receiving. Perhaps it is because we feel too unworthy.

But ever since God created humankind, He has been calling out, "I love you." And we have been flinching in the face of that declaration and saying, "Who, me? How can You love someone like me?"

If you want the sweet experience of letting God love you, then why not begin this morning by meditating on what the Lord thinks of you. As He speaks to you of His love, resolve that you will drop all your arguments and just relax.

"I have loved you with an everlasting love," He says. "I have drawn you with loving-kindness" (Jer. 31:3).

Or what about this precious reminder: "Who shall separate us from the love of Christ? Shall trouble or hardship or persecution or famine or nakedness or danger or sword?" (Rom. 8:35). And I would add: "Shall your lack of discipline, or family problems, or feelings of inferiority, or sins of the past, or temptations of the present . . . or worries and fears about the future or your failures of this morning?" And the answer is clear: Absolutely not! "In all these things we are more than conquerors through him who loved us" (v. 37).

And this promise: "He who loves me will be loved by my Father, and I too will love him and show myself to him" (John 14:21).

But this passage compels me to do something about the great love God has for me: "If anyone acknowledges that Jesus is the Son of God, God lives in him and he in God. And so we know and rely on the love God has for us. God is love. Whoever lives in love lives in God, and God in him. . . . Love is made complete among us so that we will have confidence on the day of judgment, because in this world we are like him. . . . We love because he first loved us. If anyone says, 'I love God,' yet hates his brother, he is a liar. For anyone who does not love his brother, whom he has seen, cannot love God, whom he has not seen. And he has given us this command: Whoever loves God must also love his brother" (1 John 4:15–17, 19–21).

After we have basked in the presence of God, reading His love letters to us, there is no way we can remain detached and uninvolved. Get up now and call someone who needs to be reminded that she is loved. Write a love note to an invalid who may feel forgotten. Share the good news that our God is love!

WEEK 20 — FRIDAY
OPEN YOUR MOUTH WIDE

It is interesting to probe beneath the surface of a particular Scripture passage to discover the picture God is drawing for us. In doing so, I sometimes find that becoming familiar with customs of the day can help to clarify the meaning of the passage.

One such verse is Psalm 81:10, where God says through the psalmist Asaph: "Open wide your mouth and I will fill it."

One can best understand these words if he is acquainted with a strange custom that existed in the days when Asaph wrote this psalm. At that time when a benevolent king wished to extend a favor to a visitor, or give an ambassador a special honor, he would request him to open his mouth wide. The king would then cram it full of sweetmeats. On occasion he would even put in a handful of jewels.[1]

What a shock, I should think, to bite down on a fig newton and discover a mouth full of jewels! But what a picture of the bounty of God's provision!

First, I think it's significant to note that if my mouth is open wide, I can't be talking. Coming into the presence of the King of Kings is a complete experience only when we listen as well as talk. He can never delight us with surprise delicacies if we never stop talking. So I intend to spend some time in silence today, with my mouth open wide, in the expectancy of good things.

Have you watched a nest of hungry birds lately? Do they sit serenely, chirping at one another occasionally while they wait patiently for their meal? No indeed. When you look in the nest, all you see is wide-open mouths, eager

104

for every morsel their mama bird will bring. They are expecting her to fill their mouths, and that expectation keeps them ready!

How many times do you go to the Lord out of obligation and with non-existent expectations? Do you reluctantly read a chapter in your Bible every day? Do you do what's right because you should, or do you come to God with expectation and excitement because you never know what jewel He is going to drop into your mouth next?

What fun it is to come into God's presence and say, "Lord I wait before You with an open mouth. I'm not here to make any requests or to try to figure out any answers, or to be spiritual. I am here for You to fill my mouth with sweetmeats and treasures that I can relish because they come from You."

There was a time when all I could do was open my mouth. I had no answers and I had exhausted myself telling God all about my problem. So, I just opened my mouth and waited in expectancy. This is the jewel I found in the midst of the sweetmeats He dropped in my mouth: "The Lord longs to be gracious to you; he rises to show you compassion" (Isa. 30:18).

What a many-faceted diamond that verse turned out to be! In His goodness, God gave me a jewel that I would treasure the rest of my days. It was unexpected, given freely, and is cherished beyond measure.

Today, He is waiting to drop a jewel into your open mouth. Why not take Him at His Word, dare to open your mouth, and wait in silent expectation?

WEEK 21 — MONDAY
THIS THING IS FROM ME

In her essay, "This Thing Is from Me," Laura Snow says,

> This day I place in your hands this pot of holy oil, make use of it freely, my child. Let every circumstance as it arises, every word that pains you, every interruption that would make you impatient, every revelation of your own weakness, be anointed with it! Remember, interruptions are divine instructions. The sting will go as you learn to see me in all things.

If you are feeling stretched beyond your resources . . . if you are beginning to wonder where all the pressure is coming from . . . if you are questioning whether the Lord is aware of your stress, consider that "this thing" may be from His hand.

Could it be that God is in the process of educating you? A loving Father would not leave His children ignorant, ill-prepared, and uneducated, but would see to it that they learn valuable lessons that will equip them for the complex and difficult days ahead.

Are you in financial straits because of the failing economy or because you have more needs than you can cover? Could God be teaching you a lesson in High Finance? Could He be saying, "I want you to depend on Me . . . to come to Me for your needs . . . I want to teach you how to use what I give you?"

What about your relationships? Has someone betrayed your confidence? Put a knife in your back and slandered you? Could God be teaching you that He is the only One you can count on? He alone will never leave you nor forsake you, nor will He be your accuser.

Are you under the stress of plans that have gone awry? Are you struggling because you were just sure that God wanted you to tackle that problem? Could it be that in your independence you have bitten off too much and He is trying to teach you, "The work is too heavy for you; you cannot handle it alone" (Exod. 18:18).

Whatever it is, my friend, you may feel that you are under stress, but I assure you that you are in school. God knows every assignment you are facing and what it will take for you to graduate with honors!

WEEK 21 — TUESDAY
WHAT IF THEY DON'T BELIEVE ME?

"If there is a God, why is there so much pain and suffering in the world?" "How could a loving God allow a little child to starve to death?" "Would a just God have permitted such atrocities as the Holocaust?"

I confront these and other hard questions about God with weak knees, feeling that at any moment someone is going to shoot holes through my explanations. Though I know that what I believe is true, I get cold feet when someone decides to challenge my faith.

Moses understood this apprehension. Read Exodus 3 and 4 if you doubt that this great father of the faith had shaky knees. He even had the audacity to question God's judgment in choosing him: "Who am I, that I should go to Pharaoh and bring the Israelites out of Egypt?"

"And God said, 'I will be with you. . . .'"

"Moses said to the Lord, 'O Lord, I have never been eloquent, neither in the past nor since you have spoken to your servant. I am slow of speech and tongue.'

"The Lord said to him, 'Who gave man his mouth? Who makes him deaf or mute? . . . Is it not I, the Lord? Now go; I will help you speak and will teach you what to say'" (Exod. 3:11–12; 4:10–12).

Surely, then, He understands our reluctance:

"Lord, today I'll be in class with that professor who makes mincemeat out of Christians. Will You be with me?"

"God, You know how some of the people at work laugh at Christians. Will you stand by me as I take a stand for You?"

"Lord, You know my husband makes fun of Christianity. Will you help me love him and minister to him for Your sake?"

Do you think for one moment that God would deny you His presence and His power in such situations? No way. Even if you feel inadequate, and maybe even stupid, when the intellectual skeptics make fun, you will be amazed at what will come out of your mouth if you simply ask God to speak through you.

Even with all of Moses' insecurities and doubts, God reassured him, "Now go, and I will help you speak and will teach you what to say." He says, "Your job is to go. My job is to provide the appropriate words for the occasion."

What does your day hold? What kind of intellectual battles will you face? Do you feel ignorant or inadequate for the task? My friend, God says He will be with you and supply the words. You have only one responsibility, and that is to be his representative to people who, despite their skepticism, desperately need to know the Lord who indwells you.

WEEK 21 — WEDNESDAY
OUT OF CONTROL

I don't like roller coaster rides because they are designed to give the sensation of being out of control. And one of our greatest fears is losing control. At such times anything could happen!

This is exactly the helpless feeling produced by runaway people and circumstances in our lives. It's frightening to learn that you may be facing major surgery with an uncertain outcome, or when you realize that your teenager is blatantly rebelling, or when a headstrong mate is determined to make a business decision you honestly believe to be wrong.

I've found an unlikely principle in Scripture to be tailor-made for such difficult situations: "Rejoice in the Lord always. I will say it again: Rejoice! . . . Do not be anxious about anything, but in everything, by prayer and petition, with thanksgiving, present your requests to God. And the peace of God, which transcends all understanding, will guard your hearts and your minds in Christ Jesus" (Phil. 4:4–7).

Impossible?

Not at all. He is saying that, if you are taking delight in who God is, then your eyes are focused on the only One who can help. Although you may feel utterly helpless, you can rejoice that there is Someone who has everything under control.

Stress often surfaces in complaints and worry that spill over onto others. God says, "Let your forbearing spirit (sweet reasonableness) be known to all men."

If you fear losing your job, thank the Lord for promising to supply your needs and then thank Him in advance for salvaging your job, providing you with another, or meeting your needs for an income in some other creative way. Remember, you can't pick and choose how God will answer. You can only be sure that He will!

If your child is giving you nothing but grief, pray very specifically that God will grant him wisdom, understanding, and spiritual maturity. Give the control of your situation to the Lord, and ask Him to guide both you and your child.

We live on an out-of-control planet that marvels when one of God's children is peaceful in the midst of incredible crisis and change. You speak well of your heavenly Father in an earthly world gone mad when you demonstrate His perfect peace.

WEEK 21 — THURSDAY
SET IN YOUR SPIRITUAL WAYS?

Okay. I admit it. I'm set in my ways about some things. I like to shower and wash my hair in the morning. I pass up cookies with raisins. And I have a real hangup about men who keep their hats on at the table!

We all have our preferences, even if it sometimes seems a little inconvenient to hang on to them. We also have our ideas about how things should be done.

In the spiritual realm, preferences and tendencies are no different. I have a precious friend who measures spirituality by a person's regularity in having a quiet time. I have another friend who doesn't feel a relationship is really all it should be unless you pray together. Still another friend believes that a table blessing doesn't count unless you mention the food. Oddly enough, the friend who wants to pray with me doesn't have a regular quiet time, and doesn't ever mention the food when she asks the blessing. The friend who wouldn't think of missing her quiet time has never prayed with me, nor has the one who always mentions the food when she prays at the table.

Are you set in your spiritual ways? Do certain acts make you feel more spiritual, yet you pass over others? Do you have certain rituals that you hold to as Truth?

Even some folks in Bible times couldn't believe that true worshipers would deviate from established religious practices. In Matthew 12, such an incident is recorded: "At that time Jesus went through the grainfields on the Sabbath. His disciples were hungry and began to pick some heads of grain and eat them. When the Pharisees saw this, they said to him, 'Look! Your disciples are doing what is unlawful on the Sabbath' " (vv. 1–2).

Jesus, always the radical, said, "If you had known what these words mean, 'I desire mercy, not sacrifice,' you would not have condemned the innocent. For the Son of Man is Lord of the Sabbath" (vv. 7–8).

Often, the things we hold to most rigidly tend to bring condemnation on others because we're convinced our way is the right way. The Lord knows this tendency and cautions us: "Be transformed by the renewing of your mind" (Rom. 12:2). Unfortunately, that change of mind will come only when we acknowledge that our views are distorted and need changing.

If this is the case, and you are stuck in the rut of tendencies that are harshly critical of others, Jesus invites: "Take my yoke upon you and learn from me, for I am gentle and humble in heart, and you will find rest for your souls. For my yoke is easy and my burden is light" (Matt. 11:29–30).

In other words, He is saying, "Please join with Me and learn from Me . . . for I am gentle and humble. There is no place for harshness and judgmentalism in the lives of my children. My yoke will be easy for you, and it will be easy for your friend. Just make sure it is My yoke you are wearing and not another."

You may be set in your ways, but as your mind is gradually renewed, ask God to show you the bondage of your ruts and the freedom of His Word. You'll be amazed at the good things He has in store for you and the sweet release He has for your friend. The Truth that Jesus gives is liberating.

WEEK 21 — FRIDAY
THE PARENTS' COMMAND

I recently talked with a parent who said, "I have been so hurt by my daughter's choices that it is hard for me to talk to her, much less love her."

On the same day I talked with another mother who said, "My son has been estranged from me, but I love him. He has taken me to court and vowed never to speak to me again, but he is still my son. Last week, he called and said, 'Mother, I'm coming by the house to see you and spend the night with you . . . is that okay?' "

Two women, two broken hearts, but one right perspective—unconditional love. We may have to let our children go from our presence and protection, but we are never called upon to release them from our love.

Unconditional love is the kind of love that makes no requirements before extending favor. The child can be pretty or ugly, hateful or kind, considerate or rude, yet your love never diminishes. Unconditional love seeks another's highest good. To love your child unconditionally is to determine that no matter what, you will always seek his highest good, not your own.

Erma Bombeck, the syndicated columnist, puts it this way:

> I'll tell you what parenting is in one word: longevity. That's right, the long haul. And here's the kicker; it's being there when your kids don't want you to be there. There is no other job in this world where there is more rejection, where you are dismissed with more regularity and where the people you are sworn to serve tell you "I don't need you. I don't even like you."

I think Erma hit the nail on the head in describing many parent/child situations. Yet God says to seek the highest good of this person no matter how self-defeating that action may be.

There's a perfect picture of unconditional love in 1 Corinthians 13:

1. *"Love is patient."* Short tempers never help anyone. Although you may be hurt and offended, blowing up and lashing back only gives the child a reason to think you are unreasonable.
2. *"Love is kind."* Playing tit for tat with sarcasm and personal jibes only creates an atmosphere of tension. Kindness finds a way to serve—a favorite meal, a load of clean laundry, gentle words in return for cutting ones.
3. *"Love believes, hopes, and endures all things."* Unconditional love never gives up. It believes the best is possible, that pain is endurable, and that things will be better in the morning.

WEEK 22 — MONDAY
PEOPLE ADDICTION

We hear much today about dependencies. Every few months, some celebrity or politician's wife goes public with the announcement that he or she is being treated for some kind of chemical dependency, usually alcohol or drugs. But there is another form of dependency currently under discussion by many people—emotional dependency, or "people addiction."

It is becoming evident that the nineties will be the decade of people addiction. But because contemporary society gives its stamp of approval to deviant relationships, I doubt that it will ever be widely acceptable to say, "I am at the Susie Smith Center being treated for the devastating results of my affair [or my homosexuality, or my obsession with my children, or my worship of my husband, or my endless search for parental approval, or my love-hate relationship with a friend]."

Whether acceptable or not, the reality is that these are problems confronting people everywhere, in the body of Christ and outside. This subtle form of dependency knows no boundaries.

Pain is the first sign of dependency in a relationship. I have yet to talk with a homosexual who will honestly admit that the gay life is good. Instead, if one probes deeply enough, you will find pain and guilt. I've never met anyone involved in an affair who, deep down inside, believes, "This is what I want out of life." Mothers and grown children caught in the control cycle inevitably show signs of bitterness, and the woman who is abused but unwilling to make a change is fearful and miserable, if paralyzed by her dependency. Even friends on the love-hate seesaw often go their separate ways because friendship cannot sustain prolonged pain.

The root of all this tragedy is idolatry, dating back to the couple in the Garden of Eden.

Everyone is hungry for union with someone or something to fill an incomplete part of himself. God created man with a hunger for relationship when he was still in perfect communion with Him. Before the serpent ever slithered onto the scene, God said, "It is not good for the man to be alone. I will make a helper suitable for him" (Gen. 2:18).

But Adam and Eve chose to defy the Lord God, and when they did, they severed the only relationship that could keep every other relationship balanced, controlled, and meaningful. They broke their intimacy with God, tainted their openness with one another, and found themselves castaway grandparents to a race of dependency-prone descendents.

The discontent, rebellion, idolatry, and mistrust of our first parents have been visited on every generation with increasing furor since the day they left the Garden. And now, in our time, we see the full-blown effect of their fall in the dependencies and addictions enslaving our generation.

If you or someone you love is trapped in the pain of people addiction, there is hope and help with the Lord. The process is slow, but you can get better. It will take time.

WEEK 22 — TUESDAY
A SENSE OF WONDER

A few days ago I heard a remarkable woman describe the last days she spent with her husband. Though he was dying and in great pain, as the hours ticked by they enjoyed a heightened sense of wonder in little things—the veins on the leaves of the floral arrangements sent to his room, the delicate colors of the flowers, the sweetness of shared silence. While they had their careers and their busy home to run, they had missed much of the very essence of all that makes up life . . . until it was ebbing away.

There is an interesting verse in 1 Timothy that speaks of the worth-whileness of little things: "For everything God created is good, and nothing is to be rejected if it is received with thanksgiving" (4:4). Though this is a passage referring to apostasy, it states a truth that is applicable to your life today. Everything created by God is good and is to be gratefully received.

Recently, while planting some flowers, I moved a rock and found a strange worm-like creature. Inspecting it more closely, I discovered that it was bigger than an earthworm and had feet and a tail. It was a chameleon, glorying in trying to make himself invisible by changing colors and blending into the earth beneath that rock. Intrigued with God's creative artistry, I rejoiced for a moment in one of His lesser creations, realizing once again how seldom I take time to sense the wonder of life.

If you have found your zest for life flagging lately, or if you are struggling with burdens that seem too heavy to bear, why not take a nature break and exercise your sense of wonder in the good things God has made.

I love these words written by an older person who has discovered a great truth that could change the rest of your days:

If I had my life to live over again . . . I would take more trips, I would climb more mountains, swim more rivers and watch more sunsets. I would do more walking and looking. I would eat more ice cream and less beans. I would start barefooted earlier in the Spring and stay that way later in the Fall. I would play more, I would ride more merry-go-rounds, I'd pick more daisies.

It's not too late. Begin today to open your eyes wider. See the incredible loveliness planned and executed by the Master Designer. Rejoice in the smallest creature or the greatest and grandest display of nature. It was all created to be received with thanksgiving. This world and everything in it was created to be an accurate reflection of our God and His creative genius.

WEEK 22 — WEDNESDAY
SPIRIT OF FEAR

Think about your greatest fear. Can you identify it? Do you fear being left alone? Do you fear illness and death? Do you fear losing your job? Do you fear being ridiculed or not taken seriously?

Fear often motivates behaviors that are incompatible with trust and obedience to God. If you fear loneliness, you may try to cling to those who are dear to you. If you fear illness, you will be panic-stricken at every twinge of pain or possible symptom of disease. If you fear financial insecurity, you may compromise your ethics just to guarantee a salary.

Second Timothy 1:7 states: "God did not give us a spirit of timidity [fear], but a spirit of power, of love and of self-discipline." If you are afraid, God didn't do it!

Power to cope with anxious moments, love to deal with difficult people, and self-discipline are the marks of a man or woman who walks in faith. Since fear is the opposite of faith, one of the healthiest things you can do is to face the fact that you are fearful, name your fear, and then tackle it head on.

Try talking about the thing you fear. Denying that you are fearful will merely provide fertile ground for a whole crop of fearful thoughts.

I confess, I have an irrational fear of elevators, the result of having been stuck in one. Consequently, whenever I have to ride in an elevator, I do a lot of talking to myself and to the Lord. "Yes, indeed," I say. "I'm afraid of this elevator, but I know that God rides in elevators, too. So, since He has promised never to leave me or forsake me, and since He has not given me a spirit of fear but the power to cope with this situation, then why am I making such a big deal about getting on?"

God has not made me fearful. My choice is to avoid riding in elevators altogether or to put my fears aside and trust Him to ride with me!

What are you fearful of today? What keeps you from becoming the full-of-faith man or woman God intends for you to be? Whatever it is, God says, "That fear is not from me."

If fear seems to dominate your life, I would encourage you to memorize 2 Timothy 1:7. The next time you begin to feel fear get a grip on you, remind yourself that it is not from God and that He can replace it with an overcoming faith.

WEEK 22 — THURSDAY
JUST LIKE MAMA

Lately there has been a proliferation of books on quotable quotes from mothers. One author calls them "momilies": "This hurts me more than it hurts you"; or "As long as I'm around, I'll be your mother"; or "If somebody else's mother lets him jump off the Empire State Building, would you want me to let you do it, too?"

Those are some of the phrases that many of us heard as kids growing up. We just couldn't believe we'd ever be repeating them to our own children!

While these are often amusing to recall, some of the more negative attitudes and behaviors embraced by our mothers seem to be equally well preserved. Many times the second or third generations never realize that the attitude that is being tenaciously held to may not be God's truth but the truth as seen and interpreted by "Mother."

For example, how do you respond to disappointment or hurt? Are you outspoken or withdrawn? Do you pout or speak your mind? Do you let it roll off or bury it inside? Whatever your style, it was probably influenced by your mother.

In the Scriptures, Paul addresses a man who was blessed by the faith that was passed down from one generation to the next: "I have been reminded of your sincere faith, which first lived in your grandmother Lois and in your mother Eunice and, I am persuaded, now lives in you also" (2 Tim. 1:5). Timothy, of course, grew up to assist the apostle Paul in his ministry.

Today, Timothys are few and far between. Instead, we are seeing adult children of alcoholics, incest victims, and many hurting grown men and women still trying to discover who they are.

Most of us reflect the attitude of our mothers. If you were blessed with a godly mother, the evidence will show in your life. Was she self-willed, manipulative, bitter? Then, unless you yourself have had a transforming experience with the Lord, you may be cursed with an attitude of rebellion, self-promotion, and bitterness.

Your mother's legacy is either a blessing or a curse. Resolve, with God's help, to break any negative cycle that may be passed on to future generations. And if you are a parent, cultivate a close walk with God, which, when all is said and done, is the greatest inheritance a child can receive.

WEEK 22 — FRIDAY
A GRACIOUS INVITATION

For me, the warmest invitation to prayer in all of Scripture is found in Hebrews 4:14–16:

> Therefore, since we have a great high priest who has gone through the heavens, Jesus the Son of God, let us hold firmly to the faith we profess. For we do not have a high priest who is unable to sympathize with our weaknesses, but we have one who has been tempted in every way, just as we are—yet was without sin. Let us then approach the throne of grace with confidence, so that we may receive mercy and find grace to help us in our time of need.

This passage describes a Priest (Jesus Christ) who is sympathetic and understanding, and a throne that is full of unmerited favor, waiting to be poured out. When you approach Him, you will walk away with mercy—a full pardon instead of what you deserve. And you will find grace—what you *don't* deserve—to help in your time of need.

Let's take a moment to look at this spectacular promise in practical, everyday, where-you-are-living terms:

Are you worried about a teenager who is giving you a fit, and you realize that a lot of his rebellion is a result of your failure to be the parent you should have been?

God says, "Come to the throne room." Jesus is a sympathetic listener. While He never sinned, He was human and knows the pull and distraction of the flesh. Tell Him about this child and how inadequate and guilty you feel. You will not be condemned or belittled for failing, but will be given God's wisdom and strength to help you through the crisis.

What about the financial jam you've gotten yourself into? Will you dare to come to the throne where Jesus, who owns the cattle on a thousand hills, is waiting to forgive your debt? Oh, you probably won't walk away with a big loan to solve your financial problems, but you won't be condemned for making that bad business deal. And you will find His wisdom for future transactions.

Or what about the marriage you're committed to? To be perfectly honest, this man you married has turned out to be a big disappointment. God says that if you really want change and not just relief, come pour out your heart to your great High Priest, who knows how difficult it is, because of sin, for men and women to live together in harmony. Mercifully, you won't be punished for not trying harder or for failing to be more spiritual before you decided to marry. But you will find grace to become the person who makes your marriage the very best it can be.

I pray that today, no matter what your burden, you will come confidently to the throne room and tell Jesus all of your troubles. He has promised mercy and grace for this very crisis.

WEEK 23 — MONDAY
UNLIVED TRUTH

Dwight L. Moody once said, "Our great problem is the problem of trafficking in unlived truth. We try to communicate what we've never experienced in our own life."

But it doesn't take long to discover when a Christian knows from experience what he is talking about. I recently read an article on suffering, written by a person who obviously knows both what it means to hurt and to be comforted by the Lord Jesus. He writes, not from theological or grammatical correctness, but from a heart that has been broken and mended again:

When you are deeply hurt—no person on this earth can shut down the inner fears and deepest agonies. Not the best of friends can really understand the battle you are going through or the wounds inflicted on you.

Only God can shut down the waves of depression and feelings of loneliness and failure that come over you. Faith in God's love alone can salvage the hurt mind. The bruised and broken heart that suffers in silence can be healed only by a supernatural work of the Holy Spirit—and nothing short of divine intervention really works.

God has to step in and take over. He has to intercept our lives at the breaking point and stretch forth His loving arms and bring that hurting body and mind under His protection and care. God must come forth as a caring Father and demonstrate that He is there, making things turn out for the good. He must by His own power dispel the storm clouds—chase away the despair and gloom—wipe away the tears—and replace the sorrow with peace of mind.

Another who knew all about pain and healing was the apostle Paul, who writes, "Endure hardship with us, like a good soldier of Christ Jesus" (2 Tim. 2:3). Paul wasn't just mouthing trite platitudes. He was communicating a living reality in his own life to which he could confidently call others.

One Sunday, when my boys were young, I apologized to them for making them sit through a sermon that was so boring and so dead that the greatest lover of Christ and His Word would have gone to sleep. Whether minister, Sunday school teacher, lay leader, or ordinary Christian, the vitality of one's relationship with the Lord Jesus Christ will show. If it doesn't, then something is dreadfully wrong.

Are you able to say, "This is what God is showing me. This is the reality of Christ in my life," or are you content to let others speak of reality while you say the usual "right things" everyone has heard a hundred times before?

My friend, why not ask God to give you a vital oneness with Him today? It is from that living relationship that you will be able to speak with the confidence, authority, and love which will convince others that you really know what you are talking about and will compel them to seek Him, too.

WEEK 23 — TUESDAY
ON THE ANVIL

The older I get, the more I realize that there is no end to the ordeals each of us has to face. Sometimes these painful trials come at the hand of someone we love.

Asking why is a normal reaction to being hurt or betrayed. And although we might be tempted to say, "This is the last thing on earth I ever expected," God says, "Do not be surprised at the painful trial you are suffering, as though something strange were happening to you. But rejoice that you participate in the sufferings of Christ, so that you may be overjoyed when his glory is revealed" (1 Peter 4:12–13).

In an article entitled "When You Hurt," by an unknown author, I found these words that seem to interpret that passage for contemporary Christians:

What has happened to you is a very common ailment among mankind. Your situation is not unique at all. It is the way of human nature. Whether you were right or wrong means absolutely nothing at this point. All that matters now is your willingness to move on in God and trust His mysterious workings in your life.

It is the mysterious workings of God in our lives—the hurt and loneliness themselves—that may someday be recognized as the tools God has used to shape character and insight in us. During these painful times of disbelief, God often does His anvil work in our lives.

One of my favorite authors, Max Lucado, writes these words about anvil time:

> Anvil time is not to be avoided; it's to be experienced. Although the tunnel is dark, it does go through the mountain. Anvil time reminds us of who we are and of who God is. We shouldn't try to escape it. To escape it could be to escape God.
>
> God sees our life from beginning to end. He may lead us through a storm at age thirty so we can endure a hurricane at age sixty. An instrument is useful only if it's in the right shape. A dull ax or a bent screwdriver needs attention, and so do we. A good blacksmith keeps his tools in shape. So does God.
>
> Should God place you on his anvil, be thankful. It means he thinks you're still worth reshaping.[1]

I talked with a woman who had been deserted by her husband and was on her way to another state to be with her son, on trial for armed robbery. With the sweetest expression in her eyes, she said, "I wouldn't want to go through all of this again, but I really don't regret it because God has been so near and so dear. I have learned to love Him in a way I've never known."

I don't know what you are going through today, but I would encourage you not to try to figure out the whys but simply to thank God that He sees you as still useful . . . and that He has a purpose for your time on the anvil.

WEEK 23 — WEDNESDAY
WHEN PRAYER DOESN'T SEEM TO HELP

I've been praying for a particular person for several years. The more intense my prayers, the more aloof and untouchable this individual seems to become. I know that God has given me a burden to pray specifically and constantly for this dear soul, but I just can't see any results.

Have you ever wondered if the Lord really understands what it's like to pray and pray and yet see nothing happening for a long period of time? Or even worse, have you prayed and seen that individual go in the opposite direction?

That thought has come to me from time to time, but I never got past the thinking stage until I read these words by Amy Carmichael in her devotional book, *Edges of His Way:*

> Our Lord Jesus prayed for Peter that his faith might not fail, and within a few hours his faith did fail.
>
> The more we think of those last hours of our Lord just before Calvary, the more we see every kind of trial compressed into them. It was not only that His cup was filled to overflowing with suffering, but that every variety of suffering was there. It is easy to escape from the intolerable sense of such suffering by saying, He was God; for example, where Peter was concerned we may say that He saw across to the victory that would be given. But we

know, though we cannot understand it, that He was man, too, and the word in Hebrews says that He suffered being tempted; to suffer means to endure or experience pain, so there is no escape by that door.

Is there one for whom we are praying who seems to be unhelped by that prayer? Are we suffering, enduring, experiencing the bitterness of disappointment? Our dear Lord has been this way before. We shall find Him there. He who "turned and looked upon Peter" will give to us, will maintain in us, His own eternal tenderness of spirit, the love that cannot be tired out of loving, the patience that will not let go.[2]

My friend, if you are tired of praying because it seems your prayers are making matters worse, I would encourage you to remember that God often has to do a stirring up and breaking down that creates pain and pressure in the life of a person in whom He intends to do a mighty work.

I spoke with a young man the other evening who was bemoaning a situation he's in that is crumbling before his eyes. While I feel compassion for him, I know that this seeming disaster in his life is a breaking that God must do before the prayers of his family and friends can possibly be answered.

Never give up, even when it seems that your prayers are achieving nothing but problems for the object of your loving concern. God is still on the throne, and though He understands and sympathizes with your feelings, He knows what He is doing. Be patient. Things are not what they seem.

WEEK 23 — THURSDAY
WOMEN'S RIGHTS ... OR WRONGS?

Sometimes it grieves me to be a woman in this generation. I think it hurts most when I see women shaking their fists in the face of God, and saying, "I'll do what I want to do with my own body." And when I hear the rhetoric of strong feminists who seem to dominate the secular media, I want to ask, "Wait a minute! Don't you know your own history? Don't you know that Christ liberated women two thousand years ago?"

In Ephesians 5:33, Paul, another of God's men who is accused by the feminists of being biased toward women, wrote these words: "Each one of you also must love his wife as he loves himself, and the wife must respect her husband."

No one in the twentieth century can fully appreciate what a radical statement this was in the day that it was written. Though we have come to accept this as a standard for marriage, it was a very different story in Paul's day. According to Barclay,

> The Jews had a low view of women. In the Jewish form of morning prayer there was a sentence in which a Jewish man every morning gave thanks that God had not made him "a Gentile, a slave or a woman." Under Jewish law, a woman was an object. She was not considered a person. And broadly speaking, a husband under Jewish law could divorce his wife for any cause; a wife could divorce her husband for no cause.

In the Greek world, the situation was more drastic. Prostitution was an essential part of Greek life. Demosthenes said, "We have courtesans for the sake of pleasure; we have concubines for the sake of daily cohabitation; we have wives for the purpose of having children legitimately, and for having a faithful guardian for all our household affairs." The Greek expected his wife to run his home, to care for his children, but he found his pleasure and his companionship elsewhere.[3]

Roman life was even worse. Seneca writes that women were married to be divorced and divorced to be married.

It was against this background that Paul writes. To compound the problem, he risked stating an unpopular view: "There is a better way."

Like the men and women of our generation, the people of the first century thought the whole concept of fidelity, love, and mutual submission was stuffy. After all, they, like we, wanted to be free to do what they wanted with their own bodies.

When I see women march for reproductive freedom and for feminist causes, I wonder what that must do to the heart of God who so long ago said if we will live in love and in mutual submission, then we will be fulfilled and blessed and experience joy.

I regularly talk with women who believe they can live any way they want, whether inside the bond of marriage or outside. But they are miserable, hurt, feel cheated, and depressed. I believe it all goes back to the fact that we are either going to do things God's way or we are going to reap a bitter harvest.

Oh, my dear sister, let us not be duped by the lie of "doing it my way." God sent His Son to deliver an "emancipation proclamation" from every form of bondage. Women—and men— who will accept His saving grace are liberated from the tyranny of sin.

WEEK 23 — FRIDAY
WHAT COMES OUT OF A MAN

I have been reminded once again of how much emphasis we put on the outward appearance. During the sixties and seventies, there was enormous emphasis on the dress code for Christians, including the length of a haircut. But when I turned on a Christian television program last week, I was amused to see that, whereas several years ago, the men on this particular program were required to keep their hair short, most of them now wear their hair long in back.

Now that the styles in hair and clothing have eased, we are getting legalistic about other things, still failing to focus on those things God says are important.

Recently I met a woman who loves the Lord with all her heart. She works hard for Him, is concerned about His kingdom, and never misses a church service. But as I got to know her a little better, I have had to ponder her perspective. All I have ever heard her say is tinged with negativism. And while I know she is sincere, she is in a constant state of agitation and worry.

As Jesus taught His disciples, then and now:

"What goes into a man's mouth does not make him 'unclean,' but what comes out of his mouth, that is what makes him 'unclean.' " Then the disciples came to him and asked, "Do you know that the Pharisees were offended when they heard this?" (Matt. 15:11–12)

Isn't that a picture of human nature at its most human? "Lord, you're giving us truth . . . but did you know the Pharisees are offended because they emphasize the externals? They have quiet times, they say prayers in public, they even tithe . . . and every time the temple doors are open . . . there they are."

In our humanity, we are so prone to mislabel things. We are big on what we can see, feel, touch, and do that will prove our standing in God's sight. And yet He says, "You've got that backwards. Whatever comes out of you is really *in* you . . . and that's what proves what you are really made of."

What do you hang on to as being very important to God? Is there some ritual, some service, some article of clothing that you associate with spirituality? If so, there's nothing wrong with that . . . unless you are harboring feelings of anger, worry, bitterness, or even hatred for yourself or someone else. These are the things that defile you, the issues that concern God most.

Why not take stock of what is coming out in your attitudes and actions. Those are the things that tell the world you're a Christian. Man-made standards of dress and conduct mean nothing if your thoughts and attitudes fail to meet God's standard.

WEEK 24 — MONDAY
FRUSTRATION

Trying to get across Chattanooga late on a Friday afternoon has to be one of the most frustrating experiences of my life. Suddenly every car and truck in the city emerges from hidden garages and clogs the major thoroughfares. Traffic slows to a snail's pace, and drivers bite their fingernails or sit and fume.

Frustration is having your plans thwarted. It is thinking things will be one way when they turn out another, or experiencing delay after delay while something vitally important seems to be slipping away.

Circumstances are not the only source of frustration. You can be frustrated by someone who promises to take out the garbage and never gets around to it. You can be frustrated by a family member who has to be told to pick up his shoes out of the den every single night. You can be frustrated by an employer's poor planning that results in unnecessary late-night hours. You can be frustrated by a friend who is always late.

Most of us take the normal frustrations of life pretty much in stride, until it comes to some dream we have always hoped or planned for.

I have a friend who was very athletic until she had knee surgery. Since then, she has been unable to return to her usual rigorous activities.

Another friend dreamed of getting married. Last summer she was sure she had found her mate. But two months before the wedding, he became controlling and domineering, and she saw they would never be able to make a life together. So she called off the wedding. For her, this has been a terrible frustration.

A third friend desperately wants to have a baby, but so far has been unable to conceive. All she wants is to be a mother, but her hopes have been frustrated.

These frustrations can only be placed in perspective as God's truth spotlights the deeper work and eternal purpose that is being worked out in a life "The Lord will fulfill his purpose for me; your love, O Lord, endures forever—do not abandon the works of your hands" (Ps. 138:8).

If you can remember that God will perfect everything He has willed for you, no plan will be ultimately frustrated. In the waiting and chafing that accompany feelings of frustration, there is always the promise of God's eternal purpose. He is working out that purpose in love.

WEEK 24 — TUESDAY
HOW TO FIGHT DEPRESSION

A friend of mine who has battled depression all her life recently pointed to this Scripture passage and said, "These words have made a difference in my life."

For though we live in the world, we do not wage war as the world does. The weapons we fight with are not the weapons of the world. On the contrary, they have divine power to demolish strongholds. We demolish arguments and every pretension that sets itself up against the knowledge of God, and we take captive every thought to make it obedient to Christ. (2 Cor. 10:3–5)

For those who are afflicted with depression—that all-pervasive state of gloom and hopelessness that hover over a person like a black cloud, this passage speaks of three keys to overcoming.

1. *Demolish strongholds.* God says that we have the power to tear down strongholds—those protective measures we use to keep ourselves from being hurt again, those thoughts that justify an attitude of defensiveness or anger or bitterness. Strongholds are walls that keep other people out. What walls have you erected to keep your love contained and your heart untouched?

2. *Destroy arguments and every pretension that sets itself up against the knowledge of God.* In our weakness of faith, we sometimes question God—His sovereignty, His love, His care. But the depressed person focuses inwardly: Is God's love sufficient to overcome my worthlessness? Is His blood sufficient to cleanse my sin?

   These "pretensions and arguments" are raised against the truth He has revealed—that His love is eternal and that nothing can separate us from that love, that Jesus came to shed His blood for the sins of the whole world. Yet, in his lofty speculations, the depressed person manages to make himself an exception to every rule.

3. *Take captive every thought.* Thoughts can be deceptive and cunning and need to be brought under control. The only way to do that is to say, "I choose for Christ's thoughts to be my thoughts even if I have trouble believing them to be true." Mercifully, He has given us the power to believe the unbelievable and to recognize truth in the midst of great deception.

If you are battling depression today, I pray that you will act on this Scripture passage and ask God to set you free.

WEEK 24 — WEDNESDAY
GODLY REPENTANCE

The story is told of a man who stole an ox. In punishment, he was placed in a large wooden collar. A friend came along and asked him what crime he had committed to merit such treatment. The thief replied, "I was just walking across the street when I saw on the ground a grass rope. Thinking it was of no use, I made the mistake of picking it up and taking it home, and so I got into this trouble."

"But what could be wrong with picking up a grass rope?" the friend wanted to know.

"Well, something was tied to the other end of the rope."

"And what was that?"

To which the thief replied, "A very small ox."

What "small oxen" have you picked up lately? Have you ever justified an angry outburst, for example, on the basis of the other person's rude behavior? In other words, if they had not left their string dangling, you would not have walked off with their ox!

An interesting Scripture passage deals with this kind of situation in a very practical way. Paul, in writing to some Corinthian believers who had blown it and were aware of their sin, says:

> I am happy, not because you were made sorry, but because your sorrow led you to repentance. For you became sorrowful as God intended and so were not harmed in any way by us. Godly sorrow brings repentance that leads to salvation and leaves no regret, but worldly sorrow brings death. See what this godly sorrow has produced in you: what earnestness, what eagerness to clear yourselves, what indignation, what alarm, what longing, what concern, what readiness to see justice done. (2 Cor. 7:9–11)

When we are truly repentant, there is an attitude of brokenness, an earnestness, a hatred for what has been done; there is a zeal and a longing to avoid any further taint of the sin. And it only comes when we see our sin the way God sees it. Eventually, we realize that our anger, our bitterness, or backbiting, our lack of forgiveness—all these and more grieve God. He is grieved because He knows that sin leads to a death in us—death to our ability to be useful, death to our fellowship with Him, death to the peace and freedom that is every believer's heritage.

Ask God to show you what is at the end of your rope. If you ask Him to be specific, you'll be surprised at just how specific He will be. Then ask Him to give you a heart for godly repentance—not only changing your mind but your direction. Viewing your sin as God views it is the first step toward true repentance.

WEEK 24 — THURSDAY
GETTING ALONG WITH OTHERS

Getting along with other people when they are different and difficult, at least to our way of thinking, is one of the biggest challenges we face as God's children.

Amy Carmichael, the wonderful missionary to India, spent the last twenty years of her life confined to bed due to an accident. During those years she occupied herself writing words of encouragement to her children in the faith. Her thoughts have been recorded in a little volume entitled *Candles in the Dark*.

> I have a canary all by himself in a big cage in my room. His name is Cymbal because he sings beautifully. But he can't get on with other canaries. That is why he is alone in my room. He doesn't like to sing with them, or eat with them, or play with them.
>
> Is there anyone with whom you don't get on? With whom you don't like to work, or play or do anything? Perhaps you haven't actually quarrelled, but if you can avoid it, you don't talk together, and you don't care to pray together.
>
> If there be such a one, will you do this? Every day will you name that one to your Lord? (Don't mention faults, but just ask for a blessing.) I do earnestly ask you to do this. Will you do it?[1]

What a challenge to go to the Lord with the name of someone you don't even like, and ask for a blessing!

Yet this is the essence of Jesus' teaching: "I tell you: Love your enemies and pray for those who persecute you, that you may be sons of your Father in heaven. He causes his sun to rise on the evil and the good, and sends rain on the righteous and the unrighteous" (Matt. 5:44).

In other words, if we want to look and act like our heavenly Father, we cannot choose who receives the blessing. He gives rain to the good and the bad. So why should we be so picky?

Mentally, I can see the face of someone right now who is really not an enemy; neither is she a special favorite of mine. I don't look for opportunities to spend time with this person. In fact, if the truth were known, I don't want to spend time with her at all. She irritates me. Maybe such a person comes to your mind. Instead of ignoring these people in our lives, God wants us to do something radical—to pray that they will receive a blessing!

Join me this week as I pray God's blessing on this irritating person in my life. And will you dare to pray for that difficult person in your life? In so doing, we prove that we are "sons [and daughters] of our Father."

WEEK 24 — FRIDAY
LESSON FROM THE HAWK

It is said that when a hawk is attacked by crows or kingbirds, he does not make a counterattack, but soars higher and higher in ever-widening circles until his tormentors leave him alone.

The hawk is a powerful adversary. If he chose to fight, no doubt he

121

would win. But he chooses to fly above all the clatter and fuss by spiraling upward.

In Proverbs 20:3, God says, "It is to a man's honor to avoid strife, but every fool is quick to quarrel."

All of us have people who make our lives difficult, either directly or subtly. Perhaps you are under fire today. Someone has unleashed an all-out attack, or has picked at some very sensitive area in your life. You would like to retaliate. But God's children are called to deal with such people through uncommon means.

Maybe you can identify with the woman who wrote:

Seems like we think we've nailed our behaviors to the Cross, only to find we only nailed the part I saw to the Cross, and that old way of acting spirals around on me. I'm going through, "You make me so angry when you tease me!" And I wish he would stop teasing me, because I've had forty years of it and I don't think I need any more. I know it's not his teasing but my reaction to it that needs changing. It's just so much easier to gripe at him, pout, stomp, and glare than it is to sit up, shut up, and carry on.

In the sitting up, shutting up, and carrying on, there is an opportunity to soar above it all. To give back as good as you get is only an invitation to get more.

The hawk teaches a valuable lesson. The better part of valor is avoiding strife . . . flying above your tormentors. Just drop the whole matter and leave the scene. Fighting even when someone else initiates the fight, might exact a greater price than you want to pay in defense and counterattacks. If you choose to soar above it all, then you have focused on a loftier goal and have left your opponents to their own devices.

Why not resolve to spiral upward—above and beyond the conflict—into the very presence of God. Time spent with Him makes tense situations more bearable.

WEEK 25 — MONDAY
MY SALAD DAYS

Shakespeare talks about "my salad days, when I was green in judgment."

"Salad days" are those days of our lives when we assume we know what is right, jump into the project, the relationship, the move, or the job, and then look back and wonder what on earth went wrong. Usually, it was because our judgment was "green," untested and untried.

When I had been married only a short time, I decided to paint a room and all the furniture in it. The fact that this was a first for me didn't deter me at all! I started early in the morning with my bucket of pink paint, and by evening, I had finished, furniture and all. Seeing one spot I had missed, I climbed up on a chair. But in my fatigue, I failed to notice where I had left the paint bucket, and when I stepped down off the chair, I landed in the bucket and turned it over on the carpet. Now, not only did I have a pink room and furniture, but a pink carpet! I could have cried, but there was no time. I had to get busy and clean up the paint!

Needless to say, if there is a room to paint these days, my husband does it. He doesn't want me near a paintbrush!

In our "salad days," we learn valuable lessons, if sometimes very costly ones. Still, it is during those times that we explore the limits of our own judgment and realize how much more we have to learn.

In his book *The Saving Life of Christ,* Major Ian Thomas writes, "If there is any situation from which you are not prepared to step back, in recognition of the total adequacy of Christ who is in you, then you are out of the will of God." And in reality, until we realize our own inadequacy of judgment, that we can be wrong with the best of motives, then we will be unwilling to step back, lay down our judgment and let Christ call the shots for us.

I have had to admit that I spent a lot of "salad days," days when I depended upon my own wisdom, my own sense of what was right, never even considering what God might think of my decisions. Yet, He has caused some of my worst decisions to work for good, and He is in the process of doing that in your life, as well.

If you are on the brink of making a decision today, yet have not consulted God, take time to step back for a long look. Ask God to give you wisdom and knowledge to judge as He would judge, and thank Him for helping you mature past the "salad days."

WEEK 25 — TUESDAY
FRET NOT

A recent PBS telecast featured six families who occupy a ghetto tenement in Harlem. As the reporter moved from apartment to apartment, his camera lens zoomed in on unbelievable squalor, mirrored in the dark, despairing eyes of the tenants.

Then the scene changed abruptly. In the last apartment, a woman and four neatly dressed children sat at a simple table. A hot breakfast was being served. Each child bowed his head as the mother gave thanks to God for the meal. The contrast with the families in the other units was remarkable. In the midst of decadence, filth, and hopelessness, here was cleanliness, hope, and reverence.

The reason for this difference was soon evident. In an interview with the widowed mother, she quoted some words from Psalm 37: "Do not fret because of evil men" (v. 1). Though this woman lived in an unjust and oppressive society, where people were breaking the law with impunity, she had found a way to hold on to truth that could stabilize and protect her children.

In Psalm 37, that precious psalm for people with a reason to fret, David deals with how to handle feelings when all the bad guys are winning and all the good guys are losing. If God is really in control of the universe and the government is really on His shoulders, then how come the righteous seem to be getting such a raw deal? David tackled the first response: "Fret not." In the Hebrew, that means, "Don't incense yourself." The English translation is, roughly, "Don't stew in your own juice."

If you are stewing in your own juice because someone has succeeded in walking away with a job, a prize, a raise, and you know they have done it by unscrupulous means, God has a word for you: No matter how evil and unjust the deed that has been perpetrated, no matter how unpunished the evil-doer, you may be sure that God, the righteous Judge, will hear and vindicate your case.

We live in a fallen world which has been summed up by the cynic in these words: "Life's tough, then you die." But we have a fair and loving Father who will see that justice prevails. Stewing in our own juice leads only to ulcers.

WEEK 25 — WEDNESDAY
PERFECT PEACE

While eating out last week, I found myself at the salad bar behind the classic spoiled child. Before I had the lettuce on my plate, I had learned that the child's name was Daniel and that fixing a salad in his wake was going to be a challenge!

Only about five years of age, Daniel was not tall enough to help himself conveniently, though he could see the contents of every container and personally examined every onion, green pepper, beet, pickled bean, and tomato. Despite his mother's assurance that he would not eat those things, so there was no need to take them on his plate, he grabbed for the ladles in the salad dressings and splashed French and bleu cheese on the counter with one last defiant comment. As his exasperated mother tugged him toward his seat, he continued to complain loudly.

We are a lot like Daniel, making ourselves and everyone around us miserable when we fret over what we cannot have and demand things that God knows we do not need. His remedy for this kind of confusion is found in Isaiah 26:3: "You will keep in perfect peace him whose mind is steadfast, because he trusts in you."

We all want the "perfect peace," but "a steadfast mind" is hard to come by. Often when we come to prayer, we find ourselves so caught up in our circumstances that focusing on God seems impossible.

Amy Carmichael writes: "I think distractions in prayer are often because we have let ourselves wander too far from the things that matter most at common times, and so we have slipped into an easily interrupted, easily distracted frame of mind. We need to live more at home. 'In Him we live, and move, and have our being' means simply this: God is our home."[1]

If God is our home, then He is the one to whom we naturally return again and again. What do you think about in your idle hours—when you are driving, when you fall asleep at night, when you take a break? If your mind strays to things you want to own, successes you want to achieve, goals you have set, you will feel only a sense of frustration, and the peace that is your heritage as God's child will always be just beyond your grasp.

The little Daniel I mentioned earlier was a frustrated, frantic little boy for one reason: He wanted what he wanted, but he wasn't willing to trust his mother and rest in her wise care of him. So, he stirred up a ruckus with every step he took.

Are you easily distracted today? Do the things you want but can't have for now obsess your thinking? Then, my friend, focus on the One who cares about every facet of your life. He knows what you think you want and, in reality, what is best for you.

Trust in Him steadfastly—with 'undeviating constancy and resolution." Your reward will be perfect peace—"excellent, exactly and completely fitting your need, beyond practical and theoretical improvement."

WEEK 25 — THURSDAY
FELLOWSHIP OF SUFFERING

There are verses in Psalm 37 that I dearly love: "The days of the blameless are known to the Lord, and their inheritance will endure forever. In times of disaster they will not wither; in days of famine they will enjoy plenty" (vv. 18–19).

If Helen Rosevere, a missionary doctor to the Congo, had read those words the night rebel soldiers took her captive, there may have been some doubt in her mind that they were really true. But as she endured the atrocities, God Himself taught her she could trust Him. The time was evil, but she did not know shame. Listen to an excerpt from her book, *Living Sacrifice:*

> Beaten, flung on the ground, kicked—teeth broken, mouth and nose gashed, ribs bruised—driven at gunpoint back to my home, jeered at, insulted, threatened . . . It was a very dark night. I felt unutterably alone. For a brief moment, I felt God had failed me. He could have stepped in and prevented this rising crescendo of wickedness and cruelty. He could have saved me out of their hands. Why didn't He speak? Why didn't He intervene? And in desperation, I almost cried out against Him: "It is too much to pay!"
>
> In the darkness and loneliness, He met with me. He was right there, a great, wonderful, almighty God. His love enveloped me. Suddenly the "Why?" dropped away from me, and an unbelievable peace flowed in, even in the midst of wickedness. And He breathed a word into my troubled mind; the word *privilege* . . .
>
> For twenty years, anything I had needed, I had asked of God and He had provided. Now, this night, the Almighty had stooped to ask of me something that He condescended to appear to need, and He offered me the privilege of responding . . . He offered me the inestimable privilege of sharing with Him in some little measure, at least, in the edge of the fellowship of His sufferings. And it was all privilege.

My friend, the Lord knows your days—the stresses, the strains, the sufferings—and He has promised that no matter how much you have to suffer at the hands of an evil person, you don't have to be ashamed because He is with you in it, taking the abuse and injustice right alongside of you.

Thank God today for knowing what is going on in your life, for His purpose in your pain, and for the comfort of His presence. And while you are offering Him your sacrifice of praise, ask Him to give you eyes to see that He really understands.

WEEK 25 — FRIDAY
THE LORD IS MERCIFUL

The Scriptures say in Psalm 37, "The steps of a man are established by the LORD; and He delights in his way. When he falls, he shall not be hurled headlong; because the LORD is the One who holds his hand" (vv. 23–24 NASB).

Back in 1971, when I came into a personal relationship with the Lord, it seemed that I did more falling than walking. It got to be discouraging because just about the time I thought I was on a consistently righteous walk, I'd fall. I was around a lot of Christians who were older in the Lord, and I was watching a lot of Christian television programs and reading a lot of Christian books but I just wasn't measuring up to what I knew I should be. Frankly, I despaired that I ever could be the kind of Christian I wanted to be. I had played the church game for years and I couldn't stand to think of just playing at being a Christian and never becoming what I thought a real Christian was.

One day I sat down on my sofa and my eyes fell on the big Bible that was open for decoration on my coffee table. (It was of the gilded variety that comes as a bonus with a set of encyclopedias. Terribly impractical, but attractive, nonetheless.) I looked down and it was opened to Psalm 56:12–13. And for the first time, it was as if God said these words directly to me: "Thy vows are upon me, O God: I will render praises unto thee. For thou hast delivered my soul from death; wilt not thou deliver my feet from falling, that I may walk before God in the light of the living?" (KJV).

My eyes nearly popped out of my head. This verse was for me! His vows were on me. Having taken wedding vows I knew the seriousness of a vow, so I knew that if His vows were on me I was a Christian whether I happened to feel like one that day or not. Then He said my soul had been delivered from death. He had saved me from eternal damnation, so surely He could keep my feet from falling. I had been underestimating the power of God in my life to "keep" me. I could believe that He would save me, but I just couldn't believe that I could walk without falling down and permanently blowing it as a Christian. In Psalm 37, God says, "He shall not be utterly cast down; for the LORD upholdeth him with his hand" (v. 24 KJV). The very hand of God is there to hold you—you may not feel it, but God says it is there.

As each of my three boys learned to walk, our hands were always there. They fell to their knees, many times, but we never let them fall on their heads or get permanently hurt. In the same way, the Lord is always there to keep us. He will not let us be cast down. "For though a righteous man falls seven times, he rises again" (Prov. 24:16).

My friend, if you feel as if you're going down for the eighth time, hold on. God is holding you with His hand. And His goal for you is strength and confidence in the face of the rough spots in the road. So hang on . . . you cannot fall headlong.

WEEK 26 — MONDAY
NOTHING IN RETURN

As a Sunday school teacher and conference speaker who teaches the Word of God to others, I have sometimes found myself in the hot seat being tested on lessons I have taught!

One such occasion occurred shortly after I had delivered a thorough exposition of Luke 6:34: "And if you lend to those from whom you expect repayment, what credit is that to you? Even 'sinners' lend to 'sinners,' expecting to be repaid in full."

Then the Lord said to me, "OK, Jan, let's see what you have learned."

Since it was my practice to pick up one of my sons after football practice, we inevitably ended up with a carful of youngsters. Giving the other boys a ride never bothered me until I observed them piling into another car one day when I picked up my son.

"Did they ask if *you* needed a ride?" I asked. And when he replied that they had not, I proceeded to blow a fuse, telling him that unless they could share rides equally, his friends would just have to find another way home. Amidst instructions that he was to tell his friends, "No more free rides!" my son was obviously relieved when we pulled into the driveway and he could escape my preaching.

By the next day I had forgotten all about my irritation. But when I arrived at school to pick up my son, our former hitchhikers walked right past my car and across the parking lot.

Bewildered, I asked my son, "Where are they going?"

"They're going to walk the six miles, Mom. Remember? I told them what you said."

At that point, the Holy Spirit put His finger on my heart and brought to mind the very lesson I had just taught: "Lend . . . without expecting to get anything back. Then your reward will be great" (v. 35). Needless to say, I went after the boys and insisted on giving them a ride. And when we got home, I confessed to my son that I had been wrong and that if anyone ever needed transportation, we would gladly provide it, "expecting nothing in return." My mercy has been stretched to the limit a time or two, but I know I am acting in obedience.

Is there an area in your life that does not truly reflect righteousness? Often it is the "little things" that trip us up, that others can point out as inconsistent with our claim to be Christian.

Ask God to reveal the cracks and crevices of your heart where the little things are hidden. And while you're at it, why not ask Him for the courage to bring them out into the Son-light and expose them for what they are.

WEEK 26 — TUESDAY
A TIME FOR TEARS

When one of my dearest friends lost her young son, I was appalled to hear someone say to her, "I don't know what I would do if I ever lost one of *my* children."

How I cringed for my friend! But I regretted even more the fact that some people seem incapable of offering comfort in times of distress.

Joseph Bayly, a man who has known the deep sorrow of losing three sons, has written a book, *The View from the Hearse,* in which he gives these words of instruction to those who are interested in learning how to meet the needs of a grieving friend:

> Don't try to prove anything to a survivor. An arm about the shoulder, a firm grip of the hand, a kiss: these are the proofs grief needs, not logical reasoning.
>
> I was sitting, torn by grief. Someone came and talked to me of God's dealings, of why it happened, of hope beyond the grave. He talked constantly, he said things I knew were true.
>
> I was unmoved, except to wish he'd go away. He finally did. Another came and sat beside me. He didn't talk. He didn't ask leading questions. He just sat beside me for an hour or more,

listened when I said something, answered briefly, prayed simply, left.

I was moved. I was comforted. I hated to see him go.[1]

In ministering to a grieving friend, I would encourage you to lay aside your need to explain death and God's dealings with us. The Scriptures say we are to "weep with those who weep." Just as Jesus wept at the tomb of his friend Lazarus, so we are to be present, to listen, to focus on another's hurt and pain. We are to offer comfort, not answers; silence, not sermons; a shoulder to cry on, not a push to hurry past the grief.

A grieving person does best when he is allowed time to feel the grief, and can receive the assurance of friends that they will be there with him as long as it takes him to heal.

William Blake, an eighteenth-century poet, said it well in his poem "On Another's Sorrow":

> Can I see another's woe,
> And not be in sorrow, too?
> Can I see another's grief
> And not seek for kind relief?

That is what God calls us to do for each other. Simply sit quietly by and feel your friend's pain, offering no explanations or exhortations, but only the compassion of one who cries with him.

WEEK 26 — WEDNESDAY
THE HOLY BALANCE

I know an elderly woman who is an eternal optimist, emphasizing the happy aspect of any circumstance. One day, in talking about the death of her husband, she became aware that the conversation had taken a turn toward the morbid, including too many painful details of his last days. "This is really so unpleasant," she said. "I'd much rather remember the happy days."

Another dear woman can take the happiest of circumstances and, before she is through relating the details, it has become a sad, often tragic, event.

Which kind of person are you? Do you look for the positive, or do you have a tendency to take the most unfavorable view of situations or actions?

Actually, too much optimism can set one up for a fall. Life can often be brutal, and every situation does not have a happy ending. We must be prepared to trust that God is at work and will ultimately cause everything to work for our good, but everything is *not* good, and sometimes the breaking and molding He has to do in our lives is anything but a carefree matter.

On the other hand, pessimism creates such a dispirited mental attitude that the word *hope,* the happy anticipation of good, loses its promise. If you are always expecting the worst, then you lose the vision of God's purpose in pain and His strength to stand every test.

I honestly believe that God intends for us to live balanced lives—to realistically assess the grave nature of many difficult situations, and to have hope in the midst of the sobering realities.

Both the optimist and the pessimist must realize that, although we may experience depression, difficulty, disappointment and even death, there is a counterbalance that gives us stability: "When you walk through the fire, you will not be burned; the flames will not set you ablaze" (Isa. 43:2).

The truth, which is always balanced, is: "You [will] walk through the fire." The pessimist yells, "See, I told you! Fire, fire! Fire everywhere!" The optimist responds, "Yes, but I am not being burned. Watch me! I'll sit down in the fire. . . ."

God says, "You are both right to a point. You will walk through fire, my beloved pessimist, but there will be an end to your fire-walk. And, yes, my precious optimist, the flames will not harm you, but don't just sit there to prove my protection. Persevere, keep on walking . . . and my purpose for you and your more sober, pessimistic brother will be accomplished."

No matter what your inclination, God says you can be a balanced individual, a person who finds purpose in the happy times and God's hand in time of trouble.

WEEK 26 — THURSDAY
FEAR OF WHAT PEOPLE THINK

Do you worry about what other people think of you? Do you struggle with what someone else will do with your reputation?

I have always been slightly amused at folks who say things like "I would love to have a red dress, but what would people think?" Or "I could never live in house in that neighborhood; people might think we were uppity." Or "I couldn't possibly drive a new car; someone might think I was rich."

"What people think" is the bane of many folks' existence; in fact, it controls every move they make. The truth is that the only one you have to please is the Lord.

The Scriptures say to beware "when all men speak well of you" (Luke 6:26). So if you are living your life shadowed by what other people think or what other people say, then you are probably doing something wrong.

Of course, you must strike a balance. If you live your life only to please yourself and you don't care how it affects other people, that is just as dangerous. The balance, the happy medium, is found in the confidence of having the Lord's approval.

Do you remember the movie *Chariots of Fire*? The main character, Eric Liddell, was a star runner who went against everyone's opinion and chose not to run on Sunday. There was quite a stir about it, but he didn't care. He had only one person to please, and that was the Lord.

In fact, his most famous line was, "When I run I feel His pleasure." He had no fear of what other people said about him because he was confident that he was pleasing to the Lord.

If you are sure that your heart belongs totally to the Lord and your greatest desire is to please Him, then you have no reason to fear other people's opinions. Everyone has an opinion, but God's is the only opinion that counts.

WEEK 26 — FRIDAY
DON'T QUIT!

When my boys were very small, they loved to wrestle with their daddy. They would brag about how brave they were and how they could pin him to the floor. They entered every bout with great gusto, but sometimes when the going got tough, they would cry, get angry, and want to give up. Their brave talk wasn't proven in battle.

God says we're the same way. Sometimes we want to run from the very process that He is using to allow us to know Him better. When it hurts too much or when we feel defeated, we pout and want to quit.

In James, we find this practical piece of advice:

> When all kinds of trials and temptations crowd into your lives, my brothers, don't resent them as intruders, but welcome them as friends! Realize that they come to test your faith and to produce in you the quality of endurance. But let the process go on until that endurance is fully developed, and you will find you have become men of mature character with the right sort of independence." (James 1:2–4, PHILLIPS)

According to this Scripture, God permits the tough times to test the validity of our faith. The way we react in a crisis is a barometer of how much we really believe God is in control and is doing what is necessary to build strong character in us.

In the passage in James, God also tells us to "Let the process go on until that endurance is fully developed." I believe there is a quality of strength that is evident in the life of the believer who has chosen not to abandon a hard situation or to shortcut the long haul. There is a confidence that comes from finishing the course and keeping the faith.

The situations we are most prone to give up on are close relationships. There may come a time when the greatest temptation will be to walk away. Leaving seems the simplest way to cope. No more problems. No more hassle. And I might add, no more maturing. The process is brought to an abrupt halt when you opt out.

I understand the temptation to give up, to say, "I've had it!" At times like these, let's remember the promise recorded in the James passage: "You will find you have become [people] of mature character with the right sort of independence." Such a guarantee for the future is worth some temporary pain and hardship.

WEEK 27 — MONDAY
POLITENESS

One of the nicest compliments a mother can hear is that her children are polite. In our day, it seems like that compliment can be given less and less. Politeness seems to have taken a back seat not only for our children but also for many of us. However, the story is told about one little boy whose mother had made quite an impression on him about being polite. He was told that when visitors came to the house it was his duty to pay them some attention.

Shortly afterward, a Mrs. Daniel called. The small boy shook hands with her politely and exclaimed in his best, most polite manner, "How do you do, Mrs. Daniel? I've just been reading about your husband in the den of lions."

You have to give the little guy an "A" for trying!

When I was a little girl, I can remember that my parents were always telling me, "When you are at church or at school, speak to adults. Don't just walk by and ignore them." I guess they told me that fifty times before it finally sank in and I began to say, "Hello. How are you?" to the grown folks. Now, since I am grown, I see the importance of speaking to people, of concentrating on them, of finding out how they are doing.

It is such a small thing to say, "Hi, how are you?" but it shows another person they have value and that they matter. Let's face it, we all want to matter.

Another way to be polite is to say, "Please." You know where that fits in. "Please pass the butter," or "Please pass the bread." I think a lot of people don't realize that what you are really saying is "If it pleases you, please pass the butter." In other words, the focus on the other person. You are showing them that they matter and have value.

Valuing another person is really the root of all of our politeness. When we treat someone with politeness which, as Webster says, "shows by speech and behavior a considerate regard for others," then we are saying, "You are a valuable person, you are worth this little extra effort that it will take to say please or thank you or to speak to you when I am in a hurry."

Parents, that works both ways for us. Many times we expect our children to be polite to us and to other adults but we don't take the time to be polite to them. Don't confuse being polite with being a pushover. Politeness says, "Please clean your room," one time and if it isn't done, it says, "Please meet me in the kitchen. There are some things you need to understand." A pushover says, "Please clean your room, please clean your room, please clean your room."

"Politeness is to do and say the kindest things in the kindest ways." Sometimes the kindest thing we can do is to correct one another, but it is most effective when you do it in kindness.

The Bible says that for a man to have friends he must be friendly, and it is impossible to be friendly without letting another person know that he is valuable . . . so valuable that you will be polite to him.

There is a little chorus that says, "To be like Jesus, this hope possesses me." You know, I can't imagine Jesus ever being impolite even to those who were impolite to Him.

To the young people, why not surprise your family by being polite to everyone, even your little sister, this weekend.

To the parents, why don't you give the whole family a surprise and determine you will be polite to everyone, even the most difficult person in your household.

What a gift that will be to your family and to the Lord.

WEEK 27 — TUESDAY
JESUS FOR HELP

On a major thoroughfare of my town, someone has crudely scrawled these words on one of the stone pillars of an overpass: "Jesus or hell?" Every time I pass that sign, I am disturbed by this insensitive presentation of the Savior who died that we might have eternal life. And while it is true that there is no other way to the Father except through Jesus, and the alternative is hell, the message of this graffiti seems harsh and condemning.

Apparently I am not the only one who has had a negative reaction to that sign because, when I drove by last week, someone had used a can of spray paint to alter the message from "Jesus or hell?" to "Jesus for help." That's

131

better! The message a dying world needs to hear is, "There is help." I believe that people will consider the claims of Christ if we will allow them the dignity of asking questions without condemnation.

A story in Mark, chapter 9, describes an incident in which Jesus walked up on a group of scribes who were arguing with His disciples. When all the confusion was brought under control, we see a man who has brought his demon-possessed son for help. The disciples had tried, without success, to heal the boy, and now his father turns to Jesus:

> Jesus asked the boy's father, "How long has he been like this?"
>
> "From childhood," he answered. "It has often thrown him into fire or water to kill him. But if you can do anything, take pity on us and help us."
>
> "'If you can'?" said Jesus. "Everything is possible for him who believes."
>
> Immediately the boy's father exclaimed, "I do believe; help me overcome my unbelief!" (vv. 21–24)

This man uttered the words that any of us might have said in a similar situation: "Help me overcome my unbelief." And that is why I like the change of the sign on the overpass from "Jesus or Hell?" to "Jesus for Help." He doesn't condemn, but simply invites us to come, even with our questions and doubts.

Even though you are a believer, you may feel condemned when confronted by spiritual harshness. I know I feel hell-bound at such times, despite my conviction that I am a child of God. Still, because signs that scream ultimatums condemn me, I am sure they must crush the hearts of those who are struggling to believe.

Jesus came, not to condemn the world, but to provide a means whereby all people could be saved. What message are you giving today: "Jesus or Hell?" or "Jesus for Help"?

WEEK 27 — WEDNESDAY
NO REQUEST TOO SMALL

Shortly after I became a Christian, I was helping my husband with his uniform for a National Guard drill when we discovered that his belt was missing. We looked everywhere, but no belt. Slipping off by myself, I asked the Lord to help me find it. At that moment, the words *the bottom of the closet* came to mind. Hurrying to the closet, I moved all of the shoes, felt around in the very back, and fished out the belt! Thanking the Lord, I went to show Charlie the answer to my prayer.

As I grew older in the faith, I found that some people believe it is presumptuous to talk with God about small, insignificant matters when there are so many more weighty issues. So I began searching the Scriptures to see if I was out of line.

In John 2:1–11, I read about a wedding feast where the hostess ran short of wine, and Jesus provided more. Now, that situation was certainly not of monumental proportions, but Jesus apparently thought it was significant enough to do something about it.

In fact, I remembered that act of kindness a few weeks ago when I was putting together a fiftieth wedding anniversary reception for my parents. As the only child, I was handling all the details myself. "Lord," I prayed. "You have told us to honor our parents, and this party is being held in their honor. So please guide the arrangements and bring to mind anything I might have forgotten." The party went off without a hitch. "Silly," you might say. But for me, this is where the reality of walking with Christ is seen most clearly.

In Matthew 10:29, we read of God's concern for a dying sparrow, and, in Luke 15, for a lost lamb. Several years ago, I had an old dog named Andrew. Andy was a special favorite of a dear lady who worked for me. I told her that since he had been sick and couldn't walk, and since he was almost eighteen years old, we felt it would be best to put him to sleep. She was visibly upset with this news and, after I left the room, I could hear her muttering under her breath. As I looked back in on her, she was on her knees, praying for my crippled pet. Soon, I heard the click of nails on the kitchen floor. Andy was up walking around, and we had him with us for several more months before he died!

Now, I'm not saying that God will always extend the life of a pet, or find the things you have lost, or coordinate your next party. Each of those falls within the realm of His choice. But I do believe that He invites us to come to our heavenly Father in an attitude of trust that leaves the outcome to Him. He never limits our topics of discussion. There is no request too small for your Father to consider.

Don't hold back today because you think your concerns are too trivial or unworthy. Your Father delights in hearing your least impressive thought because He cares for you with an everlasting love.

WEEK 27 — THURSDAY
THE HOLY SPIRIT

On the night Jesus was betrayed, He left a legacy of love to all His disciples through all the ages:

"Now I am going to him who sent me. . . . It is for your good that I
am going away. Unless I go away, the Counselor will not come to
you; but if I go I will send him to you." (John 16:5–7)

The Amplified Bible gives these names to the Holy Spirit: Comforter, Counselor, Helper, Advocate, Intercessor, and Strengthener. Let's look at what each of these names mean.

1. *The Holy Spirit is our Comforter.* We live in a time when the popularity of Christianity is at an all-time low. There are many people in the world who are almost militantly anti-Christian. We don't have to watch too many marches to realize the hatred the world has for the standards we uphold. And yet, Jesus says, "Don't panic. I have not left you comfortless and unprotected. I have sent you the Comforter."
2. *The Holy Spirit is our Counselor.* If you don't know what to do, ask. He will give inner direction in a still, small voice that plants an idea in your mind. This idea will always be consistent with the Scriptures.
3. *The Holy Spirit is our Helper.* In times of crisis and decision, we have residing within us the very One who can deliver us safely on the

other side. How else could Paul sing while in prison chains? How else could Peter, the original coward, preach with such great power on the day of Pentecost?

4. *The Holy Spirit is our Advocate.* Is the Adversary whispering lies to you again? Is he threatening to overcome you with negative thoughts about your past? Then call on the Advocate, who will always be on your side, pleading your case.

5. *The Holy Spirit is our Intercessor.* We can always be confident that at least two are praying for us—Jesus and the Holy Spirit. They stand before the throne of grace, praying with groanings that cannot be uttered.

6. *The Holy Spirit is our Strength.* When our own strength is exhausted and we feel we can't make it through another day, the Holy Spirit provides strength to go on. He will give us an extra measure of energy to do His will today.

I don't know what you are facing. Maybe you are at the hospital keeping a night-time vigil with someone you love. Maybe you are reporting for work that drains you dry and is unfulfilling. Maybe you are sitting in a house that has never been a home because of broken relationships. Maybe the one you pledged to love and honor has turned out to be an enemy who would like to destroy you.

Whatever it is, my friend, Jesus says, "You have a Comforter, a Counselor, a Helper, an Advocate, an Intercessor. And when your own strength is gone, He will give you what you need."

WEEK 27 — FRIDAY
MY THOUGHTS ARE NOT YOUR THOUGHTS

Several years ago at a conference, I met a woman named Pat who made a real impression on me. As the coordinator, she interacted with me as guest speaker and with the other women present with poise and confidence. Pat was one of those people who stands out in any gathering.

At lunch that day, someone sitting at the table told me her story. When Pat's son was about twelve years old, he accidentally shot and killed his father while on a hunting trip. Now twenty-one, the boy has recovered from this tragedy, largely through his mother's efforts.

Later that day, Pat confided, "My husband was a man who loved God with all his heart. In fact, right before he was killed, he had encouraged each of us to choose a verse for the year that we might be held by God's Word, no matter what happened." She went on to confess, "For a long time, I looked forward to going to be with the Lord so I could ask Him why my husband was taken from us in such a tragic way. But, you know, I have come to understand that when I finally see my Lord, it really won't matter why."

Since that time, I have thought often of Pat's statement as I have seen good men who love the Lord taken home prematurely and evil men who have nothing but contempt for God left here to make life miserable for their families.

In the face of these inequities, we can turn to Isaiah 55:8: "For my thoughts are not your thoughts, neither are your ways my ways."

Are you wrestling with some "whys" today? If you are, don't worry. Nowhere does God tell us that we cannot ask "Why?" or that it is a sin to wonder. In times of deep hurt, there is always the hope that we will receive an answer that will somehow bring peace.

People have always asked questions:

Why did Abraham's faith have to be tested in such a dramatic way?

Why was Joseph left to languish in that Egyptian prison after being falsely accused?

Why did Moses have to stay on the back side of the desert so long?

Why do our bodies grow old?

Why are little babies born deformed?

Why do some clean-cut young men die after using drugs only once, while hardened drug pushers live, never seeming to suffer the ill effects of their wares?

Our finite minds can never comprehend the ways of God. And when we see Him face to face, all the "whys" won't really matter. He will be enough to satisfy the hurt and longing of our souls.

WEEK 28 — MONDAY
PEOPLE-PLEASERS

Do you make decisions based on what other people will think of you? Are you strongly motivated by the opinions of others? Then you could be a people-pleaser. And pleasing people puts you at risk of compromising in order to gain their approval and favor.

Several months ago I was in a meeting with a man who was trying to impress several of us with all the Christian leaders he knew. During the conversation, he moved from trying to impress to slandering the characters of some of these leaders. Because the room was full of people I did not know, I did not speak up in defense of these brothers and sisters, fearful that people would think I was merely a hothead. The truth is, I was being a people-pleaser.

There is nothing wrong with wanting the approval of people as long as it is not at the expense of God's approval. But when a brother or sister is unjustly accused, I don't think Christ appreciates my silence. And when an inappropriate joke is told, I don't think He would approve of my laughter.

The time has come for those of us who are serious about being followers of Christ to stand firm when it would be more comfortable to go with the flow.

Paul addressed this issue when he wrote to the believers in Galatia who had reverted to some of their former beliefs although Paul had given them the gospel: "I am astonished that you are so quickly deserting the one who called you by the grace of Christ and are turning to a different gospel. . . . If anybody is preaching to you a gospel other than what you accepted, let him be eternally condemned! Am I now trying to win the approval of men, or of God? Or am I trying to please men? If I were still trying to please men, I would not be a servant of Christ" (Gal. 1:6–10).

If we are going to be bondservants of the Lord, we cannot be concerned with pleasing people. Yes, we should try to get along with others. But if the way they react affects the stands we take or the things we don't say, then we need to examine our penchant for pleasing people.

What is your situation in the office, in the club, in your church? Do you go with the flow in order to keep the peace and curry favor for yourself? If so, today is a good time to examine your motives and choose to please God rather than people.

WEEK 28 — TUESDAY
MAKING COMPARISONS

If you are feeling distant from the Lord, maybe you need to be reminded of how God looks at you. The Bible gives us many pictures of our relationship to God. As you reflect on the comparisons that God makes between his children and things in nature, ask God to show you how precious you are to Him today.

He calls us his sheep. Sheep were never meant to be burden-bearing animals. They were meant to be cared for by the shepherd, to produce wool, to hear their shepherd's voice, and to stay close to him (Ps. 23).

He says we are to be like the birds of the field. Remember what He says about the birds. They don't have to worry about their next meal or what they will wear or where they are going to spend the night. He takes care of all that. Birds never have to strategize for a recession or an upswing in the economy. Birds just enjoy being birds (Matt. 6:26).

He calls us branches of the vine. The branches draw their life from the vine (John 15).

He says we are like trees who will bring forth leaves in due time. In fact, he says we are like trees planted by a river. We never have to worry about drought or heat, for we have a never-ending stream of water that flows from the heart of God (Ps. 1).

He compares us to flowers that neither toil nor spin. Flowers don't go to work every day. They just stay in the field and bloom where God planted them (Matt. 6:28).

He calls us clay—moldable, usable, and pliable as long as we are under the watchful, artistic eye of the potter. Clay can be wonderfully flexible or hard and brittle. The potter has only one goal for the clay on his board: to make it usable and beautiful. It's His job and He won't fail (Jer. 18:6).

He calls us vessels. Although on the outside we are as plain and unremarkable as an earthen vessel, inside we carry the precious treasure of Christ (2 Cor. 4:7).

May your heart be encouraged by the comparisons God makes with you.

WEEK 28 — WEDNESDAY
ANXIETY

I read recently that anxiety has now surpassed depression as the most common emotional affliction in the country. On one hand, depression is the feeling that nothing is right, nor will it ever be. And now we must cope with the ominous feeling of uneasiness about what might happen in the future.

Do you ever have irrational fears that something bad is going to happen? If so, you are in the majority. At times, I have to fight off a sense of disaster, especially when my family is scattered or I am away from home. So what do we do with these feelings of doom and imminent danger?

136

First, I pray: "Father, today I am feeling uneasy and anxious. I don't know why. Only You know what this day holds, where my loved ones are and what they need, and You love them more than I. So I release my anxiety to You and ask You to release me from this emotion."

Second, each time the emotion comes back, I say aloud, "I have released that situation to You and I have no intention of carrying it around any longer."

In her book, *A Closer Walk*, Catherine Marshall recorded her thoughts on anxiety in an entry called, "Worry, Be Gone":

This morning I awoke full of worry about the future, with Len having resigned from his job as editor of *Guideposts*. Len and I were in agreement about this step, and he is enthusiastic about going into book publishing, but I see so many obstacles ahead, especially when his salary check stops coming.

Then the Lord directed me to the fourth chapter of Philippians, particularly to verse 8 in the Amplified Bible.

. . . Whatever is worthy of reverence . . .
is honorable and seemly . . .
is just
is pure
is lovely [and lovable]
is kind [and winsome and gracious]
if there is any virtue
[excellence]
anything worthy of praise
we are to think on
[and weigh
and take account of] these things.
[Fix your minds on them.][1]

When anxiety creeps in and takes over, then there must be a concentrated effort to fix your mind. That means, set it in cement with the determination to think about the things that really matter.

Anxiety is miserable, but you don't have to keep on being anxious. You have a heavenly Father who has promised that if you will bring all your anxiety to Him, and fix your mind on the things He says, He will give you peace which no one can take away.

WEEK 28 — THURSDAY
LOVE IS PATIENT

In 1 Corinthians 13:4, God makes the statement through the apostle Paul that "Love is patient."

According to Barclay, "The word which is used in the Greek *makrothu-mein* in the New Testament always describes patience with people and not patience with circumstances." Chrysostom said that it is the word which is used of the man who is wronged and who has it easily in his power to avenge himself, yet will not. It describes the man who is slow to anger. It is used of God Himself and His relationship with people.

The story is told that no one treated Lincoln with more contempt than did Edwin McMasters Stanton. Stanton called him "a low, cunning clown" and "the original gorilla." Lincoln never retaliated, but made Stanton his war minister because he felt he was the best man for the job, always treating Stanton with every courtesy.

The years wore on, and the night came when an assassin's bullet felled President Lincoln. In the little room to which the President's body was taken, Stanton stood looking down on that silent face in all its ruggedness. "There lies the greatest ruler of men the world has ever seen," said Stanton through his tears. The patience of love conquered in the end.

There is probably someone in your life who tries your patience to the utmost. Perhaps it would be a good idea to prepare yourself before your next encounter with this person by recalling, "Love is patient" and "God is love." God is patient with me; therefore, I must be patient with others.

I was reminded of God's patience recently. While driving down a North Carolina freeway, I passed another car on a curve. The driver pulled out, nearly causing a collision. I swerved, slammed on my brakes, and blew the horn. He seemed oblivious to the danger he was putting us both in, and went on down the freeway. About six seconds later, in the adrenaline surge that such situations create in me, I was overcome with a rage that demanded revenge. Since I was alone, I chased the other car down the freeway, blowing my horn. As I caught up with him, God seemed to say, "Now what? Do you think he did it on purpose? Could you have been in his blind spot right at that moment?"

Instantly convicted, I had to confess that I was way out of line. Fortunately, no one else saw the incident, and I could settle it with the One who is infinitely patient with me.

If you and I are to reflect the character of God, we must cultivate patience. Our claims of love for our fellow men and women will not ring true without it!

WEEK 28 — FRIDAY
KNOWING WHO YOU ARE KEEPS YOU FROM BEING AFRAID

Have you ever thought about who you are, about what that really means in fearful times?

If you are having a hard time grasping who you really are, think about the names that God has called us.

First of all, He chose to call us children, which in itself is a term of endearment (Rom. 8:16).

He calls us heirs. We have an inheritance, something to look forward to, that is guaranteed not by what we do or who we are but by who *He* is (Rom. 8:17).

He calls us friends. He says He will think the best of us, He will enjoy our company, and He will treat us as a fond companion in our times of communion with Him (John 15:14–15).

He calls us his brethren. He says that we are family. No one can get to us without first passing by the watchful eye of our elder brother. No one will be allowed to bully us—test us perhaps, but never harass us enough to make us lose out on all that God has for us. We are in the family to stay, whether or not we make Him proud all the time (Rom. 8:29).

With that kind of relationship, how can you feel down and out? You are closely related to the King of Kings, the Lord of Lords, and nothing can ever break that relationship!

WEEK 29 — MONDAY
FORGETTING THE THINGS THAT ARE BEHIND

Is there a song, a fragrance, a picture, or a place that can elicit hurtful memories for you?

When I first became a Christian, I was not long removed from the days of coffee houses and college nightclubs. As part of the generation that came of age in the era of Viet Nam, my life was pretty much governed by "eat, drink, and be merry, for tomorrow we die."

A few years later, when I committed my life to Jesus Christ and started to walk with Him, things began to change. Still, certain restaurants that smelled like the old coffee houses or college pubs had the power to whisk me back to the former days. And the memories of how life used to be would blot out the reality of what life is now.

It occurred to me that I never thought about those things unless my memory was jogged in some way. And I began to realize that my responsibility was to guard my heart and mind against the invasion of memories that would surface old patterns of relating.

For example, I have a suitcase full of letters and several boxes of pictures and memorabilia that remind me of old friends and fine experiences. But I have made a choice to do away with some some items because they bring back memories of events that need to be forgotten. To keep pictures of a faithless boyfriend is only to preserve a painful past. As Paul says, "Forgetting what is behind . . . I press on" (Phil. 3:13–14).

In counseling, I always encourage the person who is having difficulty forgetting the past or who is easily tempted to return to an ungodly lifestyle to get rid of anything that speaks of the past. For the person who has been involved in an affair, holding on to gifts, pictures, or letters is nothing more than nurturing the bond. And for the person who has had a compulsive, addictive problem, to get rid of all paraphernalia connected with the addiction is a must.

When Paul said, "I press on," I believe he is exhorting us to make a clean sweep of anything in our lives that would draw us back into a harmful relationship or habit.

Why not determine to destroy today anything that is binding you to the past. Clean it out! Throw it away! Affirm your belief that God has given you a future and a hope. My friend, press on, but remember that God wants His children to travel light.

WEEK 29 — TUESDAY
JESUS, OUR AVENGER

Do you remember when someone got the best of you in a childish scuffle and left a cut or a bruise? Pulling off your Band-Aid to show your friends became a badge of courage. The gorier the wound, the more sympathy you got. But every time you pulled the bandage off, you disturbed the healing process. And many a wise parent has said, "Honey, leave your sore alone, or it will never heal."

Our heavenly Father knows that if we continue to pick at our scabs, they will never heal. So He wisely instructs us to take our attention off ourselves and turn it to the one who inflicted the wound: "Do not take revenge, my friends, but leave room for God's wrath, for it is written, 'It is mine to avenge; I will repay,' says the Lord" (Rom. 12:19).

Getting even never works; it just causes the sore to fester. The Lord has promised to settle old scores if we turn the problem over to Him. In the meantime, He has given us something therapeutic and tangible to do about the matter: "If your enemy is hungry, feed him; if he is thirsty, give him something to drink. In doing this, you will heap burning coals on his head" (v. 20).

One of the most outstanding principles of the Christian life is forgiveness, blessing those who wrong us. And yet, most people struggle with forgiving—giving up the right to punish, to bring up the hurt, to remind the perpetrator that he or she has inflicted a wound that is very hard to forget.

In ancient days, hot coals for cooking and heating fires were a precious commodity. People would often have to borrow live coals from another's hearth in order to have fire in their homes. "Heaping coals of fire" thus means to bless abundantly. How like the Lord to tell us to bless our "enemies" with food, drink, and fuel. When we are blessing someone, we are not spending time in useless self-pity or in plotting vengeance.

Besides, God has promised to avenge every wrong if it becomes necessary. These words by an unknown author are reassuring:

Jesus is the Avenger. His blood was given to avenge every wrong done to us, His brothers and sisters. Now He says to us, "When someone hurts you or those you love, release the wound to Me for healing. Give the one who hurt you to Me; pray for him to be forgiven. Say, "Father forgive him; he didn't know he was dealing with You." That prayer releases My power to work in his life to bring him to Me. In Me your only motivation is that all men everywhere come to know My love.[1]

When the memory of a past hurt comes to mind, do you replay the scene and then have to forgive all over again? Or are you still picking at the scabs? Surrender the problem and the offending person to God, thus releasing His power to work in both your lives.

WEEK 29 — WEDNESDAY
THE HAMMER

There are times when I let the pressures of life harden my heart, and I know that I am in for an encounter with the hammer of the Word.

Jeremiah 23:29 says, " 'Is not my word like fire?' declares the LORD, 'and like a hammer that breaks a rock in pieces?' "

Now, I have walked with the Lord long enough to know that His preferred way of dealing with me is like the potter who patiently forms the soft clay into the vessel He needs. He is gentle in His conforming work. I know when I am pliable and I know when I am hardened.

You probably know that about yourself as well.

Do you have days when you can't get enough of the Word?
Do you have days when you just don't want to hear it?
Do you have days when you have an abundance of patience and people are a joy?
Do you have days when you are short-tempered and easily irritated and woe be to the one who gets in your way?
Do you have days you want to change?
Do you have days when you want to be left alone to just live life until it's over?
Maybe you feel that way today.

If you relate, then no doubt you are near to an encounter with the fire and hammer of the Word. If you are one of God's precious children, a hardened attitude will not go unnoticed and unattended.

He will discipline, and it is most gentle when we are willing to yield. God tells us that no discipline for the moment is pleasant, but afterwards it yields the peaceable fruit of righteousness.

Not long ago, I had to have the hammer of the Word come against my hardness of heart in a situation where I believed I had been done wrong . . . just plain done dirty. I didn't like it. I knew it was unjust. I knew that it did not have to happen, and when it did, I was not exactly straining at the bit to apply biblical principles. My preference would have been to let my displeasure be known in no uncertain terms.

But I had an encounter with the hammer of the Word, and a little bit of the fire as well. You know how it is at times like that—every other word you read jumps out and strikes at the core of your fleshly reasoning. Scriptures like:

"For it has been granted to you on behalf of Christ not only to believe on him, but also to suffer for him" (Phil. 1:29) and "Do everything without complaining or arguing, so that you may become blameless and pure, children of God without fault in a crooked and depraved generation, in which you shine like stars in the universe" (Phil. 2:14–15).

There is no way to fight the hammer of the Word. It will crush the hardest part of your heart if you are a child of God. He is committed to bringing you into conformity to His Son, so for Him the hammer and the fire are just necessary tools of the conforming work. For you and for me though, they are instruments to which we need never submit ourselves if, when we see the clay of our attitudes hardening, we will yield our wills to God.

How is your heart today? Do you feel the clay hardening? You have a choice—the gentle hand of the Potter or the crushing hammer of His Word.

WEEK 29 — THURSDAY
THE WISE MAN

One night several years ago, a friend and I were dinner guests in the home of a Christian woman. Her purpose in inviting us was the hope that we might be able to influence her husband and brother-in-law who were both antagonistic toward Christianity.

I was curious as to what would happen at mealtime. Would one of the men pray? Or would we begin eating without a blessing for the food?

To my amazement, the host, a very educated man, bowed his head and quoted these words from Jeremiah:

> This is what the Lord says: "Let not the wise man boast of his wisdom or the strong man boast of his strength or the rich man boast of his riches, but let him who boasts boast about this: that he understands and knows me, that I am the Lord, who exercises kindness, justice and righteousness on earth, for in these I delight" (Jer. 9:23–24).

As the night wore on, it was evident that my host and his brother-in-law were both condemned by the very words that had been spoken as a blessing over the meal. Neither of these men knew God. They had truth in their own mouths, but they refused it.

I learned some important lessons that night:

1. *Prearranged "witnessing arrangements" are usually unprofitable.* If the Spirit of God arranges a meeting, it is usually spontaneous and without a third party orchestrating the events.
2. *The Word of God speaks for itself.* Nothing my friend or I could have said would have spoken more powerfully.
3. *When a person already knows truth but has rejected it, most conversations will end in arguments.* That night we could not get past the fact that in the mind of these two men, the burning bush that Moses encountered was just a natural phenomenon, very common in the desert today.

The older I grow in the Lord, the more I realize that I serve a God who doesn't need my help, my ideas, or my arrangements, but values my willingness to walk in my understanding and knowledge of Him. I serve a God who will see that His Son is never robbed of one person who will follow Him, and that I am not needed to arrange and manipulate what only God can do.

That agnostic spoke truth that night. If he is a "wise man," he will realize that not only does the Lord delight in kindness, justice, and righteousness, but He delights in saving people and in giving them eternal life with Him.

WEEK 29 — FRIDAY
FEAR OF TOMORROW

How are things in your life tomorrow? I know that seems like a silly question because you haven't lived tomorrow yet. But have you worried about how it will be?

The fear of what will happen tomorrow is a subtle thing. The cares and burdens of tomorrow's load are more than you or I can carry today. We are fearful because of all the ominous world events, because of disease and the aging process and the economy—all things that will catch up with us tomorrow. But don't you have trouble enjoying the blessings of today when all you can see are the things that loom so large in the future?

I am learning this whole principle in an interesting school. I have my calendar planned out through the end of next year. I have places to be, opportunities that I have looked forward to, people I know are counting on me to be at certain places. But the last few months have taught me to say, "If the Lord wills I'll be there; if not, then we will just have to see what He has in mind." I always think of this passage in James:

Now listen, you who say, "Today or tomorrow we will go to this or that city, spend a year there, carry on business and make money." Why, you do not even know what will happen tomorrow. What is your life? You are a mist that appears for a little while and then vanishes. Instead, you ought to say, "If it is the Lord's will, we will live and do this or that." As it is, you boast and brag. All such boasting is evil (4:13–16).

Sometimes it's hard to think about what may be coming tomorrow: the pain, the suffering, the loss, the struggle. But when we get caught up in what may or may not happen, we miss the point. Whatever comes, we will take it one day at a time. His grace will be sufficient for that day.

If the future holds loss, there will be grace for times of losing; if the future holds rejection, there will be grace for times of not being accepted. No matter what happens, you can be sure that the Lord will be right there in the middle of it acting as a buffer, a gracious covering, a provider, a shield, a defender in the midst of all that you have to face.

Is today starting out as a day to dread? Remember, there will be grace to get through. There is great comfort in resting in the Lord's will.

WEEK 30 — MONDAY
HOW TO PRAY FOR YOUR CHILDREN

My three sons range in age from sixteen to almost twenty-three years of age. I love my boys, pray for them, and often tell the Lord I would die for them. And the Lord always gently reminds me that there is One who has already died for my children. My death is not what He is asking. Rather, He is calling me to love and to pray. As they grow and as my understanding develops, I realize more and more the power a parent wields through prayer.

In a booklet by Jean Fleming entitled A Woman of Influence, the author cites three specifics when praying for your children:

1. Pray for them to have a place in the kingdom—pray for each child's salvation.
2. Pray that they would be a credit to the kingdom—that each child will develop a godly character.
3. Pray that they would be used to promote the kingdom—that each child will become a servant of others.

1. A place in the kingdom—becoming a Christian. The story is told that Monica, the devout mother of Saint Augustine, prayed fervently for her son's salvation. But Augustine's non-Christian father was as zealous to lead him into sin as Monica was to introduce her son to Christ. For a time, Augustine showed little spiritual interest.

After he became a Christian, however, Augustine wrote a prayer, citing his indebtedness to his mother's intercession:

And now didst thou stretch forth thy hand from above and didst draw up my soul out of that profound darkness because my mother, thy faithful one, wept to thee on my behalf more than mothers are accustomed to weep for the bodily deaths of their children.

Prayer has the power to circumvent the unfavorable circumstances that seem to stand in the way of your child's salvation.

2. *A credit to the kingdom—developing godly character.* In our world, we cannot protect our children from the presence of evil. They are bombarded at every turn with temptation and enticement to shortcuts—physically, emotionally and spiritually. But prayer often releases the power to stand firm and the wisdom to turn from evil.

3. *A promoter of the kingdom—becoming a servant.* Servanthood might seem like the most remote possibility in your mind right now if your child has no interest in spiritual matters, but we serve a mighty God who delights in answering big prayers. His desire is to conform every believer to the image of His Son, creating His character in each one.

Our prayers for our children—their salvation, the development of a godly character, and servanthood—are in perfect accord with the heart of the Father. We may be confident that He cares about our children even more than we do and will work to answer our prayers in keeping with His divine purpose for their lives.

WEEK 30 — TUESDAY
WORKING MOMS

A recent statistic states that sixty-eight percent of women who work would prefer not to be working. Though some women have an alternative, others are forced to work and must not only juggle many tasks, but must deal with the guilt they feel as well.

I speak to this issue as a woman whose mother worked out of necessity. When I was two years old, my parents moved to Washington, D.C., believing they could find a better economic opportunity for our family there. I remember living in one room, sleeping in a couple of overstuffed chairs pushed together, and keeping our milk and juice cold on the windowsill because we had no refrigerator.

I was unaware of what my parents were going through at the time, but later learned of my mother's determination not to be separated from me and her persistence in looking for a job where we could be together. When she found one as director of a day-care center, she enrolled me and I spent my pre-school years there. When I was in the fourth grade, she pursued a job as a schoolteacher. Therefore, I was with her every day until I was thirteen years old.

My mother had to work, but she made the most of it. And once my dad's situation stabilized, she continued to work out of enjoyment.

I believe our Christian bias against working mothers can put women as well as men in bondage. But God has given us some principles to live by that will make the difference in our family relationships, whether a mother works in or outside the home. The issue is not the *location* of one's job, but the *attitude* one has:

Whether a woman is a single parent, or is helping her husband with the financial load, attitude is vital. Ephesians 5:15–21 provides a platform for a successful home life:

> Be very careful, then, how you live—not as unwise but as wise, making the most of every opportunity, because the days are evil. Therefore do not be foolish, but understand what the Lord's will is. Do not get drunk on wine, which leads to debauchery. Instead, be filled with the Spirit. Speak to one another with psalms, hymns and spiritual songs. Sing and make music in your heart to the Lord, always giving thanks to God the Father for everything, in the name of our Lord Jesus Christ. Submit to one another out of reverence for Christ.

Using time wisely, keeping God's Word prominent in daily conversation, walking in the Spirit, and singing songs of praise with your children will ensure a happy home. When the "poor me" syndrome strikes those who have to be both mother and breadwinner, count your blessings. Thank the Lord for the gift of children and for the gift of a job to support them.

And last, all who live in a family—moms, dads, and children—should be willing to be subject to one another in the fear of Christ. Learn how to blend and bend in order to meet one another's needs, whether or not Mom goes to work outside the home.

WEEK 30 — WEDNESDAY
BEFORE YOU FALL

I recently attended a workshop on emotions, in which the guest speaker made this statement: "Every emotional difficulty can be traced to pride."

He documented his statement with the fall of man as recorded in Genesis 3:4, when the serpent tempted Eve to eat the forbidden fruit: "You will not surely die," he said. "For God knows that when you eat of it your eyes will be opened, and you will be like God, knowing good and evil." The rest is history. The man and woman disobeyed God, and we have been dealing with the consequences ever since.

This same speaker, Dr. Les Carter of the Minirth-Meier Clinic, went on to explain: "Pride is preoccupation with self, preoccupation with our own desires, and a craving to be in control."

As I listened, I thought of the emotional difficulties I hear about from women all over the country. And I began to recognize this pattern:

Preoccupation with self. I have a recurring struggle with having been made to look foolish by a friend. The more I think about the events in which I ended up looking like a fool, the more I stew over the situation and the more I become absorbed with myself. This negative emotion which is rooted in pride robs me of much joy and creativity.

Preoccupation with our own desires. When we don't get what we want, we are prime candidates for depression, frustration, and disappointment. In our rights-conscious society, it is a challenge to admit, "This is only a desire,

145

not something I must have." It is helpful to remind ourselves that the root of this struggle with our "want to's" is pride.

Craving to be in control. This is one of the most powerful and destructive of all, destroying relationships within the family, among friends, and in the workplace—husbands and wives trying to control the behavior of the other . . . parents trying to control the attitudes of their children . . . friends trying to control the actions and reactions of peers.

Ultimately, this pattern ends in destruction: "Pride goes before destruction, a haughty spirit before a fall" (Prov. 16:18).

To ignore the warning signs of preoccupation with self, preoccupation with your own desires, and a craving to be in control is to drive past the caution signs that shout, "You are headed for a fall!"

WEEK 30 — THURSDAY
KEEP ON PRAYING!

I love the story about the little boy named Tim who included this request in his bedtime prayers: "And please make Tommy stop throwing things at me. By the way, I've mentioned this before!"

I understand exactly how little Tim feels! I have prayed for some persons and situations over a long period of time and felt that I might as well have been talking to the wall! Prayer is some of the most difficult work we do. It requires concentration, determination, and a whole lot of persistence.

Persistence in prayer often seems grueling, partly because we have to cover the same territory over and over again. Yet this is exactly what Jesus exhorts His disciples to do: "Then Jesus told his disciples a parable to show them that they should *always pray and not give up* [keep praying until the answer comes]" (Luke 18:1).

In writing to the Thessalonian believers, Paul encouraged them to "pray continually" (1 Thess. 5:17). No doubt he meant both that they should pray for the same things until the answer came, *and* that they should pray about a variety of needs and concerns. But our flesh is weak. Keeping on praying, asking, and seeking is sometimes hard for us. We are motivated by answers and action, not necessarily by having to do more of the same with no apparent response.

In her book, *Candles in the Dark,* Amy Carmichael makes this point:

> One of the hardest things in our secret prayer life is to accept with joy and not with grief the answers to our deepest prayers. At least I have found it so. It was a long time before I discovered that whatever came was the answer. I had expected something so different that I did not recognize it when it came.[1]

If you are asking God for direction, and things seem to be going in the opposite direction, you either need to keep praying until God releases your burden, or you need to recognize that your answer is already here. If you are praying with a sincere heart and desire His will above all else, He will be faithful to show you which it is.

François Fenelon, a seventeenth-century believer, sums up prayer in these words:

Tell God all that is in your heart, as one unloads one's heart, its pleasures and its pains, to a dear friend. Tell Him your troubles, that He may comfort you. Tell Him your joys, that He may sober them; tell Him your longings that He may purify them. Tell Him how self-love makes you unjust to others, how vanity tempts you to be insincere, how pride disguises you to yourself and others. . . .

If you thus pour out all your weaknesses, needs, and troubles, there will be no lack of what to say. You will never exhaust the subject.

Don't resist or resent God's call to persistent prayer. Thank Him for deeming you worthy of intimate fellowship with Him. As you seek His face often for the answers you need, praise Him for His loving concern for you and His attention to your request. Thank Him in advance for the solution you know is coming and ask for patience to wait until the answer comes.

WEEK 30 — FRIDAY
THERE IS A FUTURE

Alexander Solzhenitsyn, the Russian dissident and survivor of a concentration camp, said: "All that the downtrodden can do is go on hoping. After every disappointment they must find fresh reason to hope."

Reason to hope is as vital to life as blood is to the body. Without it, life cannot be sustained. Hope anticipates good. It is the belief that relief is on its way and that soon the pain will be over.

Jeremiah 29:11 was written to encourage God's people who were in exile in Babylon. Banished from their homeland, they had no hope, apart from the promise God was giving them. This promise is for us as well: " 'For I know the plans I have for you,' declares the Lord, 'plans to prosper you and not to harm you, plans to give you hope and a future.' "

Because our tendency is to look at the present dilemma and not at the hope of the future, we sometimes give up on someone or some problem too soon. As Charles Allen, author of God's Psychiatry, writes: "When you say a situation or person is hopeless, you are slamming the door in the face of God."

Iris Blue spent seven years in jail for armed robbery. After her release, she became a prostitute and a drug dealer, and was physically near death. Despite the hopelessness of her situation, a young street preacher kept telling her that Jesus loved her. Although the evangelistic association he worked for discouraged his interest in Iris, insisting that there was no hope for this degenerate drug addict who walked the streets, he did not give up on her. Finally one day, Iris knelt in front of the house of prostitution she was running and gave her life to the Lord. She testifies: "I knelt down a tramp and stood up a lady!"

Today Iris Blue brings a message of hope to people in churches and prisons around the world. Though she did her best to destroy God's plans for her, in the end she claimed the future and the hope that He had ordained for her all along.

What condition or crisis has caused you to despair? What person seems beyond God's reach? Is that person you? Do you feel hopeless, at the end of your rope, that you will never escape the self-defeating cycle in which you are trapped?

Do you struggle with a situation you hate, but have no power to change? Then you need to remember God's promise of hope. And He is the God who keeps His promises.

As His child, His plans for you are to bring about ultimate good. In that promise there is hope to go on, to run the extra mile, to trust that there is something good just around the corner.

WEEK 31 — MONDAY
GOD IS WATCHING

A young boy was told that the eye of God is always watching us. He thought a moment and then he said, "I'd like to know what kind of watching it is. Tim Brown watches me in school so he can tell Teacher if I whisper and get me bad marks. But Father watches me in a different way. When I am on the beach, he keeps watch so I won't get in too deep. I like that kind of watching!"

What kind of watching do you believe God is doing in your life? Do you feel that He is waiting for you to make a mistake so He can straighten you out? Or do you believe He is watching to protect you from harm, to keep you from getting into a situation that is over your head? The perspective you have of God will affect the way you live in every other area of your life.

Think about it:

Do you dress modestly to serve as a protection from lustful looks or because you think God might not approve?

Do you avoid certain kinds of entertainment because God has shown you that keeping your mind clean is for your protection? Or do you stay away because he doesn't want His children associating with sinners?

Unless you can relax in the presence of God, you will always feel as if He is checking up on you.

In 2 Chronicles 16:9, we read: "For the eyes of the Lord range throughout the earth to strengthen those whose hearts are fully committed to him."

Does that statement sound as if God is looking for someone to punish or harass? No, of course not! God Himself is saying, "I want to support you. I want to keep you out of the deep parts of the ocean of life where you will find yourself in over your head. I want to rescue you from drowning."

If you will notice again God's dealings with the people He used to bring about His purposes, you will see that He didn't hover over them, waiting to catch them in some foul deed. Consider Abraham, the friend of God, and David, the man after God's own heart—men who lived as men on this earth, but who, in all their humanity, knew that God was in control.

These fathers of our faith made mistakes. They wandered into deep waters. But God pulled them out and gave them another chance to become the leaders He intended them to be.

God loves you and longs to find in you a heart that is completely His . . . so He can fully support you. If you will trust Him, I believe you will begin to experience the joy of knowing that He is watching you through the eyes of a loving Friend.

WEEK 31 — TUESDAY
LITTLE WHITE LIES

How honest are you? Oh, I doubt that you would rob a bank or cheat on your income tax. You might not even lie about your age. But what about shading the truth just a little in order to project yourself in the best possible light? Some people call this kind of indirect dishonesty, "little white lies." Check yourself out:

- Do you always try to fit into every situation so you will not make waves and call negative attention to yourself?
- Do you keep your ideas to yourself because someone might think you are odd?
- Do you hide your hurt feelings, yet drop sarcastic hints that something is wrong?
- Do you keep quiet if someone asks you a question that makes you feel vulnerable?

If you answered yes to any of these questions, you may have developed an intricate pattern of deception which, on the surface, appears almost righteous!

Telling a blatant falsehood is not the only way to lie. In a pamphlet from Last Days Ministries entitled *Openness and Honesty,* Melody Green gives us a new perspective on the subject:

> Many who are consistently dishonest about their true feelings would jump up in self-righteousness if anyone dared accuse them of being a liar. But let's take a closer look at what lying really is.
>
> The American Heritage Dictionary defines lying as: "A false statement or piece of information deliberately presented as being true; anything meant to deceive or give a wrong impression."

For most of us, myself included, there is a fear that the person you really are would not be loved as much as the person everyone thinks you are. So, to protect yourself from discovery, you paint a very different picture of what is going on inside. This kind of self-protective cover-up is rooted in the fear of rejection, the fear of others.

The Scriptures have something to say about that: "The fear of others lays a snare, but one who trusts in the LORD is secure" (Prov. 29:25 NRSV). If you have fallen into habitual lying because you fear what others will think of you, ask God to show you how subtle and insidious it can be.

Satan is the father of lies. Therefore, all lying is sin and has no place in the life of a believer. Repent today of all the "little white lies" of which you have been guilty. And then resolve to be scrupulously honest in all your dealings. Ask God, by His Holy Spirit, to tap you on the shoulder if you slip into patterns of telling white lies. He is faithful. You can count on Him to do it.

WEEK 31 — WEDNESDAY
FRANK OR FOOLISH?

In the Scriptures, there is a frequent comparison made between a wise and a foolish person. In Proverbs 17:27–28, God says, "A man of knowledge uses words with restraint, and a man of understanding is even-tempered. Even a fool is thought wise if he keeps silent, and discerning if he holds his tongue."

There is a time when silence is golden, and there are other times for carefully considered words. But the appropriateness of speech or silence is found in our motivation. Before we speak or fail to speak, a healthy question to ask is: "Is this motivated by my fear of what others will think, or does it come from a desire to abide by God's wisdom in this situation?"

The motivation of the heart is everything to God. There is no virtue in keeping silent about our feelings or our concerns if we are motivated by the fear of others. On the other hand, there is no virtue in being frank if the motivation is "to be heard without regard for the feelings of others."

Richard Shelly Taylor, in his book, *The Disciplined Life,* writes:

> Some people pride themselves on their frankness. "I say what I think," they boast. So does the fool, according to the Bible: "A fool uttereth all his mind" (Prov. 29:11). Frankness is indeed a virtue when mixed with intelligence, loving tact and discretion. However, it becomes a sadistic vice when it is merely the unbridled erupting of opinions, without regard to times, places or human feelings.[1]

Again, the Scriptures say: "Reckless words pierce like a sword, but the tongue of the wise brings healing" (Prov. 12:18).

There must be balance in our lives. Holding back because of the fear of others or unleashing our words under the banner of frankness and free speech can be equally injurious.

I once worked with someone who felt the need to speak frankly. He was a man of integrity, so his speech was usually appropriate and thoughtful. On one occasion, however, he was driven by his frustration with me as a fellow worker to speak openly and honestly. Unfortunately, he chose to address this issue in front of several of our co-workers. While I don't deny the truth of his message, his forum was all wrong. Consequently, he ended up having to defend his methods while his message was lost in the turmoil.

Have you ever experienced a situation where you spoke the truth but ended up the loser? Could it have been that your timing was off, or that you used the wrong approach?

God's Word teaches us a no-fail method: "Speaking the truth in love" (Eph. 4:15). If love seeks the other person's highest good, then we will look for ways to make that truth palatable as we serve it to another. The old grandma who said, "You draw more flies with honey than with vinegar," had a point. Think about it today!

WEEK 31 — THURSDAY
AS LONG AS WE BOTH SHALL LIVE

Sometimes I think I don't want to read another book or take another course on marriage, much less teach one. It's too depressing. The sad fact is that, despite all the literature written on helping people achieve happy homes, at least half of all marriages in this country end in divorce. Even Christian marriage is not exempt.

This poem by Ruth Harms Calkin summarizes the truth about many marriages in today's world:

Another marriage is shattered, Lord, the divorce
*   will be final next week.*
He said it was the breakdown of communication and the
*   subtle infiltration of boredom.*
She said it was an accumulation of things.
He said she was unnecessarily preoccupied with home,
*   children and activities.*
She said he stifled her dreams and ignored her
*   achievements.*
He said he felt in prison, restricted; that
*   night after night he got the old pushaway.*
She said he was harsh and brutal and often
*   embarrassed her in public.*
He said her critical attitude contributed to
*   his sense of inadequacy.*
She said she felt lonely and unappreciated
*   with no claim to personal identity.*
He said she wallowed in self-pity and
*   refused to acknowledge her benefits.*
She said he was shiftless and irresponsible.
He said she didn't understand.
She said he didn't care.
Lord, how tragic that through all the wasted years,
*   neither of them asked what You said.*[2]

Few of us have not been caught up in the old "he said, she said" game. Perhaps it's time to stop the escalation of verbal war and go back to that quiet moment you shared at the altar when you promised, "till death do us part." The simplicity and sincerity of that vow is the stopping place for all your arguments.

Marriage is a lifetime commitment. Your discussions will be fruitful only if they are based on that promise: "No matter what happens, what you say, or how you act, I am committed to you for the rest of my life." Suddenly all other issues fall into perspective: "Somehow we have to work this out."

If you have threatened your mate by saying, "If you say or do that one more time, then I am finished . . . no more . . . this marriage is over," ask him or her to forgive you. Tell your husband or wife that you will never, for any reason, break the covenant you have pledged. Then ask God to show you what you need to change and ask Him to give you the grace to change it.

Your promise for a lifetime was made before God. It is His responsibility and great pleasure to empower you to become the husband or wife He intends for you to be.

WEEK 31 — FRIDAY
NOT VICTIMS BUT VICTORS

How often do you feel as if you are victim? And how often does that lead you to feel self-pity? You know what I mean. The days when you are under stress and no one seems the least bit interested. Or the days when you feel alone, and you have too much time on your hands to think. Is this one of those days for you?

One of the things that makes it particularly hard is when you just can't seem to feel the presence of God. You pray and it seems that He just isn't there. It doesn't take many times like that to begin to feel like a victim, even a victim of God.

A victim's way of thinking is, "Everything happens to me," usually followed by the thought, "Because something tragic happened once, I must accept tragedy as a way of life. Nothing will ever be on the victory side for me."

In her book *Staying Happy in an Unhappy World*, Dr. Marie Chapian says, "A characteristic of the victim is he or she does not realize that though things might be unpleasant or downright bad, things are also good. Blessings do exist. You can't be victimized by disaster twenty-four hours a day every day of your life without even one glimmer of relief. Nobody is a victim all the time. You can be hurt by others, mistreated, cheated and downright abused, but if you look truthfully at yourself, you'll see you have been a winner at times, too. Many times in your life you have been blessed."[3]

But, it seems when you are feeling victimized, it is hard to remember that you have been blessed.

I have found that this root of feeling like a victim is often the inability to release our hurt through forgiveness. When I let myself begin to feel that way then I begin to "but God." You know, "But God . . . look at what she did?" "But God, look at what she's getting by with?" "But God, how long am I going to have to be dogged by this situation?" And the "But God's . . . " go on and on.

But you don't have to stay in the role of a victim. You don't have to carry around that brand on your thinking the rest of your days.

From Marie Chapian again, listen to these words:

I've never met a person lacking in forgiveness who leads a truly happy life. Even his or her pleasant moments are shadowed by bitterness and anger. Unforgiveness always hurts you more than the person or persons you are infuriated with. Disordered thinking and physical problems develop because of unforgiveness. I've stood at the deathbeds of people who have wasted precious years in bitterness and unforgiveness and experienced their moment of freedom and joy when they have finally breathed forgiveness and mercy to others. . . . Jesus made a way of escape for every problem we meet, even hate. No matter what heinous thing someone has done to you, freedom and happiness can be yours.

If you are feeling sorry for yourself today, feeling that you are living in a rotten situation because someone else has done wrong, you have a choice. You can either be a victim or a victor. You can choose to take Jesus' offer of escape from the many ills of a victim mentality or you can remain in a state of self-pity.

The closing question is very simple. Are you a victim of your own unwillingness to forgive, or are you a victor who has discovered the liberty of escape from the chains of unforgiveness?

WEEK 32 — MONDAY
FORGIVING YOURSELF

Do you still feel as if you deserve to be punished even after you have been forgiven by another?

Do you put yourself down, saying, "I've made too many mistakes for God to use me!"

Do you assume that others will be blessed by God, but believe that you have forfeited His blessings because of your sin?

Do you believe that joy may come to some, but that kind of reward is permanently out of your reach?

If you can identify with any of these feelings, you need to forgive yourself and release yourself from the bondage that has imprisoned you.

There is a wonderful passage in the Psalms that is full of liberty for us, if we will only seize it: "If you, O Lord, kept a record of sins, O Lord, who could stand? But with you there is forgiveness" (130:3–4).

If you are a child of God, you are forgiven. You have been set free from the penalty of sin. He has told us that because we are human, we are sinners (Rom. 5:12). But He has also said that when we become a child of God, we are a new creation (2 Cor. 5:17), the righteousness of God in Christ (1 Cor. 1:30).

As long as you continue to hold a grudge against yourself for having been born a sinner and for having acted like a sinner in some painful situations, you will walk around with a burden God never intended you to bear.

There is a difference between godly guilt and guilt one assumes voluntarily. Godly guilt is very specific. You will feel convicted in a particular area. As you respond in obedience, the conviction will be replaced by the pure joy of knowing that everything is clear between you and the Lord, and that your sin is remembered no more (Jer. 31:34). Nor will there be any residual ugly feelings to torment and punish you.

Ungodly guilt, or condemnation, will feel like a heavy, wet blanket that stifles your peace and your sense of being right with God. Depression, irritability, and self-hate will escalate, often manifesting themselves as fatigue, bothersome physical ailments, and a general sense of unworthiness. If you have experienced any of these symptoms, I would encourage you to begin to inventory the specific sins you know about but have been unwilling to take to the Lord for cleansing.

It may be too painful to tell a friend, a counselor, or your doctor just what is bothering you. But God says we have a great High Priest who is touched by the feeling of our infirmities. You can tell Him everything:

You can tell Him everything! "I have wanted another woman's husband, Lord . . . " or, "I have lived in a world of gossip or lies to make myself look better . . . " or, "I have been jealous and vengeful."

Say it. Don't shrink back. The promise of cleansing and freedom is your birthright as a child of God. Then confess: "I am forgiven by the blood of the Lord Jesus Christ and there is no condemnation for me" (Rom. 8:1).

My friend, that is your birthright as His precious child. Claim it and live in the light of it today.

WEEK 32 — TUESDAY
TROUBLE WITH TRUST

In our high-stress society, certain prolonged pressures will sometimes make it difficult to trust God.

When you are exhausted, you may doubt God's provision. There are times when fatigue will rob you of your ability to relax in God's providence. Your sense of responsibility in providing for the needs of those you love can keep you on a treadmill. You know you should relinquish their care to God, but trusting Him to provide seems like a copout.

There was a man in the Scriptures who understood that feeling. His name was Moses. And he was in charge of 600,000 grumbling, complaining Jews who were tired of eating manna and wanted meat. Moses could see only that the task was overwhelming until God answered him with the same question He poses to you and me: "Is the Lord's power limited? Now you can see whether my word will come true for you or not" (Num. 11:23 NASB).

When you are pressed on every side, letting go and letting God is tough. But I would remind you that He is trustworthy even when you are too tired to trust Him.

When you are in an impossible situation, you may forget what God has said. John the Baptist, the fiery young man from the desert who fearlessly took on the religious leaders of his day, saying, "You generation of vipers . . . repent" faltered in his faith when he was imprisoned, soon to die. He sent word to Jesus, asking, "Are you the one who was to come, or should we expect someone else?" (Matt. 11:3). John's trust was shaken, although he had been anointed in his mother's womb for this very mission.

Let's face it. Setbacks and adversity can shake anyone . . . even a John the Baptist. But Jesus saw through his temporary doubt and later told His disciples, "I tell you the truth: Among those born of women there has not risen anyone greater than John the Baptist; yet he who is least in the kingdom of heaven is greater than he" (Matt. 11:11).

Jesus didn't condemn John. He simply reminded his disciple of what he already knew was true. Jesus understands our doubts: He doesn't feel threatened by our questions. He merely longs to reassure us.

My friend, are you having a hard time trusting today because you are tired? He invites, "Come to me, all you who are weary and burdened, and I will give you rest" (Matt. 11:28). Are you struggling because you can't see a way out of what looks like an impossible situation? Like John, confide in the Lord your honest doubts. Tell Him how you feel. He will answer your questions, confirm your faith, and restore your joy and confidence.

WEEK 32 — WEDNESDAY
HUMILITY

Not long ago I heard Tony Melendez play his guitar and sing. Now that is of no interest to you unless you know that Tony has no arms. He was a Thalidomide baby who came into this world with missing and deformed limbs. Tony has a club foot and one normal foot. But it only takes a moment in his presence to forget what he doesn't have and concentrate on the great gift of humility that God has given him.

By being humbly born, he has really been given the gift of humility.

Tony slips his sandals off of his feet and begins to strum his guitar with his toes . . . a humbling thing for anyone to do . . . and yet the beauty that comes from the strings and the radiance that comes from his voice somehow put a supernatural glow around his deficiencies. And little by little, you realize that this young man has been gifted . . . gifted with humility.

That's the way it is in the kingdom of God. But when we put our interpretation on circumstances and events, we can never bring ourselves to see these humbling situations as gifts.

154

Then there is this reminder from Proverbs. "Humility and the fear of the LORD bring wealth and honor and life" (Prov. 22:4).

There is the key. In our society, riches and honor and life have such a different definition that the word *humility* seems distasteful.

If you are like me, the word *humility* and the word *doormat* are often interchangeable. For a person to be described as humble has a connotation of weakness and no power, but in God's eyes, it is just the opposite. Humility is bursting with God-infused power that is able to stand taller than circumstances and endure the toughest tests, all the while radiating confidence.

If you are going to face an office situation where you have felt that you have had to fight and scrap for every promotion you have had, then maybe the word *humility* is frightening to you because it seems to leave you as an easy prey for the office jackals who are out to pull the unguarded apart limb from limb. If you feel that way, I understand. There have been times I have felt the same way, but in God's economy things just aren't that way.

I would encourage you to take a few moments to pray before you enter the situation where you feel vulnerable and ask God to show you what humility is. Jot down this short verse and put it where you can see it all day. "Humble yourselves, therefore, under God's mighty hand, that he may lift you up in due time. Cast all your anxiety on him because he cares for you" (1 Peter 5:6–7).

He really does care for you, more than you could ever know.

WEEK 32 — THURSDAY
WHO'S RESPONSIBLE?

One of the qualities that marks our lives as adults is responsibility. No longer can we depend on someone else to look out for us, to make sure we keep up with our umbrellas, get the proper rest, and eat the right foods. That's something adults do for themselves. But even those of us who are independent types often fail to assume responsibility for our own emotions.

I know a dear woman who refuses to let go of the pain she feels because her father abandoned her family when she was a child. She is a capable, functioning adult who has a husband and children of her own, but she has never assumed responsibility for her own happiness. No matter what encouragement she is given, she uses her past hurt to fuel her present emotional state. Her father left his family; therefore, she is bound to the belief that she can never be happy.

The Bible says, "For as [a man] thinketh in his heart, so is he" (Prov. 23:7 KJV). If you are what you think, then you will have to take the responsibility for what you allow to lodge in your mind. Old patterns die hard, but if you are the kind of person who harbors hurts and insults and is habitually offended by real or imagined slights, then, like my friend, you probably carry around a lot of unnecessary pain.

Do you feel obligated to be unhappy because you have experienced pain in the past? Do you feel that it would be wrong to take responsibility for your pain and choose to be happy?

When God says, "A cheerful heart is good medicine" (Prov. 17:22), I believe He is saying that choosing to have a cheerful attitude rather than a gloomy one promotes health and healing.

The theologian Kierkegaard once wrote:

If an Arab in the desert were suddenly to discover a spring in his tent, and so would always be able to have water in abundance, how fortunate he would consider himself—so too, when a man, who as a physical being is always turned toward the outside, thinking that his happiness lies outside him, finally turns inward and discovers that the source is within him, not to mention his discovery that the source is his relation to God.[1]

Examine yourself. Ask, "Am I assuming responsibility for the health of my emotions? Am I looking at the power I have, because of Christ who lives in me, to choose my feelings? Or do I feel consigned to a life of pain and grief?

If you encounter a painful situation today with a family member, a fellow employee, or a friend, ask yourself right away if you can assume responsibility for your emotions by acknowledging the pain, by addressing it with the person who has caused it, and by accepting the fact that you have a choice. You can choose to walk around with hurt feelings, or you can choose to feel good. You have a choice, but more than that, you have a responsibility for your emotions.

WEEK 32 — FRIDAY
A SOUND INVESTMENT

For some parents whose children are grown and are making a life for themselves, the investment of love, care, and prayers has been worth it all. For others, there is some doubt as to whether the investment will ever pay off.

In an article by Dr. Harold Bussell of Gordon College, this point was made:

> Consider the struggles Moses' mother must have faced. She had invested her life in this young miracle, had seen God deliver him and provide the best training for him and the first thing Moses did after identifying with God's people was commit a murder and run. How embarrassing!
>
> He was not even seen for another forty years. There were no verses to claim (the Bible hadn't been written yet), no seminars to attend, no telephone hot lines to call, not even a cassette ministry to help. Moses disappeared for forty years and was forty when he ran. Chances are his mother never saw the answer to her prayers. She could easily have questioned her investment in this gift of God.
>
> But encouragement and hope are to be found in a sovereign God. God knew where Moses went. He raised up another family to minister to him and did not discard Moses because of his earlier failures. If your child has strayed, God knows where he or she is and knows that child by name.

Have you forgotten that every hair on your child's head is numbered, and that the sovereign God of the universe is watching every step he or she takes?

Moses' mother would have held to this promise in Proverbs: "Train up a child in the way he should go, and when he is old, he will not depart from it" (Prov. 22:6 NASB). I'm sure Andrew's mother did.

Andrew has AIDS. But his letter of testimony is encouraging:

I have begun to think like a parent (if that is possible) and I've been thinking about . . . the open wound caused by my venture into the homosexual lifestyle (ten years ago) I thought would never heal.

I'm sure you've heard before that God answers prayer, but not always how we expect Him to. My family can sure say "Amen" to that.

The open wound has been sewn with the glorious thread of God's love for His children. I can now sing "Jesus loves even me," and know that He does! I am His child. I am not perfect, I still stumble; but I am His and He is mine.

With AIDS in the picture, I know that a difficult time may still be before us. But I can't help thinking . . . I could still be out there drowning, just far enough from the lighthouse that I couldn't be helped. Praise Jesus! I am safe in His arms and if He desires to take me home—I desire to go! And for my family—as the song says, "To multiplied trials, His multiplied grace."

Andrew's parents are singers who have given their lives to praising God through their music. Their hearts must be full of gratitude to a loving Lord who redeemed their son from such a pit, though the consequences linger on.

Friend, don't give up praying or loving . . . you never know the day or the hour your investment will begin to pay off.

WEEK 33 — MONDAY
THE DAY PRECIOUS DIED

A couple of years ago I met an incredible young woman named Amy Harwell who has terminal cancer. She is single, thirty-eight years old, and at the time, had just had a lung removed in her second cancer surgery.

As the author of a book, *When Your Friend Gets Cancer,* Amy has a lot to say about ministry to those who are faced with terminal illness. In her book, she talks about the day she planned her own funeral and the thoughts that went through her mind:

A flood of memories swept over me. I had never attended the funeral of a close relative. However, I found myself reliving an event that had happened a year before.

On a beautiful summer day, I put my dog Precious in the car and drove back to where he and I used to live, for a farewell picnic. He was a five-dollar-from-the-pound dog, and I loved him dearly. After several happy years together, I found out that Precious had cancer—of a type that did not permit him to lie down. "He can't rest," the vet told me. "He's too sore." So I had made the hard decision to put Precious to sleep. Today was the day.

I chose for the picnic a spot where Precious used to walk morning, noon and night on the golf course tucked in between the woods and the creek. As I set up the picnic of his favorite people foods—salami, cheeses and chocolate chip cookies—he scampered off to renew his acquaintance with ducks, squirrels, and rabbits, then hurried back to sniff and inhale the goods.

157

After about an hour-and-a-half, I knew the picnic couldn't go on forever. I watched him run up that long fairway with his customary crooked gallop for the last time. Ears flying, tail wagging, he clambered in the car and, as my co-pilot, stuck his head out of the window as we headed for the vet.

I held him as he was injected. I held him as he fell. I held him as he cooled down.

Then I walked out.

My first stop was a local florist where I bought a rose and went into the cool sanctuary of my church. I just stopped and thanked God that my dog had been part of my life.

My next stop was a music store where I bought a tape of the Canadian Brass playing Vivaldi. I returned to the old neighborhood and I rolled back the sunroof. I pealed those trumpets as loudly as I could as I criss-crossed every block Precious and I had walked on our evening walks.

And then I went home.

Alone.

He was a wonderful friend. In my mind, I had this replay as I sat there with my empty pad of paper. I realized that what I had done for Precious was what I wanted done for me. Then the writing of my own funeral just flowed.[1]

To be alive is a gift to be cherished. Amy Harwell has learned how to live, so she will be ready to die when the time comes. But for many of us, life and all of its experiences have become routine and bland. We have forgotten how to feel, how to absorb, how to process life.

Make this a day to remember. Really see the people around you. Hear the music. Feel the rhythm of life. Relish the rain or the sun on your face. Thank God that you have this day. Give it back to Him.

WEEK 33 — TUESDAY
"I WILL NEVER LEAVE YOU"

In the escalating pressures of life in modern America, promises of forever are becoming more and more fragile and rare. But we all need the security of knowing that there is someone who will stick with us to the end.

I have seen women look to husbands for security, only to be abandoned in the most vulnerable years of their lives. I have seen mothers cling to grown children until the relationship has been strained to the breaking point. I know a woman who has pursued an immoral lifestyle with other women for the past twenty-five years. She knows it is wrong, hates herself for what she had done, and cries out for release. But in her desperation for someone to love, she just can't relinquish old relationships. She remains totally unconvinced that there is one who will never leave her nor forsake her.

There is Someone who promises to stay with us forever—Jesus Christ. "I will never leave thee nor forsake thee" (Heb. 13:5 KJV). In the Greek the word *never* is stated in five negatives. Jesus is saying, "I will never, never, never, no, not ever forsake you!"

One devotional writer, Amy Carmichael, explains further:

158

Many years ago someone told me that *forsake* is a compound of three words in the Greek, *leave behind in*. It conveys the thought of leaving comrades exposed to peril in the conflict, or forsaking them in some crisis or danger. Westcott interprets this verse, "I will in no wise desert you or leave you alone in the field of contest, or in a position of suffering. I will in no wise let go—loose hold— my sustaining grasp."[2]

Sometimes I feel that I have been left behind in the battle to fight it out alone. Do you ever feel that way? Abandoned? Unprotected? Alone and vulnerable? Then this reminder is for you.

Jot down the promise—"I will never leave you"—and put it where you can see it often—on your desk, the refrigerator, the sun visor. Learn to recognize feelings that get in the way of truth. Begin to fight those whimsical and untrustworthy feelings.

When the battle begins to rage, remind yourself that you are not alone. You have the King of kings standing with you and you have His promise that He will never leave you nor forsake you!

WEEK 33 — WEDNESDAY
TEMPTATION IN THE WORK PLACE

I talk with women all the time who tell me the same story: "I had no idea anything was wrong until he came home and said he was moving out!" Ninety percent of the time, the person he is moving *to* is someone he met in the office.

The work place, whether secular or Christian, is a fertile field for romance to blossom. The proximity, the everyday contact, the frequent opportunities to talk—all nurture relationships. Unfortunately, they also often open the door to tragedy.

The cycle often sounds like a soap opera:

"I need someone to understand."
    "I understand you."
"I need more time to talk."
    "I'll give you the time."
"I feel so alone."
    "I'll hold you. I'm here."
"I've never known anyone like you."
    "Really?"
"I know it's late, but I need to talk."
    "I'll be right there."
"I never meant for it to go this far."
    "I didn't either."
"I don't think we should keep seeing each other."
    "I can't leave you."
"What if your wife finds out?"
    "We haven't been getting along lately anyway."

An extramarital affair often begins with a genuine desire to meet a legitimate longing. When loneliness is eased, value is restored, and longings are being fulfilled in two people's lives, the affair can seem so right.

The need to be loved and accepted is not sin. The desire to feel acceptable and approved is not sin. But to seek fulfillment of these needs outside marriage is dangerous and may lead to a violation of one or more of God's laws, and *that* is sin. James warns: "But each one is tempted when, by his own evil desire, he is dragged away and enticed. Then, after desire has conceived, it gives birth to sin; and sin, when it is full-grown, gives birth to death" (1:14).

My friend, no one wins when a need is met in an ungodly way. Adultery has never ended in anything but death to relationship, death to a good conscience, death to trust, death to dreams, and for the Christian, death to effective ministry.

If you can see yourself slowly being ensnared by an illicit relationship, remember that it is a matter of life and death! Stop! Consider the consequences. And let the Lord release you from this bittersweet bondage.

WEEK 33 — THURSDAY
THE TRIAL-PIECE

In 1608, a new dictionary was published that gave a new twist to the word *trial:* "Something that serves as an example or proof of a manufacture or material, the skill of an operator, and especially in pottery manufacture, a piece of clay, or the like, by which the progress of the process may be judged a trial-piece."

The progress of the process is shown in the strength of the clay to withstand the heat. If the clay breaks, the pot is discarded and the whole process begins again on another piece. If we apply that principle to our lives, most of us would be on a shelf or in a heap of rubble somewhere!

But our Potter takes us through a process that is never terminal: "So I went down to the potter's house, and I saw him working at the wheel. But the pot he was shaping from the clay was marred in his hands; so the potter formed it into another pot, shaping it as seemed best to him" (Jer. 18:3–4). This Potter chooses to remake the vessel rather than discarding it!

In her book, *Edges of His Way,* Amy Carmichael writes:

> There is a difference between clay in the hands of the potter and clay in the fire. If the trial-piece cracks, it is the end of it, so far as the earthly potter is concerned; but thank God, not so when He is the Potter. He is the God of the Impossible. So if the devil of discouragement is whispering discouraging lies, do not listen to them. Even if we have failed in some supreme test, our God is not done with us.[3]

Have you ever thought of yourself as a trial-piece, an earthly representative of the Potter who has formed you? If you have blown it, you may feel as if you have lost your testimony and are embarrassed. Embarrassment is one of those emotions that seems to hover over the pots and vessels that have cracked in the fire. Although they may be patched and remade, they tend to feel others are viewing them as cracked pots!

Simon Peter was a man who knew what is was to fail under fire. When the heat was at its hottest, he denied the Lord before a crowd of unbelievers. Everyone looking on wondered. Later, when he confronted his Master, the

Potter who had made him, Peter was astonished to find that he was still valued as a usable vessel. He had failed the first thrust into the fire, but he had a Lord who was willing to work with him again.

My friend, if you have failed your first firing, confess your sin to the Lord and to all the witnesses who are aware of your transgression. Ask forgiveness, and then determine to let Him remold you and make of you a trial-piece worthy of the Master Potter.

WEEK 33 — FRIDAY
AVOIDING THE APPEARANCE OF EVIL

Have you ever heard anyone say, "No matter what I do, someone isn't going to like it! So I'm just going to go ahead and do what I want to do!"

This adolescent reaction is often used to rationalize rebellious behavior. Unfortunately, immature young people are not the only ones who respond in this way.

When it comes to our relationship with God, we are sometimes guilty. For example, when He gives such clear-cut commands as "Abstain from all appearance of evil" (1 Thess. 5:22 KJV), we want to argue and debate rather than obey unconditionally. If everyone else is doing it, we reason, then it must be okay.

I have a single friend who frequently has lunch with married men. She tells me that they often chat about spiritual matters. I believe her heart is pure and that the gentlemen she has lunch with are pure, but I have often wondered if others who see them in the restaurant together believe it!

What kind of "appearance" do you present to the world? If you work outside the home, review your own situation, and answer the following questions. Then let your answers dictate the boundaries of your activities:

1. Will it appear evil if I work late with a co-worker of the opposite sex if he (or she) is the only other person in the office?
2. Will it appear evil if I go to lunch alone with a co-worker of the opposite sex?
3. Will it appear evil if I hug my secretary or my boss?
4. Will it appear evil if _____ ? (You fill in the blank.)

While it is true that there are some folks who will always find something wrong with anything we do, the object is not to please others. The object is to obey God so that, as His children, we will not find ourselves in a compromising position that would reflection on His purity.

God calls us to be a holy, set-apart people. The rewards of obedience are rich and abundant!

WEEK 34 — MONDAY
SATAN'S FIERY DARTS

When I am troubled by tormenting thoughts, there is a wonderful verse in Ephesians that is a reminder to me that I am not powerless: "Take up the shield of faith, with which you can extinguish all the flaming arrows of the evil one" (6:16).

The devil's "flaming arrows" or fiery darts are those accusing thoughts that plague you about some past sin that you know Jesus has forgiven and which God says He has forgotten. He promises that He has separated us from our sin "as far as the east is from the west." On the other hand, Satan keeps a missile trained on our minds, programmed to smash into our memories at the most inopportune times, just to remind us of an embarrassing or potentially damaging situation from our past.

When Jesus died on the cross, He died for all our sins—past, present and future. There is nothing that He did not foreknow. If you have aborted an unwanted child, Jesus died for that sin. If you have had an adulterous affair, He knew you would fall and He bled for your sin before you were born. If you have lied, stolen, cheated, gossiped, been sexually promiscuous, abusive, or just plain mean . . . Jesus has already died for those sins. And if you have cleared your record with Him by confessing and receiving His forgiveness, then you are free. No one can accuse you.

In Romans 8, we read: "If God is for us, who can be against us? He who did not spare his own Son, but gave him up for us all—how will he not also, along with him, graciously give us all things? Who will bring any charge against those whom God has chosen? It is God who justifies. Who is he that condemns? Christ Jesus, who died—more than that, who was raised to life— is at the right hand of God and is also interceding for us" (vv. 31–34).

Even with that kind of powerful reminder of our forgiven state, there is one who likes to make us squirm. Satan will goad us at the point of our sin, spotlighting it in our minds. But if you are a believer, he has no authority over you. He is intruding on blood-bought ground.

God says we don't have to put up with that kind of harassment. We are equipped with a shield of faith to deflect Satan's blows. That shield of faith is our belief that God's Word is true and that we can rely on it. When thoughts condemn us, we can say, "I recognize you, Satan, as the one who has shot a flaming arrow into my mind and disrupted my peace and joy. I will not stand for it any longer. I raise my shield of faith and say, 'If God is for us, who can be against us?' And I remind you that you are the one who is defeated and I am victorious in Christ. My sin is covered by His blood, and you have no right there. So be gone . . . and be gone now!"

I find that singing or playing praise music and reading the Psalms help to erase the lingering effects of Satan's latest attack.

If you are bothered with haunting thoughts of the past and have cleared your conscience before God through confession and repentance, then you have the authority to stand against any of the fiery darts or flaming missiles that Satan sends your way. Jesus is your Shield and Defender!

WEEK 34 — TUESDAY
WHAT MATTERS MOST?

Recently I went through an experience with my mother that taught me a great deal about our priorities.

After taking her to the hospital for some tests, we were told she must have emergency bypass surgery. The doctors were blunt as they told her, "You can have a stroke or even die. The chances of surviving this surgery are about ninety-five percent, but in your case, the risk is greater, so we just don't know.

We are preparing the operating room now and after we put a balloon pump in your heart, we will take you into surgery."

There it was. No warning. No idea when we got up that morning that we would have to face this kind of trauma before the day was over.

My mother is a healthy woman who has never been seriously ill. Now I was standing by her bedside and hearing the doctor say, "This is very serious. . . . There is not time to fly you by helicopter to a major medical center. We will have to do the surgery here . . . and soon!"

I had often wondered what one said at a time like that. What words do you speak that will bind you together forever, whether forever is tomorrow or sometime in the distant future when you meet in heaven?

I know now, because I have lived through such an hour. I said, "I love you . . . I love you . . . I love you . . . I'll take care of Daddy . . . I love you. You know God has you in His hand. I love you, I love you." And too soon the last "I love you" was said and there was no more time.

The hours in surgery ticked away. As my mother lay in the Coronary Care Unit attached to tubes, a respirator keeping a steady beat as it breathed for her, I took her swollen hand in mind. "I'm here," I said. "I love you. Squeeze my hand if you can hear me." And there it was! The unmistakable sign of life . . . the encouraging tug that said, "I love you, too!"

I learned that when everything is stripped away and a person you love is leaving you, whether for a day at work or school, or on an extended trip, or forever, the words "I love you" are a cord that hold you close . . . for a day or for a lifetime.

What is the last thing you said to your child before he left for school this morning? What did you say to your husband or wife before you went your separate ways for the day? What did you say to that son who lives far away or the daughter who never comes home any more? Did she hear a reassuring "I love you," or did she leave the house or hang up the phone with stinging words of rebuke or indifference ringing in her ears?

When all the trivia is stripped away, when all the things that don't matter anyway are laid to rest, there is one thing left—"I love you." Let's don't forget to say it often. The Lord says it, too: "You are precious and honored in my sight, and . . . I love you!" (Isa. 43:4).

WEEK 34 — WEDNESDAY
WHEN YOU DON'T KNOW HOW TO PRAY

Sometimes we simply don't know how to pray. When a loved one is ill, we don't whether to pray for supernatural healing or healing through conventional channels. We don't know if we are to pray to land a certain job . . . or whether we are to move . . . or whether we are to have that operation we've been putting off. You and I can't foretell the future, so our specific prayers are often merely weak cries for help!

We have a God who understands our dilemma. "In the same way, the Spirit helps us in our weakness. We do not know what we ought to pray for, but the Spirit himself intercedes for us with groans that words cannot express. And he who searches our hearts knows the mind of the Spirit, because the Spirit intercedes for the saints in accordance with God's will" (Rom. 8:26–27).

God says His Spirit *helps* in our weakness. The Greek word for *help* depicts someone who shoulders one end of a heavy log that another person has been struggling to carry alone. When you don't know how to pray, you are entering a work you can't handle alone. God has given us His Spirit who will pick up the other end of our prayer burden and help us pray what needs to be prayed.

He explains how this works: Jesus, who searches the heart, knows what the Spirit is praying because He prays for us according to the will of God. Father, Son, and Holy Spirit go to work in our behalf.

We may wonder why God asks us to pray if we don't know what to ask for. Catherine Marshall wrote:

God insists that we ask, not because *He* needs to know our situation, but because *we* need the spiritual discipline of asking.

Are you praying for a difficult relationship or a tough work situation or a wayward child . . . and don't know how to pray? Then just cry out, "Help!" You will find a merciful response, the help that you need, and you will know that you have One who is interceding for you.

WEEK 34 — THURSDAY
FEAR AND ANXIETY—DOUBLE TROUBLE

God has said, "Do not fear." But how, in a practical way, can we actually live out that command?

The last couple of years my parents have gone through major health problems. In those trying times, I have learned that I can either chew my fingernails fearfully, or I can apply the truths God gave me for days like those.

During the most desperate, nerve-wracking times, the Scripture that always came to me was Philippians 4:6–7: "Do not be anxious about anything, but in everything, by prayer and petition, with thanksgiving, present your requests to God. And the peace of God, which transcends all understanding, will guard your hearts and your minds in Christ Jesus."

I began to apply that truth in a methodical way. Every time I needed to make a decision I would go through a certain thought process. I would tell myself, "Be anxious for nothing . . . *nothing* means *nothing*."

My emotions told me I was a fool not to be anxious, but in my heart I knew that God had said I didn't have to be anxious. So I made a conscious choice not to be anxious.

Then I told myself, "In everything present your requests to God." Again, *everything* meant *everything*. I was to pray, to supplicate, to ask specifically about *everything*.

My dad was critical: hemorrhaging, lungs full of fluid, and heartbeat out of rhythm. I went through my thought process step by step, asking God to answer my prayers. The only answer I received from the Lord was "Do nothing."

After giving my father a barrage of tests, the doctor came back and said my father needed a pacemaker but was too weak for the operation. The doctors could do nothing for him.

Two days later, my father's heart began to beat normally. The doctor couldn't believe it. He said this sort of thing rarely, if ever, happened. In fact, textbooks say ninety percent of patients with irregular heartbeats do not recover their heart rhythm.

God's answer to my prayers was "Do nothing." I didn't know what that meant. I only knew it meant that we were to do nothing.

Therefore, when the doctors said there was nothing they could do to save my father, I knew we had done all we could humanly do. I did not need to fear that we had made a wrong decision. Whether my father lived or died, I knew he was in the Lord's hands.

What are you fearful of today? God has shown us a very simple method for handling today's troubles: Be anxious about *nothing* and pray about *everything*.

WEEK 34 — FRIDAY
FIXER-FOLKS

Do you feel compelled to try to fix things for other people—their marriages, their health, their finances? I must confess this is one of my failings. Uninvited, we fixer-folks have a tendency to try to second-guess God and bring about solutions to other people's problems!

We are especially interested in fixing the circumstances of those we love. If a child, especially a daughter, is at a marriageable age with no prospects in sight, some moms can't resist matchmaking. I know two mothers who have thrown their young adult children together in the hope that they will get married. The young people went along with this thinly disguised scheme for a while, but they are beginning to feel manipulated and resentful.

We fixer-folks also like to know what's going to happen before it happens. We wish God would tell us what He is going to do, when He is going to do it, and how much we can count on Him to supply our needs.

Do you have a young person in your family who is looking for a job? Have you caught yourself offering to help him work up a resume? Have you contacted some of your friends in the business world . . . just to give him some connections? Have you gone so far as to suggest that he shouldn't worry, you'll take care of everything, even to subsidizing him if, for any reason, he doesn't get a job right away? If you have ever had these feelings, whether you verbalize them or not, then you are a "fixer."

You may reason, "Well, someone has to be concerned about this kid, or this husband, or this brother!"

The issue is not compassion. The issue is presumption—taking things into your own hands without regard for what the Lord may be doing in the life of the other person.

I know a woman who is wonderfully compassionate and generous, but whose kindness backfired when the people she was trying to help became resentful and demanding. When God's work is interrupted by human intervention, inevitably there is a problem.

Simon Peter is the prime example of a biblical Mr. Fixit. When Jesus was betrayed in the Garden of Gethsemane, Peter moved quickly to protect his Lord. Whipping out his sword, he cut off the ear of the servant of the high priest. "Put your sword away!" Jesus commanded Peter. "Shall I not drink the cup the Father has given me?"

Jesus knew that there was something going on that transcended the momentary threat. The will of the Father would lead to the cross, but the victory of the resurrection could never happen apart from that experience. To "fix" it would have been to destroy the most significant event in history.

165

My friend, what "cup" may your friend or loved one be required to drink in order to gain a victory? Might your "help" actually hinder God's work in their lives? Ask Him: "Teach me the difference between ministering with compassion and interfering in Your work. Open my eyes and give me faith to trust You to cause all things, even the tough things, to work together for good."

WEEK 35 — MONDAY
SOMEBODY PRAYED

Have you ever considered the fact that your prayers will affect the lives of those you love long after you are dead and gone? That thought boggles my mind! Yet, since God is not limited by time, then when our earthly lives end, death will not be able to stop His work in response to our prayers.

In John 17, Jesus prayed for you and for me: "My prayer is not for them alone [speaking of the disciples]. I pray also for those who will believe in me through their message" (v. 20). Think of that! We may never have known Him if those early disciples had not spread the Word. Jesus prayed for us, knowing that, through the centuries, the Word would be passed on, and millions of us would believe and come to Him.

If we believed the power of prayer in the lives of our children and unborn grandchildren, would we dare let a day go by without interceding for them? God will not turn a deaf ear to a prayer just because it is prayed years before the fact.

In a family of three children, the dad was an alcoholic who left them to be brought up by the mother and grandmother. The grandmother believed in prayer and made her grandchildren a priority. She died when they were young teenagers, and the three moved into adulthood as nominal churchgoers. One by one, each of the teenagers came to know Christ personally, and are all now actively serving Him in the ministry. There is no way to explain the human influence on their lives apart from the prayers of this godly grandmother. Think what their reunion in heaven will be like as she welcomes those children she prayed for so long ago!

When I was a young mother, I had a terrible fear of dying before my children were old enough to take care of themselves. "O Lord, just let me live until my kids are grown!" was an almost daily prayer. But what a comfort it is to know that we can pray *now* for our children's future, and those prayers will continue to be answered throughout their lives!

Recently I attended the funeral of one of the godliest young Christian men I have ever known. He loved his wife and children and served God with a wholehearted devotion before he was stricken with cancer. After a long battle with pain, he died. At his funeral, one of the most comforting words that could have been shared with his family was this: "The prayers that he prayed for you have yet to be answered."

If you are weary of praying because the answers to your prayers seem so long in coming, may I encourage you to keep on keeping on. "By faith he still speaks, even though he is dead" (Heb. 11:4) is as true of you as it was true of Abel and my young friend. Your prayers will live on long after you have gone to be with the Lord, to influence those for whom you are praying now!

WEEK 35 — TUESDAY
THE FOOL RAGES/LAUGHS

Have you ever tried to communicate something that was very important to you, only to have the person you were talking to become angry and walk away? Or have you tried to explain something that was heavy on your heart and had the other person laugh, as if you were making a big thing out of nothing?

If you have ever experienced any of these reactions, you have encountered one of the biggest blocks to communication in any relationship. It is frustrating. It is irksome. And it leaves you feeling absolutely helpless.

I have talked with many women who speak out of deep pain because they have repeatedly been rebuffed when trying to communicate with their spouse: "If I say anything, he just gets angry!" or "If I try to tell him how I feel, he just laughs and tells me I'm silly!"

While reading in the book of Proverbs, I found a verse that aptly describes this scenario: "If a wise man [has a controversy with] a fool, the fool rages and scoffs, and there is no peace" (29:9). The person who won't listen, and reacts by getting angry or ridiculing is a foolish person, and trying to talk to a person like that brings no rest.

If you can identify with this kind of frustration, whether it be with your mate, your employer, a parent, or a child, please consider the following suggestions:

1. *Talk to God about your feelings.* Pour out your heart to Him. Present every situation that has caused you frustration. Talk to Him just as openly as you would like to talk to the person who will not listen without anger or mockery.
2. *Ask Him to send other people into your life who will take you seriously.* That is the value of a good friend. A friend will listen and accept you for who you are.
3. *Be kind, tenderhearted, and forgiving toward the person who refuses to listen to you.* Don't bring up any of the old issues that have incurred his wrath or scorn, but express genuine interest in anything he might have to say. Let God do His work in the other person's life, although the answer may not come according to your timing or in your way.

In the meantime, you can rest in the fact that you are in communication with the One who understands you best of all.

WEEK 35 — WEDNESDAY
DON'T BOAST ABOUT TOMORROW

Living one day at a time is not a new concept. We are hearing more and more these days about programs that encourage people recovering from different forms of addiction to live life in small increments. Yet, for busy people involved with family and jobs, taking life one day at a time can seem almost irresponsible. So we keep complex calendars and plan our lives for months in advance.

My mother's recent heart surgery was an abrupt reminder that even the most elaborate plans can be changed. The events on my calendar, that at one moment had seemed so important, had to be cancelled or postponed. I had set aside a month to write a new book and some radio programs, and to take a week's vacation in Maine with my husband. Writing and travel immediately became secondary to my mother's recovery. Because I'm an only child, I needed to be with her. So my schedule had to be adjusted.

In the book of James, the author addresses a person like you and me: "Now listen, you who say, 'Today or tomorrow we will go to this or that city, spend a year there, carry on business and make money.' Why, you do not even know what will happen tomorrow. What is your life? You are a mist that appears for a little while and then vanishes. Instead, you ought to say, 'If it is the Lord's will, we will live and do this or that.' As it is, you boast and brag. All such boasting is evil" (4:13–16).

How easily we forget that our heavenly Father controls all circumstances. When things are going smoothly, we frequently become complacent and fail to take His sovereignty into account. Although we make plans, He is the one who allows them to occur, or alters our course.

We live in a society in which goal-setting is encouraged. "I'm going to make a million by the time I'm thirty," Or "I plan to retire at forty," or, "I will have lost twenty pounds (or some other specific goal) by this time next year." There is nothing wrong with setting goals as long as we acknowledge that we will reach the goal only if the Lord wills that we live and prosper.

Admitting that we are not the "masters of our fate" is the opposite of boastfulness. In 1 Peter 5:6, we see the "how to" of humility. Peter says: "Humble yourselves, therefore, under God's mighty hand." We humble ourselves when we acknowledge that it is God who calls the shots and that, although He allows us to make plans and to set goals, He is in control.

My friend, if you are worried about tomorrow, rest in the knowledge that God has planned every day of your life and nothing can transpire without His permission. Trust His sovereignty.

WEEK 35 — THURSDAY
HOW TO HANDLE PRAISE

Praise can bring out both the best and the worst in us. Compliments and encouragement may build self-esteem when given for a job well done. Our kids need to hear praise and so do our mates, our friends, and our colleagues at work. Praise is important. But we need to examine our motives when we're on the receiving end of praise.

I've always been a pushover for a kind word. As a child I occasionally sat with a favorite teacher in church. I was honored to be with her and basked in her praise when she commended me for sitting still during the service. Little did she know that it would have taken an earthquake to make me move after that! Her praise motivated my behavior.

When not taken to an extreme, praise can be a positive influence. But what about the people who become people-pleasers as a result? People-pleasers are those who never want to upset anyone, will say yes when they really mean no, and never express themselves freely because they live in constant fear of making someone unhappy. A "yes person" is an easy mark for manipulation.

Proverbs 27:21 says: "The crucible for silver and the furnace for gold, but man is tested by the praise he receives."

If you have to have praise in order to function well or if you avoid criticism at all costs, then you may not have high integrity or self-respect. I learned that lesson several months ago when I received a glowing letter from someone who wanted to pray for me. She was quite profuse in her praise, and I was pleased that she wanted to support my ministry through prayer. When her next letter came in answer to a letter of appreciation I had written her, I was stunned by her unexpected criticism of my stationery. She told me, in so many words, that because my name was on the letterhead, I wasn't very spiritual.

Stung by this rebuke, I fretted all the way home from the post office. But by the time I pulled into the driveway, I was reminded by that familiar still, small voice that, if another's opinion could affect my joy so drastically, I was too easily swayed by opinion.

How about you? Can someone's casual criticism or word of appreciation make or break your day? Then determine to work for God's approval only. And if praise does come to you, learn to turn it to Him. "Thank you. The Lord gave me this gift, and I enjoy singing (speaking, writing etc.) for His glory!"

WEEK 35 — FRIDAY
PONDERING THE PAST

The routine of the week will soon be over. The problems at work will be put on hold. The people with whom you spend your week will scatter to their own homes until Monday. You'll do something different this weekend—go on a picnic, wash the car, take a nap, have some time to think.

With a little more time on your hands, consider this Friday verse: "Forget the former things; do not dwell on the past" (Isa. 43:18).

It's tempting to think about "the good old days." For example, when the children were little . . . Actually, I usually recall only the good things about that era—how cute they were when they were all dressed up and on their best behavior. Then I begin to miss them, to wish I could have them back again, to yearn for a chance to make up for all my past mistakes as a mother and even to relive my young adulthood. By that time, I'm thoroughly depressed!

Do you look at old photos and miss your youth, your looks, your figure, your hair?

Do you think about all of the ways you made your parents' lives miserable and long to go back and tell them you love them, although now it may be too late?

Do you think about the choices you have made and how they have affected your life? Do you wish you had graduated from another school, married another mate, chosen another profession? Depressed? It's dangerous to ponder the past.

When you begin to replay the past, remember . . .

1. You can't do anything to change the past.
2. If there are painful memories, you will only hurt yourself by reliving them.
3. You will cease to grow if you live in the past. Talking and thinking constantly only of the past locks you in a time warp.

Determine this weekend that you will focus on the "now of life with God." He is so good, so active, so involved in the ongoing adventure of your life. If you insist on hanging on to the past, you and God will look like the dad

169

and son in the toy store. Every time they make progress toward the door where the father plans to give the child the surprise he has just bought him, the child balks and goes back to look at the "what might have beens." The father knows "what is" and is willing to give it. The child wants to ponder the past, to hold on to the "maybes," and thus forfeits the gift.

Put the past behind you and consider the hope that lies in the future.

WEEK 36 — MONDAY
AMONG FRIENDS

Friends are among our greatest gifts. Unlike families, friends choose to be with us just because they like us. And we choose our friends because we want to share a part of ourselves with them.

But friendship can suffer from mishandling. Here are some suggestions for nurturing friendships:

Conditional acceptance. Marriage and close friendship have several points in common. Once you have formed a close relationship, what happens when you begin to see the other person's flaws and phobias? It's easy to say, "I love you just the way you are" when the attraction is still new and vibrant. But when the new wears off, it's not as easy to be accepting.

Unrealistic expectations. In his book, *Quality Friendship,* Gary Inrig warns: "Friendship is built upon mutual attraction, but there is a problem with attraction we must notice. We can be attracted to others because of a lack of love in our lives. We may see the other person primarily as someone who can meet our needs. Such a negative basis can have devastating results."[1]

Some people with low self-esteem enter into a friendship with the idea that they can find positive reinforcement and affirmation to build their feelings of self-worth. Healthy friendship naturally provides some nurturing, esteem, and approval. But a person who is looking to a friendship to fulfill all of those needs is setting himself up for disappointment.

The cure for dealing with disappointment in friendship is found in Proverbs 17:17: "A friend loves at all times." I must stop looking for what I can receive from my friend, and start focusing on what I can give. Since love is seeking the other person's highest good, then it is healthy to take your eyes off the ways in which your friend fails you and to look at the ways you can be a friend. How can you be sensitive and caring? How can you demonstrate unconditional love—love that expects nothing in return?

The following, taken from Letty Pogrebin's book, *Among Friends,* is one of the best definitions of friendship I have found:

Friendship will be characterized by four qualities:

acceptance—not blind adoration;

generosity—the practical giving of one's time, effort, or money;

honesty—sincerity, which is freedom from deceit;

loyalty and trust—the ability to keep confidences.[2]

Pray today for some way in which you can express your love to a friend. Give generously, expecting nothing in return. Be honest in all your dealings, speaking the truth in love. Be trustworthy, keeping your friend's confidence. Thank the Lord for friends who stick with you because they choose to!

WEEK 36 — TUESDAY
HE MUST INCREASE

In this day of fallen heroes and Christian superstars, it is important that we get a firm grip on what our attitude should be toward those who bring Jesus to us in any form.

Many people are too easily impressed by Christian celebrities—musicians, authors, lecturers, television personalities, evangelists—and will quote their favorites almost more readily than they quote the Word of God. "John McArthur says . . ." or "Chuck Swindoll says . . ." or "Billy Graham says . . ." We honor these earthly vessels because they have ministered to us in profound ways. But none of them would want to be the only source of truth for us, nor would they want to replace Jesus in our lives.

In her devotional book, *Each New Day,* Corrie ten Boom tells a story that illustrates the importance of this principle:

> The Indian Christian, the Sadhu Sundar Singh, was once asked if he was influenced by the honor his friends gave him. He said, "When Jesus entered Jerusalem, many people spread their clothing and palm branches on the street to honor the Lord.
>
> "Jesus was riding, as the prophets foretold, on a donkey. In this way the feet of Jesus did not touch the street adorned with clothes and branches, but instead the donkey walked over them.
>
> "It would have been very stupid of the donkey if she had imagined that she was very important. It was not for her that the people threw their clothes on the streets."
>
> Stupid are those who spread the good news of Jesus and expect to receive glory themselves. The glory should go to Jesus.
>
> The more people came to this godly man after his meetings, the more he withdrew from the crowd, to be in the silence where God spoke to him.
>
> No sensation. No show.
>
> He brought them the living Word, Jesus.[3]

When you think of a man or woman who brings you Jesus in the same way you think of the donkey who carried the Lord that day so long ago, then it might be easier to keep things in perspective. The donkey was a useful tool, but it was Jesus who caused her name to be recorded for posterity.

WEEK 36 — WEDNESDAY
THE MOST HIGH

One of the most encouraging exercises we can do for one another is to rehearse the mighty works of God. I believe when we see Him doing something extraordinary, we should tell others and thus refresh their faith . . . and ours.

Corrie ten Boom tells this story of God's miraculous provision:

> Many people came to know and trust the Lord during World War II. One was an Englishman who was held in a German prison camp for a long period of time. One day he read Psalm 91:

He who dwells in the shelter of the Most High
will rest in the shadow of the Almighty.
I will say of the Lord, "He is my refuge and my
fortress,
my God, in whom I trust. . . ."
If you make the Most High your dwelling—
even the Lord, who is my refuge—
then no harm will befall you,
no disaster will come near your tent.
For he will command his angels concerning you
to guard you in all your ways. (vv. 1–2, 9–11)

"Father in heaven," he prayed, "I see all these men dying around me, one after the other. Will I also have to die here? I am still young and I very much want to work in Your kingdom here on earth."

He received the answer: "Rely on what you have just read and go home!"

Trusting in the Lord, he got up and walked into the corridor toward the gate. A guard called out, "Prisoner, where are you going?"

"I am under the protection of the Most High," he replied. The guard came to attention and let him pass, for Adolf Hitler was known as "the Most High."

He came to the gate where a group of guards stood. They commanded him to stop and asked where he was going.

"I am under the protection of the Most High." All of the guards stood at attention ⸍s he walked out the gate.

The English officer made his way through the German countryside and eventually reached England, where he told how he made his escape.

He was the only one to come out of that prison alive.[4]

If your faith is flagging, remember that the Most High is also your God— the same today as He was the day the Englishman walked out of his prison!

WEEK 36 — THURSDAY
FINDING GOD ON FLIGHT 232

For most of us, life is pretty routine. Our feelings and responses to God and people around us are quite predictable until we experience a crisis in which we almost lose that which is dearest to us—our own lives or the life of someone we love. Afterward, everything is different.

A recent issue of *Life* magazine carried this headline: "Finding God on Flight 232." Fascinated, I bought a copy and read the story of the survivors of the DC-10 that crashed near Sioux City, Iowa, in the summer of 1989. It was interesting to me to note how they coped with tragedy: Some turned to God, at least one to Buddha, and many turned to one another for support. But not one person made the comment, "Oh, it was nothing! My life is no different at all!" You just can't come that close to death and view life from the same perspective.

In studying people's reaction to tragedy, I have found that, except for the few who claim to be humanists or atheists, most people acknowledge God and

172

express love for others. Crisis has a way of establishing priorities like nothing else can.

The *Life* magazine article quoted Helen Young Hayes from Denver, Colorado: "I closed my eyes and thought, 'Dear Lord, I pray that You'll guide the pilot's hands.' I also thought that if God wanted to take my life, that it was O.K. with me. I was full of peace. Here I was sitting on the edge of eternity. I wasn't facing the end of my life." Helen survived and later said, "I think I went through this tragedy for a purpose, to show that God can still be seen and felt and glorified in the face of tragedy."

Another man said, "Though I came away with only cuts and bruises, they put me in the hospital for an irregular heartbeat. I thought, 'Well, maybe it would be nice to read the Bible.' I hadn't read it in years, and I turned to the 121st Psalm ['The Lord will keep you from all harm—he will watch over your life; the Lord will watch over your coming and going both now and forevermore' (vv. 7–8)]. It came back to me that I had memorized that Psalm, probably the only one I ever memorized, when I was four or five years old. That's about the time my heart started coming down. By the next day, it was back to normal and I could go home."

Then there was the young man named Kevin Heckman from Pandora, Ohio, who said, "My family is very reserved. There's not a lot of hugging and kissing. I think that will be different now. My dad was in the Korean War. He saw people stacked up like cords of wood. Yet, after the crash, he saw me and started to cry. That really hit me. Dad's made of iron and he cried."

Tragedy has a way of getting our attention, of making us set our priorities, of drawing us back to the basics that Jesus taught: "Love the Lord your God with all your heart and with all your soul and with all your strength" (Deut. 6:5).

The bottom line in the fiery crash of a DC-10, or in the fiery trial of your marriage, or your job, or your child who is ill or rebelling is love—love for God and love for your family and friends.

WEEK 36 — FRIDAY
THE HEAVENS

I've been enjoying the show that has been going on in the scientific community lately as the Voyager satellite, launched over twelve years ago, has neared the planet Neptune and sent back incredible pictures. Have you felt, as I have, that the scientists might be discovering something that we have too long taken for granted—that God is a great and mighty Creator and that someday we may see plants, moons, and stars we never could have imagined?

The more that is discovered, the more we realize we are but a speck in a vast creation that transcends our comprehension.

On a hillside outside of Jerusalem, the psalmist David looked out at those same marvelous stars and planets so long ago and wrote these words: "The heavens declare the glory of God; the skies proclaim the work of his hands. Day after day they pour forth speech; night after night they display knowledge" (19:1–2).

I believe that, through all of this media coverage of the Voyager, God is once again announcing to the world that He is Sovereign and there is none like Him. And once again the world is turning a deaf ear. Instead of falling to their knees, the general public yawns and the scientist returns to his microscope to probe for answers that can only be answered with, "In the beginning, God . . ."

Maybe we need to move a little closer to our own hearts. With such a great and mighty God in control, sometimes it's hard to fathom that He really cares about every little detail of our lives.

Yet He says: "Do not worry. . . . Look at the birds of the air; they do not sow or reap or store away in barns, and yet your heavenly Father feeds them. Are you not much more valuable than they?" (Matt. 6:25–26).

Yesterday morning I parked my car in a parking lot to wait for a friend. With the few trees on the periphery of the lot, I was amazed to see a flock of sparrows flitting about the cars and wondered why they had abandoned the shade for the hot concrete. I soon saw why. They were plucking insects off the headlights, enjoying the bountiful buffet provided by a heavenly Father who keeps up with all His creatures and provides for them in creative ways.

He loves you, too, for you are "much more valuable" than those sparrows. From the most farflung planet to the smallest creature, God delights in providing creatively!

WEEK 37 — MONDAY
CALVARY LOVE

A little book, If, by Amy Carmichael, recently caught my attention and stopped me in my tracks. So uncomfortable was I after one or two brief readings that I set the book aside, hoping to forget the impact it had made on my conscience. Rather than asking the Lord to show me what was hindering my obedience, I was actually willing to block that book right out of my mind!

The following excerpts illustrate the power of Miss Carmichael's message:

> If I can enjoy a joke at the expense of another, if I can in any way slight another in conversation, or even in thought, then I know nothing of Calvary love.[1]

Or try this one:

> If I take offense easily, if I am content to continue in cool unfriendliness, though friendship be possible, then I know nothing of Calvary love.[2]

Do you understand why I thought I could just leave that book safely tucked away? I didn't like some of the things I was having to face.

Then my mother came within a few minutes of death quite unexpectedly, and I discovered that love—the love I have for her, the love she has for me, the love we have for the Lord and the love He has for us—is absolutely all that matters. Everything else fades into absolute insignificance. It was at that point that I was finally willing to be honest enough with myself to compare my brand of love with Calvary love.

Read on if you want to take stock of yourself:

> If I do not give a friend "the benefit of the doubt," but put the worst construction instead of the best on what is said or done, then I know nothing of Calvary love.[3]

If I wonder why something trying is allowed and press for prayer that it may be removed; if I cannot go on in peace under any mystery, then I know nothing of Calvary love.

Loving with Calvary love means discovering a deeper level of loving that has little to do with emotions. This kind of sacrificial, unselfish love was modeled on Calvary. Calvary love puts others first and loves even when it is undeserved and uninvited! "God demonstrates his own love for us in this: While we were still sinners, Christ died for us" (Rom. 5:8).

WEEK 37 — TUESDAY
THE VALUE OF TIME

I have had friends say to me: "I just don't know where the time went!" Or "I'm so sorry I'm late. Time just got away from me!"

Time is a precious commodity. Each of us is allotted 168 hours per week—no more and no less than anyone else. We are responsible for that time. We use it, save it, spend it, waste it, and lose it. But do we guard it? Are we careful stewards of the hours God has given us?

If time is important to you and you want to get it under control, consider these helpful principles:

1. *If you respect your time, others will respect it as well.* Fred Smith, a wise and successful businessman from Dallas, Texas, says: "I don't allow other people to spend my money. Why should I let them spend my time?"

   When I was much younger, I thought I owed anyone who called me on the telephone my full attention until they were through talking. One woman who often called for counsel would put me on hold while she answered her office phone. Since she was a receptionist, the interruptions were numerous. I allowed her to spend my time freely without any consideration of its value to me, to my family, or to other duties the Lord might have had for me.

   One day when she called, my two little boys took advantage of my preoccupation to cover my bedspread with diaper-rash ointment! When I got off the phone, I couldn't believe the mess! Someone else had spent my time, but I had allowed it.

2. *The way you spend your time shows what you value most.* If we, as Christians, were more aware of how our time mirrors our values, we would probably be more careful in the expenditure.

   If I am late to meet a friend because I took too long getting ready, then I have valued my preparation more than my friend's time.

   If I am consistently tardy for meetings, church, appointments, then I am announcing, "I think more of myself and of my time than I do of this meeting or the other participants."

   When you use time to control other people, the message you are giving is: "I think I am more important than you!"

Time seems like such a small thing, and yet, we reveal so much by what we do with it. What will you do with your time today? You can choose to spend it yourself. You can let others spend it for you. You can show your regard or disregard for others. No other commodity is so equally distributed to each person or so carelessly handled.

Consider this wise word: "Be very careful, then, how you live—not as unwise but as wise, making the most of every opportunity, because the days are evil" (Eph. 5:15–16).

Only the Lord can redeem our time. Ask Him to give you discipline and show you how to use your time in a way that would bring glory to Him today.

WEEK 37 — WEDNESDAY
FALLING OUT OF LOVE

The other day I heard a woman say, "I have fallen out of love with my husband. I just don't have the feelings I used to have for him." This lament caused me to think about what it means to "fall out of love," to lose love.

Dr. Richard Meier of the Minirth-Meier Clinic says, "Love is not lost; it is simply transferred." He reports that most of us go through periods of not feeling aware of being "in love." It only becomes a problem when feeling is absent for weeks or months.

If you have experienced this very disturbing feeling, then ask yourself, "If love is gone, where did it go?"

1. *To another person?*
   a. Emotionally—because of another person, a friend, a relative? Emotional involvement requires energy, and there is just so much to go around. You can only be deeply involved emotionally with a few people at one time.
   b. Physically—because of an affair. Have you been playing with fire, thinking you wouldn't get burned? Unfaithfulness to a spouse destroys the bond and creates guilt.
2. *To a job?*
   a. Is your job on your mind all of the time?
   b. Do you work unrealistic hours? Is it easier to stay away from home than to cope with the way you feel when you're there? Do you work for feelings of accomplishment, status, recognition?
   c. Do you invest all your emotional energy in your job?
3. *To your children?*
   a. Does your child, who looks to you for his every need and makes you feel so necessary, draw love away from your mate?

Marriages don't just happen. They require nurturing and they require time. I have some tomato plants that looked great a couple of months ago. I was excited about all the big juicy tomatoes they would bear. As the weeks passed by, it became evident they would only produce little "death wads"— tiny hard tomatoes—and so I was disappointed and lost interest in my once-beautiful plants. I stopped watering and checking on them. They look pitiful now and are dying.

Marriage, too, requires nurturing. If you don't take care of it and nurture it, it will die.

If you have "fallen out of love," pray for the Lord to rekindle your feelings for your spouse. Ask Him to redirect your energies toward building strong ties with your mate and to show you how to divide your time and attention among other family members without sacrificing the marriage bond.

176

WEEK 37 — THURSDAY
A JOYFUL HEART

I consider myself a happy person. Oh, I have the usual stresses and strains as a wife and the mother of three teenage sons . . . all with different personalities. I also have some extraordinary stresses . . . the kind you just don't tell everyone. But I honestly am a happy person.

I believe there is a reason for that. Not because I don't have problems, because I do. Not because I'm superspiritual, because I'm not. My secret is this: I have learned to trust God and I have learned to laugh.

The Scripture says, "A happy heart makes the face cheerful, but heartache crushes the spirit" (Prov. 15:13).

My mother quoted that Scripture verse to me as a child. It took a long time for me to accept, though, since I didn't find the real source of joy until I accepted Christ as my Lord and Savior at the age of twenty-six.

But there is another verse that has fascinated me for years: "A cheerful heart is good medicine" (Prov. 17:22).

The concept of the medicinal value of joy is intriguing. In the Scriptures, the word *medicine* includes the meaning of wholeness, soothing and improving health. Medical researchers have proven that laughter releases a relaxing hormone, so physicians are "prescribing" laughter for critically ill patients! The best-selling author, Norman Cousins, has written of his experiences when faced with a life-theatening illness.

Since chronic unhappiness and sadness promote poor health—"I have bills to pay. My kids are sick. My husband just doesn't understand me"—it makes sense to cultivate cheerfulness.

1. *When you're in a difficult situation, remember, it will pass.* No trial lasts forever. Peter told the early Christians who were being persecuted, "In this you greatly rejoice, though now *for a little while* you may have had to suffer grief in all kinds of trials" (1 Peter 1:6).
2. *Don't fret over the past.* The past is gone. To hang on to anything but the good memories and the lessons learned is to drag a corpse around that you don't need to carry.
3. *Give the difficulty to God.* Talk to Him about it. He's the only One who can do anything about your circumstances anyway.
4. *Ask yourself if you had rather be a help or a hindrance to the people around you.* Your bright, joyful countenance will help others who are struggling.

Why not memorize this verse today and ask God to help you to remember it when you are confronted with unpleasant circumstances: "A cheerful heart is good medicine, but a crushed spirit dries up the bones" (Prov. 17:22).

WEEK 37 — FRIDAY
WHOM HAVE YOU HURT?

Making a list of people who have been harmful in your life is a good place to start the healing process. But don't forget that making a list of the people *you have harmed* and making things right with them is also a good place to start healing.

We would all like to find healthy ways to relate with other people. Often because of past hurts, we pay a great deal of attention to people who have caused us pain. In fact, many times they receive far too much attention. We often find ourselves dwelling on what the other person has done. It's so easy to relive every moment of their behavior—to relive every feeling we had—every wrong that seemed so unfair. Every time we relive the situation, its pain blocks out a truth that could set us free.

That truth is this: Until you see how you have hurt others and do everything within your power to make things right, you will never be a free person.

When you start thinking about people you have hurt, your first thought will probably be about how badly they have hurt you. Many situations are like that. The person you need to reconcile with is often the one who has done the most unforgivable things to you. But as long as you see it that way, you are a prisoner to their wrongness.

Does that make sense? As long as the person who has wronged you has the power to keep you trapped by anger and bitterness, they are still succeeding in hurting you. In fact, according to the Scriptures, you are blocked not only from forgiving, but from being forgiven by God as well (Matt. 6:14–15).

Maybe you are wondering what this has to do with going to someone and getting things straightened out between you. Well, unless you are willing to acknowledge that you might have done something wrong that was painful to that other person—even if it is something they deserved because of their bad behavior—then you have closed yourself off from God's healing and His response to your prayers.

Consider these words from Matthew 5:23: "Therefore, if you are offering your gift at the altar and there remember that your brother has something against you, leave your gift there in front of the altar. First go and be reconciled to your brother; then come and offer your gift."

Reconciliation does not mean that you have to become close, intimate companions. It does mean that you no longer bear a grudge, that you humbly ask forgiveness of the person you have hurt, and that you live at peace with yourself and that person.

Are you willing to go through this kind of process? If so, you may want to start making your list today. You might be surprised at how it begins to free the grip that other person's wrong has on your emotions. Healing from the past is never easy, but it is possible—if you are willing to look at what you have done to hurt another person. That is a humbling experience.

Sometimes it's impossible to find a person you have wronged and ask them for forgiveness. God know that and He doesn't hold that against you. He is interested only in your willingness to make things right.

WEEK 38 — MONDAY
GUILT AND REGRET

I talk with many women in their middle years who are suffering from the double whammy of guilt and regret.

They look at their children and consider the unfinished product a failure.

They look at their husband, if he is still there, and wonder what it will be like to be alone with him when the children have all left home. Will he have anything to say? Will he be around the house all day? Will they get along?

They look at themselves—middle-aged housewives minus a college degree and no experience in the workplace—and think, "Time and tide have left me in the lurch. There is no way I could start a career at my age."

By the time they have taken their morbid inventory, depression has set in.

I can relate to their dilemma. I, too, assess my adult life and realize that I could have produced so much more. I could have been a better wife. I could have been a better mother. I could have done more with my education. The possibilities would have been limitless ten years ago, but now?

That kind of thinking is a dead end. If you catch yourself thinking that way, give yourself a good shake and remember:

1. *The last chapter has not yet been written for our kids.* Would you or I have been considered a likely candidate for "teen of the year"? Has the Lord not promised: "He who began a good work in you will carry it on to completion until the day of Christ Jesus" (Phil. 1:6)?

2. *Doing is not as important as being.* Since when is "doing something" the supreme goal? God's heart for us is that we "be something." He wants us to be an accurate reflection of who He is, no matter what we are doing.

We can choose to hang on to guilt and regret, but we don't have to. Jesus said, "I have come that they may have life, and have it to the full" (John 10:10). The abundant life precludes negative emotions.

* He says that He has loved you with an everlasting love (Jer. 31:3).
* He promises you a future and a hope (Jer. 29:11)
* And He says, "Nothing can separate you from the love of God which is in Christ Jesus" (Rom. 8:31).

My friend, whatever your circumstance, the last chapter has not been written. Not only that, but we have a God who specializes in surprise endings!

Lord, forgive me for getting all wrapped up in guilt and regret. I can't change the past, but I can change the way I approach the future. If I need to ask someone's forgiveness, bring it to mind. And Lord, I'm sorry I have not been more grateful for Your goodness to me, for the free pardon of my sin. I yield everything to You. In Jesus' name. Amen.

WEEK 38 — TUESDAY
A HISTORY LESSON

I'll confess that when it came to history in high school, I was no great student. But now that I have hit the "middle ages" in my life, I wish I had paid a little more attention! Do you ever feel that way?

We are living in incredible times. While the eastern bloc countries pursue democracy, while South Africa begins to dismantle apartheid, while Russia works toward a multi-party political system, while the Middle East deals with the aftershocks of war, the privileged citizens of the United States are marching to protect fur-bearing animals, to have the right to eliminate

179

unwanted pregnancies and to marry people of the same sex! What has "civilization" come to?

In *The Lessons of History Summarized*, by Charles Beard, I found a series of quotations worth considering:

1. Whom the gods would destroy, they first make mad with power.
2. The mills of God grind slowly, but they grind exceedingly small.
3. When it is dark enough, you can see the stars.

In the events that will be tomorrow's history, we have seen evidence that these statements are true. Men *have* gone mad with power. Hitler, Mussolini, Marcos, Noriega, and many others have been corrupted by the very power they lusted for, and ultimately they were destroyed. God's mill does grind slowly, and what is left is very small. Nothing much remains of the dynasties of these men.

And now we can see the shadows falling on our own land. The scourge of drugs, of AIDS, of abortion, of blatant homosexuality, of perversions we would not have been able to name ten years ago are all taking their toll on our brightness. But there is hope that when the darkness finally descends, we will be able to see the stars.

For those of us who are believers, we can rest in the fact that we serve a God who controls all of history. In the book of Daniel, we read these words about the sovereign Lord: "Praise be to the name of God for ever and ever; wisdom and power are his. He changes times and seasons; he sets up kings and deposes them. He gives wisdom to the wise and knowledge to the discerning. He reveals deep and hidden things; he knows what lies in darkness, and light dwells with him" (2:20–22).

No matter how dark it gets, our God knows what is waiting there, and He will be the light we need to see us safely home!

WEEK 38 — WEDNESDAY
ACCEPTING ONE ANOTHER IN LOVE

Personality is a funny thing. It is what makes you unique. It is what makes you predictable or unpredictable, fun or serious, talkative or quiet. It is what determines whether you will succeed in structured situations, or whether you will be an entrepreneur who defies all the rules. Personality is distinctly and wonderfully you.

Why, then, do we so often refuse to let others be themselves? We make rules, and expect other people to follow them. We set up criteria for acceptability, and condemn those who do not meet them. We form pre-judgments, and do not bend when someone else has another opinion.

Think about it. Do you and your mate have the same ideas about vacations, spending money, raising your children? Probably not. And yet, if you are getting along, you have managed to learn the art of compromise. You have learned the give and take that is implied in the biblical word that says, "Bear with one another"—another way of saying, "Put up with one another!"

Try this exercise that might help you "put up with" someone whom the Lord has placed in your life:

If you are a quiet, unassuming person, ask the Lord to show you the good points of that talkative, brassy woman you work with. Ask Him to show you how He has created her to be expressive and funny, and how she brings drama to almost everything that happens. Then begin to thank Him for bringing her into your life. It will be hard to be irritated with her if you have just thanked God for her.

If you are a happy-go-lucky person whose lunch break is the high point of the day, begin praising God for that nit-picking neighbor who is out mowing his lawn before 8:00 on Saturday mornings. Enjoy the beauty his hard work brings to your world, and thank God for it.

If you are creative and sensitive, thank God for the hard-driving administrator you have to answer to. Ask Him to show you how to appreciate her organizational skills and the ability with which she handles her work. If you can begin to see that she is working within the framework God has given her, then you won't feel intimidated by her management style.

We all have to live together in this world, but Christians seem to be expected to live together better than other folks. Personality differences are not automatically eliminated, however, just because we belong to Jesus Christ. Nor do Christians adapt to difficult people without a struggle.

Taking the time to understand that different personalities react differently enables us to live out God's instruction to "bear with one another."

WEEK 38 — THURSDAY
GIVE ME THIS MOUNTAIN!

When was the last time you tried something new—a new taste, a new experience, a new route? And how did you respond to the challenge? Did you say, "Why not?" Or did you back out with an "Uh, uh! Not me!"?

Many people, by their mid-thirties, have stopped acquiring new skills and new attitudes in any aspect of their lives. In reality, there is much to be said for hanging on to the tried and true. If it works, why change? But much of life is unexperienced, so this may be the time in your life to give some new things a try.

While jogging in the park late one night, my husband encountered a homeless puppy who, according to the park guard, had been there all day. Charlie is a real pushover for a hard-luck story, so rather than leave the little thing there to freeze, he brought her home.

After several attempts to give her away, we decided to keep her. A new puppy is always a challenge, but particularly one that will someday hit fifty or sixty pounds! More than a challenge, there has been a change—a change in my routine, a change in the way my day begins and ends, a change in my responsibilities. But it has been fun to step out of the mold, to embark on a new adventure.

The same principle applies in the spiritual realm as well. Caleb was a man who was unafraid of a challenge: "I was forty years old when Moses the servant of the LORD sent me from Kadesh Barnea to explore the land. And I brought him back a report according to my convictions, but my brothers who went up with me made the hearts of the people melt with fear. I, however, followed the LORD my God wholeheartedly" (Josh. 14:7–9).

Many years later, we hear old Caleb saying, "Now, then, just as the Lord promised, he has kept me alive for forty-five years. . . . So here I am today, eighty-five years old! I am still as strong today as the day Moses sent me out; I'm just as vigorous to go out to battle now as I was then. Now give me this hill country that the Lord promised me that day" (vv. 10–12).

Caleb was a man who was willing to tackle something new. Ruts were not for him. How about you? Do you need to shake loose from the way things have always been? Do you need to go for the challenge God has for you today? Why not ask God to give you a heart like Caleb?

WEEK 38 — FRIDAY
GOD'S PATTERN FOR PARENTS

Not long ago I watched a moving scene between a mother and daughter as we sat at my dining room table. We adults were engrossed in our own conversation, and the little girl's plea for her mother's attention seemed almost like an intrusion. With unruffled patience, the woman drew the child close to her and began to draw pictures to distract her.

I watched them together and thought back to the days when my own children were small. As a young mother, I had prided myself on their good behavior with only a glance from me. But in looking back, I could see that I cared too much for other people's opinions of my children and of me as a parent. Unfortunately, appearances were often more important to me than my relationship with my children.

As I have come to know the Lord better over the past eighteen years, I have observed some qualities that He, as a parent, demonstrates toward His children in achieving both obedience and relationship with us:

1. *God never ceases expressing His unconditional love and commitment, even when His children are disobedient.* He repeatedly says in many ways, "I have loved you with an everlasting love; I have drawn you with loving-kindness" (Jer. 31:3).

   The Lord is never sarcastic nor does He give the silent treatment. Even when He has to administer discipline, His love is evident.

2. *God is lavish in His goodness.* He "spoils" His children with good things even when they don't deserve it.

   Listen to this Scripture: "The LORD is gracious and compassionate, slow to anger and rich in love. The LORD is good to all; he has compassion on all He has made" (Ps. 145:8–9).

   Once, when one of my children was being disciplined, he had a tough time believing that my parental restrictions were made in love. In fact, he was so angry that it was impossible to convince him that we were punishing him only because we *did* love him. Finally, I bought him a small gift and put it in his room along with a note that told him again how much we loved him. With that gesture, we were able to build a bridge and restore our relationship. The gift was a reminder that despite the fact he was being disciplined, he was still very loved.

3. *God is unashamed of His devotion to His children.* "The Lord your God . . . will take great delight in you, he will quiet you with His love, he will rejoice over you with singing" (Zeph. 3:17).

   Throughout Scripture, God's superior parenting is clearly demonstrated. He gives and gives and He loves and loves. He seems literally to enjoy His children. He "delights" in us. He loves us. He "rejoices over" us! And when the very nature of His character demands our correction, He is moved by the feelings of our weakness, and hovers close by to offer refuge to His repentant children.

For those of us who at one time may have been too harshly demanding with our own children, God is a Redeemer. He promises that He will take the mistakes we made in youthful ignorance and cause them to work for good. And that's good news!

WEEK 39 — MONDAY
THE TRUSTWORTHINESS OF GOD

Several years ago, when I suddenly lost the vision in my left eye, I experienced a crisis of faith. Though I eventually regained some of the sight in that eye, there were many weeks of waiting and wondering in which I had to search my heart and deal with the question: "Do I really trust God in this?"

It seems easy enough to trust Him for finances, for my children's future, for the amazing things He does in other people's lives, but I had a problem trusting God with this affliction.

When the unexplainable causes your faith to waver, it's important to go back and rehearse God's character. We could review all His mighty works in behalf of His people throughout history, but one event stands out as the supreme revelation of God—the suffering and death of His Son, Jesus.

The Scriptures say: "Yet it was the Lord's will to crush him and cause him to suffer" (Isa. 53:10). Imagine the agony when the Son, who had humbled himself and come to earth to carry out His Father's plan, cried out, "Father, if you are willing, take this cup from me; yet not my will, but yours be done" (Luke 22:42)!

Have you ever considered what that sacrifice cost Him, what kind of character was necessary to see it through?

Picture that scene with me. Put your human heart in the place of God's heart. Could you have heard that agonized plea and remained unyielding and resolute? For your sake and mine, God stayed with His plan and permitted His Son's suffering.

What kind of character would it take for you to sacrifice your precious only son for thieves, murderers, rapists, adulterers, child-molesters, and indifferent average sinners like you and me?

I'll have to admit that if Jesus had been my Son and had begged, "Take this cup from me," I could not have withstood the pressure. At that point, no man, woman, child, king, or ruler would have been worth His pain and suffering! If it had been within my power, I would have brought Him home in my arms and would have shielded Him from anything that could bring Him harm.

But Jesus was not my son, or your son. He was the Son of God . . . a God whose character would not permit Him to deviate from His plan, even when the raspy, agonized voice of His boy pierced His ears: "Father . . . if you are willing, take this cup from me."

If only that one moment in time had been recorded, it would be enough to prove the character of God. He chose to stay with the plan that allowed you, me, your son, my son to have eternal life and to have purpose in our pain.

How can we ever feel uneasy in the hands of a God who would not spare

183

His own Son, but would look into eternity, see you and me and our sin, and say with determination: "My Son, You must drink the cup. It is the only way."

WEEK 39 — TUESDAY
IN SICKNESS OR IN HEALTH

"In sickness or in health, till death do us part." These powerful vows have been spoken millions of times. But I wonder how many times these vows are honored.

Elisabeth Elliot, married three times and widowed twice, is a writer whose published works are always first tested in the furnace of affliction. What comes forth is a powerful and moving testament to her faith.

So when I learned of her little book, *Love Knows No Limits,* I was eager to read her candid remarks about marriage. She spoke of Jim Elliot, her first husband, who was martyred by the Auca Indians in Ecuador. After she lost Jim, she met and married Add Leitch, a godly man who later died a painful death from cancer. The Lord then brought into her life Lars Gren, a hospital chaplain. It was Lars who introduced Elisabeth to some residents of the state hospital in Milledgeville, Georgia. Some of these people were to have a profound effect on Elisabeth.

She writes:

> We eat breakfast with Mr. Smith, a very handsome man with white hair, ruddy skin, and bright blue eyes. He is wearing a blue shirt and blue sweater. He tells us a story which brings into sharp focus the words of the wedding vows, "in sickness and in health, for better, for worse." His wife has been a patient at Milledgeville for three years.
>
> "When she first got sick," he said, "I carried her everywhere, I did. The doctor said, 'She'll get worse, every week and every month. So if you want to go on any trips or anywhere, go now.' We had some good times, me and her. But the doctor said, 'You can't stand it. You won't be able to stand it.' 'Well,' I said, 'Ah'm gonna hang on long's I can.'
>
> "I took care of her for five years but I lost fifty-two pounds just from worry. I was so tense they broke three needles tryin' to put a shot in my arm. Well, I carried her to twenty-five doctors, but they couldn't do nothin. 'It's a brain deterioration,' they told me.
>
> "I did everything for her. I dressed her and fed her and everything, but it like to whup me and if it hadn't of been for the good Lord, I'da sworn I'da never lasted six months. But a lot of people were prayin' for me. Oh, yes. But finally I had to give up and put her here.
>
> "She can't do nothin'. Can't move or speak or hear. She's in the pre-birth position, legs and arms locked, heels locked up tight behind. You can't straighten her out. But I come every other day. I go in and kiss her 'bout a dozen times, jes' love her to death. I talk to her. She don't hear, but she knows my touch."

Elisabeth says, "We went later to see Mrs. Smith. If ever there was a sight to confound a man's love for a woman, to strain to the breaking point the most

184

potent human passion, we saw it in that stark white crib—a crumbled scrap of inert humanity. But there is a love that is strong as death, a love many waters cannot quench, floods cannot drown.

"But that is the love that will make marriage work. God knew it would take a remarkable love that could be called up by one's own choice . . . not according to how beautiful or pleasant or sweet the object of the love was, but rather according to a vow that was made, no matter what!"

WEEK 39 — WEDNESDAY
A TIME TO LET GO

On a panel of women whose grown children had left home, there was a discussion of the emotions they had experienced at the painful time of departure. As I listened, I noted that the mothers who had prepared to release their kids to adulthood sounded much better equipped for the transition than those who seemed to have been caught unaware.

For most parents and their maturing children, separation is inevitable, though it can feel like rejection when the child who once loved to be home no longer prefers to be around. Just as putting away the crib was a milestone when your baby mastered crawling over the sides, so is deciding to let your teen push away when the time comes.

Preparation for independence for both parents and children begins when the children are young. If a parent can't bring himself to leave a crying child in the church nursery, then it will be tough to handle unpleasant separations in the days ahead. Parents, especially moms, need to be able to entrust their children to other responsible people on occasion in order to begin to form a life outside the home.

Maybe you are struggling with letting go. Whether you are relinquishing your children to the church nursery or to college, the feelings are the same. You may feel as if you are shirking your responsibility in some way or that you are being rejected.

Here are some thoughts that might help you with your struggle:

1. *God loves your children more than you do.* Nothing can touch them that has not first been filtered through His loving hands. You can trust God to work in their lives as you release them to His care.
2. *You are a whole person apart from your mate or your children.* God has a sovereign plan for you apart from your family. He sees you as valuable in yourself. Your wholeness as a person will be a healthy example for your children as they grow up.
3. *Other people can have a positive influence on your children and can give an added dimension of understanding to their development.* Try to give them as many healthy contacts as possible with teachers, church, and community leaders. If you limit your child's contacts in his early years, you will have either a very shy and awkward young adult or one who will be determined to see the world on his own.
4. *Realize that you may lose a child to gain a cherished friend.* Don't try to keep him in a spot where he can only relate to you on a childish level. Preparation for the time when your child leaves home begins

185

on the day he or she is born. If you will let it happen, it can be a natural, rewarding process for you both.

God reminds us: "There is a time for everything . . . a time to plant and a time to uproot" (Eccl. 3:1–2). Letting go with grace can bring new blessings!

WEEK 39 — THURSDAY
GOD IS NOT "COOL"

Recently I heard a fiery young preacher speaking to high school and college students. In his desire to "relate," he was pulling out all the stops, and they were hanging on every word he was saying. Unfortunately, there was more to the message than the words!

Though his speech was eloquent, I was increasingly uncomfortable with his body language and the signals he was sending to this crowd of impressionable youngsters. The music he had chosen bordered on the raucous, and in his general attitude, he projected a slightly irreverent view of God, as if he were a rock star or a baseball player.

And I was really incensed when the young man said, "God is cool!"

I have a real problem with that image of God. God is awesome, God is sovereign, God is holy, God is love, God is a consuming fire, and it is time we all fell prostrate at His feet . . . but God is *not* cool!

Just that morning I had been reading in the book of Exodus, where the children of Israel were encamped in the desert at the foot of Mount Sinai. God invited Moses to come up and fellowship with Him:

"I am going to come to you in a dense cloud, so that the people will . . . always put their trust in you."

The Lord said to Moses, "Go to the people and consecrate them today and tomorrow. Have them wash their clothes and be ready by the third day, because on that day the Lord will come down on Mount Sinai in the sight of all the people. Put limits for the people around the mountain and tell them, 'Be careful that you do not go up the mountain or touch the foot of it. Whoever touches the mountain shall surely be put to death. He shall surely be stoned or shot with arrows.' " (Ex. 19:9–13)

Later I read, "On the morning of the third day there was thunder and lightning, with a thick cloud over the mountain, and a very loud trumpet blast. Everyone in the camp trembled" (v. 16).

My friend, I doubt that anyone that day would have dared to say casually, "God is so cool. Can't wait to see Him when He comes to the top of Mount Sinai!" No way. There was a deep awe and reverence for the holiness of God. Because of it, the people actually trembled.

We live in a generation when nothing much is sacred. People burn the flag with impunity, or wear it like a garment. The Word of God is fair game to anyone who wants to pick it apart. Laws are made to be broken. Life is cheap, and sex is easy. And very few people understand the first thing about the fear of God.

Somehow we must restore reverence for the holiness of Him who created and maintains the universe. There must be boundaries as there were on the mountain that day, a line beyond which no one dares to trespass.

We may never fully comprehend the holiness of God until we bow before His throne in heaven, but until then, may we have the wisdom to show Him the respect He deserves.

WEEK 39 — FRIDAY
THEY FORGOT HIS WORKS

Today is a good time to remember what God has done for you. I find that I am guilty of snuggling close to Him in times of crisis, but when things are going smoothly, I can become pretty independent.

The Hebrews had the same problem. In Psalm 106, God records these words about them, words in which you and I could substitute our own names: "He saved them from the hand of the foe; from the hand of the enemy he redeemed them. The waters covered their adversaries; not one of them survived. Then they believed his promises and sang his praise. But they soon forgot what he had done" (vv. 10–13).

What a powerful three-line description: "They believed His promises. They sang His praise. They soon forgot what He had done."

If there is any description of privileged America, this is it. We don't have to depend upon God for our daily bread. We don't have to pray for protection from bombs and invading troops. We are secure in all the bounty God has given us. And sometimes we quickly forget all that He has done for us.

When my mother was so very ill, every breath she breathed was a matter of intense prayer for me. Now that she's better, I already feel myself slipping from the Father's embrace. I hate that. I want to stay close to Him, even on the days when there is no crisis. I want to be so close that there is no space between us, even today when things are so normal they are almost boring.

Do you ever feel that way? I have some thoughts that I hope will help as you and I get honest with ourselves and with God.

I start to pull away when I get busy. During a crisis, one's attention—prayers, thoughts, conversations—are all focused on the situation. But as the pressure eases and you get back to a more normal routine, time seems fragmented.

The need to pray grows less urgent. Once the crisis is past, there is not the same compelling desire, the same intensity in sharing things with the Lord. I find it easier to put Him on hold.

When this happens, there is only one way to retrieve that precious relationship: Immediately recognize what is happening. Go to the Father and confess your preoccupation with other things to the exclusion of time with Him. Ask Him to give you back the fervor and excitement of communion.

Read and reflect on all the ways God has dealt with His people. Psalm 106 is a great place to start. Ask God to show you His faithfulness as you read words like these: "Many times he delivered them, but they were bent on rebellion and they wasted away in their sin. But he took note of their distress when he heard their cry; for their sake he remembered his covenant and out of his great love he relented" (vv. 43–45).

That's the kind of God we serve! How can we ever forget His great love and mercy for us, even when we least deserve it?

WEEK 40 – MONDAY
JOIN THE PARADE!

Second Corinthians, a book I have both studied and taught, is one of my favorites because of the personal insight the apostle Paul gives us into his own feelings and struggles.

In this letter, he is writing to a group of people who have been led astray by false teachers. They have questioned Paul's authority and motives and have caused him no small amount of anguish, yet he continues to love them deeply. In fact, at one point, he writes, "The less that I be loved, the more that I love." What a sad, sad commentary from a man who knew the Lord intimately and loved his brothers and sisters in Christ.

We also glimpse another aspect of Paul's nature, one that we don't see anywhere else in the Bible—depression. "Now when I went to Troas to preach the gospel of Christ and found that the Lord had opened a door for me, I still had no peace of mind, because I did not find my brother Titus there. So I said good-by to them and went on to Macedonia. But thanks be to God, who always leads us in triumphal procession in Christ and through us spreads everywhere the fragrance of the knowledge of him" (2 Cor. 2:12–14).

Paul was not only a man who preached the truth but also lived by it. He demonstrates to the Corinthians the way to deal with that panicky feeling. While he confesses that he is too upset to stay in Troas, he gives thanks to God and moves on to Macedonia.

In his letter to the Philippians, Paul writes, "Rejoice in the Lord always. I will say it again: Rejoice! . . . The Lord is near. Do not be anxious about anything, but in everything, by prayer and petition, with thanksgiving, present your requests to God. And the peace of God, which transcends all understanding, will guard your hearts and your minds in Christ Jesus. . . . Whatever you have learned or received or heard from me, or seen in me—put it into practice. And the God of peace will be with you" (4:4–7, 9).

Paul's three-fold plan for overcoming depression and panic is as effective for believers in modern-day America as it was for first-century Christians in Corinth and Philippi. When you are discouraged, when things haven't worked out and you don't know what to do next, even when you can't locate someone you love, peace is possible if you:

1. Rejoice! Be thankful that God is in control.
2. Confess your feelings, holding nothing back from Him.
3. Take action. Do something constructive.

You may not know what is going on, but God does. He is in control and will not concede His position. Join the parade—the "triumphal procession in Christ." We can celebrate because Jesus has triumphed!

WEEK 40 — TUESDAY
A DISCOURAGING WORD

The story is told that during the Boer War, at the siege of Ladysmith, a civilian was sentenced to a year's imprisonment.

The fortunes of the town and garrison were hanging in the balance. This civilian would go along the lines and speak discouraging words to the men on duty. He struck no blow for the enemy—not one. He was just a discourager, and at a critical time. The court martial judged it a crime to speak disheartening words in an hour like that.[1]

Unfortunately, discouragement—defined as dejection, low spirits, despondency, despair, or hopelessness—never affects only one person, but has a way of spreading its devastation like the Black Plague. And the infection is often transmitted orally—through the spoken word!

How about you? What kind of words do you speak in times of crisis and stress? Do you look for positive things to say, or do you automatically assume the worst, and share it? When you feel down, does it just seem easier to tell others how hopeless you feel, or do you voice hope? When folks come around, can they count on an optimistic outlook from you, or a discouraging word?

God has some encouraging words for us:

I am still confident of this: I will see the goodness of the LORD in the land of the living. Wait for the LORD; be strong and take heart and wait for the LORD. (Ps. 27:13–14)

Do not let your hearts be troubled. Trust in God; trust also in me. . . . Peace I leave with you; my peace I give you. I do not give to you as the world gives. Do not let your hearts be troubled and do not be afraid. (John 14:1, 27)

Discouraging words only spread hopelessness in an already difficult situation. But God's words are always light and life. To quote Him to others is to diffuse discouragement and lift spirits.

WEEK 40 — WEDNESDAY
WHEN CONFUSION REIGNS

Confusion, that word which is synonymous with disarray, snafu, uproar, row, agitation, or indistinctness, is a word that is part of our lives, but not by God's design.

In a remarkable book published some years ago, Canon Roger Floyd, an archdemon, instructs subordinates on an ancient and effective piece of satanic strategy. "Insert yourself into the simple situations which call for plain and obvious duties and complicate them again, until at last no one involved in them can make sense of the confusion."

Can you recognize the strategy that is so effectively being applied in our society today? The simple situations which call for "plain and obvious duties" are being twisted and turned into complex situations.

The Word of God, once accepted for what it said, is now in question. Starting in the 1700s, men began to confuse the issues with theories that have become fact in many churches. The simple, plain truth of trust and obey has been replaced with trust and obey *only if it seems right in your own eyes.*

Paul had to deal with people who allowed confusion to replace their trust and obedience. In 1 Corinthians 14, he writes, "For God is not a God of confusion, but of peace. . . . Let all things be done properly and in an orderly manner" (vv. 33, 40 NASB).

What confusing issues are you dealing with in your life today? Does it seem almost insane for you to believe that God will meet your needs? Is it confusing to hear, on the one hand, that suffering is a good thing because God can use it to conform you to His image, while being encouraged to pray for deliverance? I agree that the Christian life can be confusing. But that is exactly what the Enemy hopes. He wants to take the truth and complicate it, bringing doubt, confusion, and instability.

I've noticed that little children are pretty firm in their beliefs. They accept without question what we tell them about God. They don't have to have a lot of theological explanations or theories. They simply believe that God is with them, that they can talk to Him, and that He will take care of them.

The Enemy wants to hurt; God wants to help. It's as simple as that. When my youngest son was four years old, he was troubled with nightmares. We prayed every night, asking the Lord Jesus to protect him and to remind the Enemy that he didn't have any place in my son's dreams. With no further theological explanation, my child went to sleep, never to be bothered by nightmares again. There was no room for confusion because he decided to take God at His Word when He said, "He gives His beloved sleep." He asked for it. He got it.

Little children aren't confused by the lies of the Enemy. God is God and He is to be trusted. How about you? Can you lay aside your confusion today and come to Him as a little child?

WEEK 40 — THURSDAY
IN THE GARDEN

An unforgettable moment for me occurred on a hydrofoil between mainland China and Hong Kong, during a trip to visit with believers on the mainland.

The small group I was with was accompanied by a Chinese pastor who joined us at the dock. On the trip over, he was very quiet. I knew that he had been imprisoned for fifteen years for preaching the gospel and that he now went in and out of China to preach to his people, for a while enjoying the freedom of an open door.

On the way back, he asked, "May I share my story with you?" In wonder and deep humility, I listened as he quietly related the following:

"When I was arrested and sent to prison, we were assigned to work details. I worked many places, always under the watchful eye of a guard. Eventually I noticed that the guards carefully avoided the "night-soil" pits, the place where the human excrement was kept to be used as fertilizer on the fields. The stench was so horrible and the maggots and worms so plentiful that the guards stayed away from anyone who worked there. So I asked if I could be transferred there. Since the other prisoners didn't want that job, I was immediately given the assignment.

"I was thrilled! There I could meet with my Lord every morning without interruption. Every day I would start by singing:

I come to the garden alone
While the dew is still on the roses,
And the voice I hear falling on my ear
The Son of God discloses.

190

And He walks with me and He talks with me,
And He tells me I am His own. . . .

"That night-soil pit became my garden."

The pastor showed me his hands which were gnarled and broken from the beatings he had received. It was the meetings in the garden with His Lord that had kept him sane.

Whenever I become dissatisfied with my time with God and begin to make excuses about why it's not convenient, or why there just isn't enough quality time, the serene face of that dear man comes back to remind me that no excuse will do. Jesus will make a garden out of any place I choose to meet Him!

Another face and another garden came to mind—Jesus, in the Garden of Gethsemane. Here Jesus sweated great drops of blood in the dread anticipation of His death and burial. But He must have taken comfort in fellowship with the Father, for "an angel from heaven appeared to him and strengthened him" (Luke 22:43).

My friend, You and I will probably never be called upon to spend time in a prison camp or a night-soil pit, nor will we suffer for the sins of the world, but because we are often harried, stressed out, overworked, and strung tight, we do need to slow down and make a garden of wherever we happen to be. Jesus will meet us there!

WEEK 40 — FRIDAY
BEING REAL IN PRAYER

How free are you with God when you pray? Do you feel as if you have to address Him formally or that you have to apply a formula, some kind of confidential code, before He will hear you? Or have you discovered the joy of talking to the Lord as you would talk to a friend?

Recently I had the privilege of meeting with a group of women who were planning a conference for their area. Each person present was deeply burdened for the people who would be attending. Each one wanted God's will to be done during the weekend conference. As we prayed, the dear woman sitting next to me closed our time by saying, "Lord, we just invite you to have yourself a wonderful time this weekend!"

I nearly came up out of my chair! *That's it!* I thought to myself. *That's what it's all about!* We were there to plan a meeting for God's glory. Certainly, we were all concerned about the participants, but He was more concerned . . . and a "wonderful time" for Him would be to see those women coming into a closer relationship with Him. So, of course we should invite Him to interrupt our plans, to make Himself known, to manifest Himself!

Being real in prayer is one if the most obvious marks of a believer for me. I can remember when our family was looking for a church home. We visited a particular church on a snowy Sunday. There was no choir, and only a handful of people had shown up. But when the pastor began to pray, we knew we were home. He had a familiarity with Jesus that showed in the way He prayed. He was humble, but honest. No pretense, just a needy person seeking an all-sufficient God.

Do you talk to God as if you know He's glad to hear from you? Or do you

191

approach Him with caution, tip-toeing into His presence with your carefully worded prayers?

Romans 8:14–15 tells us: "Those who are led by the Spirit of God are sons of God. For you did not receive a spirit that makes you a slave again to fear, but you received the Spirit of sonship. And by him we cry, 'Abba, Father.'"

Abba is the Greek word for "daddy." To come into the presence of God is to approach a holy God, of course, One who is to be respected, but One who is willing to bend low to listen . . . as a loving father does with a little child. No daddy expects his children to speak to him in a formal manner. A real daddy wants his child to feel free to come to him anytime, and to discuss whatever is on his mind.

Those of us who were adults in the '60s will never forget little John-John Kennedy, who walked into cabinet meetings or played under his father's desk while the President entertained visiting heads of state. John Kennedy, Jr. was perfectly comfortable and relaxed, knowing that he had his father's ear and an open door at any time.

The same privilege is yours and mine as God's children. No "thees" and "thous" needed. No special formulas that will admit us into the throne room. Just our relationship—Father and child.

If you struggle with prayer, why not begin today with a simple petition straight from your heart? Just tell God . . . your Abba, Father . . . what's on your mind. Little by little you will find that your time with Him becomes sweeter and sweeter as you pour out your heart, simply and without pretense, to the One who loves you best.

WEEK 41 — MONDAY
CONFESSIONS OF A PARENT

No matter where I go to speak across the country, I meet and talk with parents who are concerned, hurt, befuddled, even desperate over their children.

I think of the young woman who was attending the conference with her mother. "She is a manipulator, and I am praying that God will work in her life to help her see that her manipulation is driving me away!"

I think of the mother whose daughter has chosen a lesbian lifestyle, saying nonchalantly, "It's okay . . . I'm a Christian."

I think of the woman who had been abused as a child, and in turn, had abused her own children. Now, wanting to make things right, she was struggling to say the words, "I love you," yet could not bring herself to say them.

Children, our greatest treasure, are often the source of our deepest pain. Pat Hinton expresses it well:

> My pretty one, my first born,
> I grieve at the wall of pain
> we build between us:
> a wall of glaring eyes and stopped-up ears
> built on misinterpretation,
> a wall of clenched jaws
> built on dread of a harsh answer,

a wall of cruel and cutting words
built on negative ideas
of you about me and me about you.

But today I saw some light.
I saw that walls only divide and diminish.
I saw that all this sarcasm
and negativism and harshness
is sin.
It isn't just growing pains and bad moods,
It's sin.
Because in every way, building a wall
between persons is a failure to love,
and failure to love is sin.
So I'm starting with myself to change
by acknowledging now that I have sinned
by failing to love you more as you struggle
to learn who you are.
(Did you know I have that struggle, too?)
I have given my failures to Jesus
and, in His love, I will begin again
so you can begin again.
Let's dissolve our wall with His love.

My friend, do you need to start over with your child? Do you need to say, "I love you?" To bring down a wall of pain? Give your failures to Jesus and let Him dissolve the walls with His love.

WEEK 41 — TUESDAY
ACCEPTING ADVERSITY

Some tragedies strike suddenly and without warning, leaving their mark which must be borne for the rest of one's life.

I think of the mother in her twenties who held in her arms a little four-year-old girl suffering from severe cerebral palsy. This young woman's circumstances were radically altered by the birth of this child. Her husband had left her, claiming he did not want to be saddled with that kind of burden for the rest of his days.

Has some drastic turn of events changed your life? Perhaps your comfort has been ruffled. Familiar surroundings and reliable relationships may have been altered, and you feel uncertain as to what to expect next.

Could it be that you are having trouble accepting the situation as a reality? Are you fighting the fact that a loving God could be using it for good in your life? Do you feel some sort of mandate to resist? If so, then you are in good company.

When the Job family's life savings were wiped out, all their children killed, and Job himself afflicted with a painful ailment, Mrs. Job had a tough time accepting their state. "Do you still hold fast your integrity?" she asked her husband, bewildered by their multiple tragedies. "Curse God and die!" But he, trusting God, replied, "You speak as one of the foolish women speaks. Shall we indeed accept good from God and not accept adversity?" (2:9–10, NASB).

193

According to the dictionary, acceptance means "to take something offered, in a positive way." But accepting without question the things that forever change our lives contradicts our natural striving to better our condition. Arthur Gordon gives us a memorable story about acceptance in his little book, *A Touch of Wonder:*

> It's hideously difficult. But in terms of courage and cheerfulness and ultimate happiness, the rewards can be beyond measure. I knew a man once, a minister, who through some hereditary affliction was deaf and almost blind. He went right on preaching, visiting the sick, listening to people with his hearing aid, laughing uproariously at jokes, giving away huge portions of himself and having a marvelous time.
>
> One Christmas I went with him to buy some trifle in a crowded drugstore. On the back of the entrance door was a mirror, so placed that as we turned to leave, my friend's reflection came forward to meet him. Thinking that someone else was approaching, he stepped aside. So, naturally, did the image. He moved forward and once more met himself. Again he retreated.
>
> By now an uneasy hush had fallen on the spectators. No one quite knew what to say or do. But on his third advance my companion realized that he was facing a mirror. "Why," he cried, "It's only me!" He made a grand bow. "Good to see you, old boy! Merry Christmas." The whole store exploded in delighted laughter and I heard someone murmur, "That man really has what it takes." What "it" was, surely was the gift of acceptance— acceptance of limitations that in turn brought the power to transcend them.[1]

Whatever your struggle, I would encourage you to quit fighting and accept it, recognizing that our God is greater than any circumstance. Kicking and arguing will change nothing, but once you calm down and accept God's dealings with you, then you give Him the freedom to work in you and through you to bring about your good and His glory.

WEEK 41 — WEDNESDAY
FREEDOM THROUGH ACCEPTANCE

"Once you accept the blow, the disappointment, you're free . . ."

Freedom is extremely important to me. And yet, I have discovered how easily I can become a prisoner in my mind and heart when I try to hold out for something I want, but probably will never have. We become a prisoner to disappointment when we hold unrealistic expectations for a relationship, for example. We become a prisoner to bitterness when we harbor feelings of revenge toward someone who has inflicted pain. We restrict freedom when we refuse to accept the realities of life.

You cannot make someone love you. You cannot make your child bright or talented if he has only average ability. You cannot make your mate understanding if he or she is emotionally on another level.

Try as we may, we cannot force the people or circumstances of our world to live up to our expectations. And the sooner we decide to "accept it and move on," the happier we will be.

The apostle Paul understood this principle when he wrote: "One thing I do: Forgetting what is behind and straining toward what is ahead, I press on toward the goal to win the prize for which God has called me heavenward in Christ Jesus" (Phil. 3:13–14).

Paul had to accept the fact that he would never live as the Hebrew of the Hebrews he had been groomed to be. He had to accept the fact that he was guilty of persecuting Christians, a fact that he acknowledged and hated. But to continue beating himself would only have made him a prisoner to himself.

To recognize that God has another agenda is to accept the freedom of hope and life beyond disappointment.

As Arthur Gordon writes:

> Just as acceptance has its rewards, so nonacceptance has its penalties. We knew a couple once who had three children. The oldest was a girl, sweet-tempered but very slow. It was clear that there was a degree of mental retardation, but the parents could not bring themselves to accept it. They tried to pretend that the child had normal abilities. They put her in schools where she could not keep up. They begged for performance she could not give. They tried to rearrange the world to fit her limitations, meanwhile neglecting the emotional needs of their other children. They meant well; they thought they were doing the right thing. But their refusal to accept their child as she really was made life a burden for all of them.[2]

Acceptance is not apathy. Apathy overtakes us when we lose the will to change what can be changed. Acceptance is realizing that there are things that only God can change, and we leave it to His wisdom and will as to whether or not He will change them.

There is wonderful freedom in really believing God when He says, "Cast all of your care on me . . . I care for you." As long as you understand that your expectations are held carefully in the hand of one who cares for you with an everlasting love, then you can accept your limitations, the failings of your loved ones, and the disappointment of frustrated plans.

Remember, "Once you have accepted the blow, you're free"—free to go on to new endeavors that may turn out better than you ever dreamed possible. That's my prayer today for you.

WEEK 41 — THURSDAY
POST-MORTEM MERCIES

Consider these words by an unknown author:

> Do not keep the alabaster boxes of your love and tenderness sealed up, until your friends and family are dead. Fill their lives with sweetness. Speak approving, cheering words while their ears can hear them and while their hearts can be thrilled and made happier by them. The kind things you mean to say when they are gone, say them before they go. The flowers you mean to send— use to brighten and sweeten their homes before they leave them.

195

If my friends and family have alabaster boxes laid away, full of
fragrant perfumes of sympathy and affection, I would rather they
would bring them out in my weary and troubled hours and open
them, that I may be refreshed and cheered when I need them. Let
us learn to anoint our loved ones beforehand. Post-mortem
kindnesses do not cheer the burdened spirit. Flowers cast no
fragrance backward over the weary way.[3]

The time for kind words and deeds ceases at death. How sad that we
don't take advantage of every opportunity to show and tell our loved ones,
while they are living, just how much they are loved!

When the teen-aged son of one of my closest friends was tragically
killed, I held her close and whispered, "He always knew he was loved." Jamie
was the kind of kid who was easy to have around, who freely gave love and
openly received it. His mother and dad were comforted that night, knowing
that from the first moment they held their son in their arms, that boy had
known their love. They had no regrets for loving words left unsaid or kind
deeds undone.

Love that is expressed is a love that will more readily be received. I've
talked to scores of people who confess, "I just can't say 'I love you' to my
children, my husband, my wife. . . . I'm just not used to that kind of emotional
display." I want to shake them and say, "Oh, my friend, someday it could be
too late! Standing by a casket and saying, 'I love you,' to ears that have been
closed by death could be the greatest regret of your life!"

The inability to express love may be rooted in the deep soil of hurt and
misunderstanding in the past. If you failed to receive love as a child, it will be
difficult for you to express it now. Or your silence and lack of demonstration
may be a way of telling your mate or child, "You've hurt me. Therefore, you
don't deserve my love." Whatever the case, this kind of indifference blocks the
kind of loving expression Christians are expected to model.

The Scriptures tell us that "while we were still sinners, Christ died for us"
(Rom. 5:8). He did not withhold His love because we had hurt him. Every day
since that awful day at Calvary, God has said, "I love you," to millions of people
who could care less, but that has never kept Him from saying it. When time is
ended and the tragic consequences of disbelief become evident as some are
banished from the presence of God forever, He will still be saying, "I love
you . . ."

Neither you nor I will ever have God's full capacity for love, but we can
cultivate love for others through doing and saying those things that will bless
them. Let's take out our "alabaster boxes" and anoint our loved ones with
sympathy and affection, kindness and mercy while there is still time!

WEEK 41 — FRIDAY
COMMUNION WITH GOD

Communion implies closeness, communication, sharing, exchange,
intimacy, friendship. It's the kind of mystical union that binds two hearts
together so that before a word is spoken, there is understanding.

Jesus invites us to commune with Him, just the two of us. This poem by
P. M. Snider sets the scene:

196

Quietly I enter the closet
Quietly I close the door.
Outside are the futilities,
The doubts and useless struggles;
Forgotten are the little things
That too long have shackled my mind
And held me prisoner.

Now unhurried and free
I contemplate Jesus,
His mercy and His love.
Patiently I wait.
Lo, out of the shadows
Comes His presence.
Silently we visit,
From His wounded hand
I receive His balm
And His comfort.
I rest.
The door to the world is opened!
Eagerly I pass,
No longer futile,
Nor fearful,
Nor yet alone.
No longer I,
But, WE![4]

And from the Psalms: "I waited patiently for the Lord; he turned to me and heard my cry" (40.1).

When was the last time you "waited for the Lord" and heard from Him? Maybe you're thinking, "That's okay for you, but I hold down a full-time job, and when I get home, there is a house full of kids and work to do." I understand. So does He.

Even in the midst of busyness, however, we can learn how to find islands of quiet time. Try praying in the shower—not just the "give me, I need" prayers, but "Lord, I love You and I want to commit this day to You." Cut off the radio or tape player in the car and make your drive to work or to pick up the kids a time of communion. Combine your exercise time—an aerobic workout or a walk around the block—with praise and prayer.

Resist the temptation to make a big production of time spent with the Lord. Don't try to program the moment. Instead, just slip quietly into His presence whenever you have an opportunity. You will come away refreshed and ready once more to meet the challenges of your busy life.

WEEK 42 — MONDAY
OUT IN THE OPEN

These words from Roy Hession's *The Calvary Road* have stimulated my thinking:

> The only basis for real fellowship with God and man is to live
> out in the open with both. "But if we walk in the light, as he is in

the light, we have fellowship one with another." To walk in the light is the opposite of walking in darkness. Spurgeon defines it in one of his sermons as "the willingness to know and be known." As far as God is concerned, this means that we are willing to know the whole truth about ourselves, we are open to conviction. We will bend the neck to the first twinges of conscience. . . .

We must be as willing to know the truth about ourselves from our brother as to know it from God. We must be willing not only to know, but to be known by him for what we really are . . . we are not going to window dress and put on appearances; nor are we going to whitewash and excuse ourselves. We are going to be honest about ourselves with them.[1]

At a conference where I was meeting with several women, our conversation plodded along for a while, never leaving the shallows. No one wanted to be the first to say, "I don't have it all together." After a few minutes of pleasantries, I plunged into deeper water, mentioning the pain I see in the lives of Christian women today.

Suddenly it was as if a light had been turned on in that room. The women began to open up, to be real, and to let themselves be known for who they really were—people who needed the Savior's love and redemption, just like me. At that point, we began to have real fellowship.

How willing are you to face the fact that God knows everything about you before you think or do it? If you can acknowledge that truth, you won't feel the need to be too "proper" with God. He knows already that you are a weak human being who can only function effectively with His help.

Openness with God means that we will be quick to respond to the gentle nudging of the Spirit when He convicts us of something—to ask forgiveness, to restore a relationship, to feed the poor. Openness with others may involve taking the initiative in resolving a problem with a mate: "I know I've really been unreasonable lately." Or a friend, "I'd rather not argue. Why don't we talk about something else?"

The attitudes that cause us to hide our true selves from others come from the conviction that no one would accept us if they knew what we are really like. But we can't hide from God. In His omniscience, He knows all about us . . . and loves us anyway.

WEEK 42 — TUESDAY
THE STRESS FACTOR

I just read an interesting passage in Kevin Leman's book, *Why Women Get Stressed Out and What They Can Do About It,* that tells us a great deal about the state of women in today's complex society:

> Most people blame the stress they encounter on their marriage, their children, their financial situation, their job, or some other set of circumstances. When a boss gets on your case every morning, you can perceive it as a problem or you can realize the boss has arthritis and is never very human until after lunch. Unfortunately, in your case, the boss's crabby attitude really bothers you and you are just about ready to quit.

Why is it that Marge, whose desk is next to yours, just brushes off his tirades and even seems to curry his favor? The answer lies in perception. You perceive the boss one way; Marge perceives him another way. Your perception causes you great stress. Marge sails through without a qualm.[2]

How we look at a situation directly affects our stress level.

In the Scriptures, we see the same sort of thing occurring with Mary and Martha. When Jesus came for a visit to their home, Mary's perception was, "This is a rare opportunity to learn from Him. I'm going to take advantage of it." Martha, on the other hand, "was distracted with all her preparations," and finally complained in exasperation: "Lord, do you not care that my sister has left me to do all the serving alone? . . . Tell her to help me!" (Luke 10:40 NASB).

Martha perceived that she was being neglected and used. Since, in her view, preparing a hearty meal for their guest was an obligation, she resented Mary's leaving her to do all the work. Not only was Martha bustling around in the kitchen, but she was also ticked off at her sister!

Jesus' words both soothed and corrected: "Martha, Martha, you are worried and bothered about so many things; but only a few things are necessary, really only one, for Mary has chosen the good part, which shall not be taken away from her" (vv. 41–42 NASB).

What situation confronts you at work or at home that is causing you tension and stress? If you are "worried and bothered" about many things, and your blood pressure is rising, simply ask Jesus: "Lord, I need You to show me if my perceptions are correct . . . or if I'm making big deals where little deals will do." He will be faithful to help you choose "the good part, which shall not be taken away."

WEEK 42 — WEDNESDAY
WORDS WE LIKE TO HEAR

My dad always called me "Boose"—a shortened form of baby talk for "Beautiful Baby." I loved to hear it because it was wrapped in all the love and admiration a father can give his child.

You may not have had a nickname as a child, but there are undoubtedly other words packed with meaning for you. Words that elicit feelings of warmth or security or happiness.

A newspaper columnist recently invited seventy-five fourth- and fifth-graders to submit the words they most like to hear their mothers say. Here are the five big winners:

1. I love you.
2. Yes.
3. Time to eat.
4. You can go.
5. You can stay up late.

The following were some other favorites:

I'll help you.
Your friend can spend the night.
You can go out and play.

You can sleep in.
How was your day?
You were good tonight.
I'm glad I have you.
I've got a surprise for you.
Let's go for a walk.
You're the best kid in the world.
Do you want to visit Grandma?
I'm sorry.[3]

What a very special collection of words! We can be sure they will be remembered long after "Brush your teeth!" "Clean your room!" and "It's your turn to load the dishwasher!"

When I meditate on the Lord, the words I most love to hear are words of love and consolation that encourage me to be all I can be for Him:

Thou wilt keep him in perfect peace whose mind is stayed on thee: because he trusteth in thee (Isa. 26:3 KJV).

Being confident of this very thing, that he which hath begun a good work in you will perform it until the day of Jesus Christ" (Phil. 1:6 KJV).

And this is the confidence that we have in him, that, if we ask anything according to his will, he heareth us (1 John 5:14 KJV).

Listening to the kind words of the Lord today will affect our own speech and teach us how to bless others with our mouth.

WEEK 42 — THURSDAY
EVERYONE IS DYING

Consider these words from a thoughtful writer:

Our attitude to all men would be Christian if we regarded them as though they were dying, and determined our relation to them in the light of death, both of their death and of our own. A person who is dying calls forth a special kind of feeling. Our attitude to him is at once softened and lifted on to a higher plane. We then can feel compassion for people whom we did not love. But every man is dying, I too am dying.

If you knew your wife, your husband, your child, your mother, father, friend were dying, what difference would it make in your treatment of that person today? It would be difficult, even cruel, to stay angry with a dying person, for example. Yet we forget that, with each day that passes, each of us is nearer death.

I hope these words will make a difference in your life:

Around the corner I have a friend,
In this great city that has no end;
Yet days go by, and weeks rush on,
And before I know it a year is gone,
And I never see my old friend's face,

200

For life is a swift and terrible race.
He knows I like him just as well
As in the days when I rang his bell
And he rang mine. We were younger then,
And now we are busy, tired men;
Tired with playing a foolish game,
Tired with trying to make a name.
"Tomorrow," I say, "I will call on Jim,
Just to show that I'm thinking of him."
But tomorrow comes—and tomorrow goes,
And the distance between us grows and grows
Around the corner!—yet miles away . . .
"Here's a telegram, sir . . . ."
Jim died today.
And that's what we get and deserve in the end:
Around the corner, a vanished friend.[4]

                —Charles Hanson Towne

It's really not my intention to make you feel guilty about procrastination. I put things off, too—writing that note to a sick friend, making a phone call to an old family friend in Georgia, dropping in to pay a visit to a shut-in, staying in touch. We all plan to do those things . . . "one day." But "one day" seldom comes. Maybe it would come sooner if we remembered that *each of us is dying.*

Why not choose one person who needs to hear from you today and make a contact. Say the words you want to say but have been putting off. Pray for that person, asking God to bless in a special way.

WEEK 42 — FRIDAY
BE HAPPY!

In an interview with the survivors of Hurricane Hugo, I heard several people discussing their experience. Some of them had lost everything they owned, but most of them seemed happy just to be alive. In surviving, they had discovered something about their own resilience that they could never have known apart from that event.

Are you able to be happy just because you are alive and the sun is shining? Or, if it is storming outside, are you happy to have a roof over your head?

As believers, we are encouraged, no, *commanded* to have an attitude that reflects happiness. But God doesn't tell us to do something without telling us how to do it: "Be joyful always; pray continually; give thanks in all circumstances, for this is God's will for you in Christ Jesus" (1 Thess. 5:16–18).

To be happy, we must be thankful, recognizing that God's will is being worked out in all the circumstances of our lives. Because His will is always good, acceptable, and perfect, we can be genuinely thankful . . . and happy.

Have you ever seen a spoiled child who has just been deprived of some small thing? If not, just go to a grocery store and listen to the whiners and fit-throwers who go through the check-out line demanding a candy bar from a mother who will usually give in: "Oh, go ahead. Take it and hush."

201

We must sometimes seem like spoiled children, pouting and making demands of our heavenly Father because we don't have all we think we need. When we begin to take stock, we may discover how very blessed we are.

The story is told of a woman named Jan Struthers who died a few years ago. Since her death, attention has been given to a little poem she wrote, which was read at her funeral. Not only does the poem reveal a rare spirit, but it also inspires and enlightens others:

> One day my life will end; and lest
> Some whim should prompt you to
> review it,
> Let her who knew the subject best
> Tell you the shortest way to do it:
> Then say: "Here lies one doubly blest."
> Say: "She was happy." Say: "She knew it."

That is the sharp point—"She knew it." So many people who have so many of the materials of happiness do not know it. Instead of really knowing their happiness and being grateful for it, their eyes are roving over the fence to the seemingly greener grass far away. The spirit of thankfulness will help one to know this happiness and save life from one long drawn-out sigh.

I hope your life is not "one long drawn-out sigh." But if your conversation includes, "If only . . . " and "Oh me! I wish . . . ," you can begin to turn it around.

Make a list of everything that is okay, right, enjoyable, healthy, stable in your life. And with each entry, thank God because each of those items, however simple, is a gift from Him!

WEEK 43 — MONDAY
ARE YOU A JUDGE?

When you hear the words, "Leave it to God, who judges righteously," what comes to your mind?

When I hear those words I think of security—the security of knowing that nothing escapes God's attention and that He is a fair Judge who will right every wrong.

When I am wronged, however, I forget how secure I am in God's ability to judge. His judgment never seems swift enough or severe enough. Then I am tempted to take on the job of judge and jury. I want immediately to judge the perpetrator and execute a sentence.

The apostle Peter acted as judge and jury the night of Jesus' arrest. John 18:10 says, "Then Simon Peter, who had a sword, drew it and struck the high priest's servant, cutting off his right ear." Seems only natural. The soldiers and officials had come to take away Peter's friend, his teacher, his Lord. Peter knew Jesus was innocent, and he struck out only in defense.

But what was Jesus' response? "No more of this!" He said (Luke 22:51). And immediately He touched the man, healing his ear.

If you had been Peter that night, what would you have done? Knowing how quick I am to become the judge and the jury, I'm afraid Jesus would have had to do more than heal the man's ear—He would have had to raise the man from the dead! That's how quickly I jump to a conclusion about another's sin.

In the natural realm, the judgment seems right, but in the spiritual realm that judgment rarely holds water.

Is there someone in your life whom you have already judged? Is there someone whom you have already punished, rejected, and condemned for their sin? If so, you need to give up acting as judge and jury and trust that God will judge that sin righteously.

Thomas à Kempis wrote these words many years ago: "How rarely we weigh our neighbor in the same balance in which we weigh ourselves." In other words, if we want the person who has wounded us to be judged righteously by a holy God, then we should be willing to be judged by the same standard.

If we were subjecting our own behavior to the same scrutiny that we give the behavior of others, we would not be so quick to judge. As Matthew 7:1 says, "Do not judge, or you too will be judged."

The Bible says in Romans 2:1 that we are without excuse when we pass judgment, because when we pass judgment on others we are condemning ourselves. Tough words, but true. Let them be a reminder to you when you are tempted to act as judge and jury.

WEEK 43 — TUESDAY
THE ECCENTRIC

One of the most interesting characters in the Bible is a man who was, no doubt, the laughingstock of his entire neighborhood. In an area where there was no large body of water, and where there was never an appreciable amount of rainfall, he built a boat!

"By faith Noah, when warned about things not yet seen, in holy fear built an ark to save his family. By his faith he condemned the world and became heir of the righteousness that comes by faith" (Heb. 11:7).

The scene in Noah's day was not so different from ours. Couples were marrying and setting up housekeeping. Babies were being born, and folks were dying. And all kinds of evil abounded.

"The LORD saw how great man's wickedness on the earth had become, and that every inclination of the thoughts of his heart was only evil all the time" (Gen. 6:5). And He decided to purge the world of the creation He had spoken into being. All except Noah—a man who had lived a blameless life.

I believe there are at least three lessons we can learn from Noah:

1. *You can be faithful to God, no matter what everyone else around you is doing or thinking.* Sometimes we use the ungodly environment in which we live and work as an excuse for sinful behavior on our part. But that never occurred to Noah. No matter how wicked his neighbors, or how they may have ridiculed him, "Noah did everything just as God commanded him" (Gen. 6:22).
2. *You can take God at His word, even when others try to discredit or ignore it.* Just watching the news these days can be a frightening experience. Activists for different groups are becoming more and more militant against those of us they peg as "born-again believers."
   Yet Noah, too, was branded a radical or an eccentric. I'm sure there were sarcastic comments when he kept on with his hammering and sawing, using God's specifications for a boat big enough to

203

accommodate all his family and two of every species of creature on the face of the earth. His former buddies probably thought he was crazy, but their jeers and catcalls didn't deter Noah from his divine commission as the hull of the great ship rose against a bright blue sky, with not a cloud to signal the beginning of the "rainy season."

3. *You can press on to accomplish what God has called you to do, even in the face of little evidence to support your beliefs.* When people snub you or look down on you or make cutting remarks because of your beliefs, you can look to brother Noah. He was the perfect model of persistent faith in the face of little evidence.

God says: "Never again will I curse the ground because of man. . . . As long as the earth endures, seedtime and harvest, cold and heat, summer and winter, day and night will never cease" (Gen. 8:21–22).

Take heart. Focus on the Lord. Listen to what He says to you through His Word. Then pursue what He has given you to do. As He took care of Noah, He will take care of you.

WEEK 43 — WEDNESDAY
LOVING HURTS

If you have ever felt that it hurts too much to risk loving, consider these words by C. S. Lewis:

To love at all is to be vulnerable. Love anything and your heart will certainly be wrung and possibly broken. If you want to make sure of keeping it intact, you must give your heart to no one, not even to an animal. Wrap it carefully around with hobbies and little luxuries; avoid all entanglements; lock it up safe in the casket or coffin of your selfishness. But in that casket—safe, dark, motionless, airless—it will change. It will not be broken; it will become unbreakable, impenetrable, irredeemable. . . . The only place outside heaven where you can be perfectly safe from all the dangers of love is hell.[1]

Have you been so hurt by someone you love that you have withdrawn from all caring, loving relationships? If so, my heart goes out to you, but let me warn you that I have never known anyone who has shut himself off who has succeeded in gaining anything but misery and loneliness.

It is painful to see people you love make choices that will hurt them. It is painful to watch people you love suffer physical and emotional pain. It is painful to be rejected by people you love. Loving is painful. Yet, God created us to "love one another."

Read these words from the Scriptures: "If I speak in the tongues of men and of angels, but have not love, I am only a resounding gong or a clanging cymbal. If I have the gift of prophecy and can fathom all mysteries and all knowledge, and if I have a faith that can remove mountains, but have not love, I am nothing. If I give all I possess to the poor and I surrender my body to the flames, but have not love, I gain nothing" (1 Cor. 13:1–3).

It is actually possible to be closed off from intimate loving relationships with other people and yet do many good things that will substitute for the courage and stamina it takes to be a part of someone's life on an ongoing basis. If you practice religious devotion, good works, or even sacrifice yourself for the sake of others and yet fail to allow yourself to love and be loved in a vulnerable and risky way, then according to the Scriptures, you are "nothing." You have missed the whole point of loving—giving and sacrificing.

My friend, only you know how willing you are to be vulnerable to other people. Maybe you are shut off from your family, your mate, your child, your friend because loving has caused too much discomfort. Trust God and run the risk. You may be surprised to find that in dying to yourself, you are more fully alive than you have ever been!

WEEK 43 — THURSDAY
IT MIGHT HAVE BEEN

As I move into those middle-age years, the "might have beens" are piling up in my memory: "If I had decided to go to another college, what might have been the effect on my choice of marriage partners?" "If I had chosen a different major, what might I have been doing professionally right now?" "If I had spent more time with my children, might their lives be different?"

Pondering all the "might have beens" is such a futile pastime. When we look back, it should be for the purpose of learning how to improve, how to allow the Lord to take control, how to avoid pitfalls and dangers. It should never be to punish ourselves for opportunities we should have snapped up, or poor decisions that left us with losses, or even spiritual sins.

If we need to confess sin, God has made provision for cleansing. There is a very familiar Scripture passage that reassures me at a time like that: "If we confess our sins, he is faithful and just and will forgive us our sins and purify us from all unrighteousness" (1 John 1:9).

As much as I rely on that verse, I have discovered something new. The word for *cleanse* is in the aorist tense in the Greek. That means a cleansing that begins immediately and has a continuing effect. Our confession, agreement with God, sets in motion a powerful action that leaves us clean and free of the lingering, negative "might have beens" that can make life so miserable.

One poet writes whimsically of the "might have beens":

IT MIGHT HAVE BEEN WORSE

Sometimes I pause and sadly think
Of the things that might have been;
Of the golden chances I let slip by,
And which never returned again.

Think of the joys that might have been mine,
The prizes I almost won;
The goals I missed by a mere hair's breadth,
And the things I might have done.

It fills me with gloom when I ponder thus,
Till I look on the other side,
How I might have been completely engulfed
By misfortune's surging tide.

The unknown dangers lurking about,
Which I passed safely through;
The evils and sorrows that I've been spared
Pass plainly now in review.

So when I am downcast and feeling sad,
I repeat over and over again:
Things are far from being as bad
As they easily might have been.[2]

If you are a chronic reviewer of the "might have beens" of your life, why not purposely review the events and situations that might have been *worse*. As you view your past history from this perspective, you will be able to see many blessings that have been overlooked. Thank the Lord for His mercy and protection!

WEEK 43 — FRIDAY
IMPROVING YOUR SERVE

Chuck Swindoll has written a book on the subject of servanthood that is slated to become a classic. And one of the things that fixes it in one's memory is its catchy title—*Improving Your Serve!*

Most believers would agree that we need to improve in the area of Christian service. Yet there are times when I believe the Lord is encouraging us not to try so hard . . . just to rest in Him and allow Him to do the work: "Take my yoke upon you and learn from me, for I am gentle and humble in heart, and you will find rest for your souls. For my yoke is easy and my burden is light" (Matt. 11:29–30).

This truth was beautifully illustrated by that great old saint, Roy Hession, in an experience I heard him relate. As a young preacher, he had a very busy schedule that sometimes left him little time for preparation. On one occasion he was traveling from one location to another, aware that he would have only three hours to prepare his message after he got to his destination. What he did not count on was his car breaking down along the way.

Arriving at the hall where the meeting was to be held, he learned there was only thirty minutes before he was to speak. He hurried into a little restaurant next door for a bite of supper, and began to pray about his situation.

He began by praising God for His power and might. He thanked Him for all His provisions and was lapsing into another round of verbose gratitude when God stopped Him in mid-sentence: "Why don't you just tell me what you need." And Roy replied, "Well, Lord, I need a message for tonight."

At that moment the thought occurred to him to look in the back of his Bible. There he found the notes for a message he had prepared several months before! He scanned it, thanked the Lord for His infinite care, and went into the hall to preach a message that was so powerfully anointed that many young men and women surrendered to Christ.

When we understand the grace of God, we can relax in the knowledge that our service *to* Him is *through* Him. He calls us to faithfulness, to study and discipline, but He does not call us to generate the power nor to produce the results. That's His job.

Often I have gone about my service as if it all depended upon me. I have exhausted myself trying to make it work to the extent that I have missed the freedom and joy possible when one knows she is in God's place of service, with access to all the gifts He has given.

I have some sweet friends who practice their gift of hospitality whenever there is an opportunity. I have seen them relax in God's provision both when everything is proceeding perfectly and when the pipes have burst and three hundred guests are expected in two hours!

Our serve will improve if we learn to pray: *Now Lord, we thank You for being in control. You know what we need more than we do. We're just here to serve You, so we trust You to supply whatever we need, and we will rest in Your grace.*

WEEK 44 — MONDAY
EARTHQUAKE!

In the past two years, tragedy has struck our nation on both coasts, forever altering the lives of many people, almost before our eyes.

Twice in rapid succession, a powerful natural phenomenon has resulted in property damage and loss of life, though not in large numbers. I have been deeply moved by the events we have seen, raw and unretouched, as the victims of Hurricane Hugo and the California earthquake have been paraded into our homes through the all-seeing eye of the television camera.

To see seasoned newsmen breathing deep and talking fast as they have recorded the events has given some insight into the unbelievable devastation unleashed on thousands. As one newsman said the morning after the California quake, "Isn't it amazing that, at 5:03, the most important thought on people's minds was the World Series, but at 5:04 the whole perspective changed?"

Not many days after that cataclysmic event, however, life was pretty much back to normal. Some even spoke out about their faith in God. In a way the rebuilding and recovery is a tribute to the human spirit. But what will it take to bring an entire nation to its knees? What additional pressures must God exert for each of us to realize that we are not the masters of our own fate? What will it take to bring us into submission to a holy God who has the power to give life and to destroy it without any obligatory warning?

The theologian Paul Tillich has written:

> The idea of the divine wrath has become strange to our time. We have rejected a religion which seemed to make God a furious tyrant, an individual without passions and desires who committed arbitrary acts. This is not what the wrath of God means.
>
> It means the inescapable and unavoidable reaction against every distortion of the law of life, and above all against human pride and arrogance. That reaction, through which man is thrown back into his limits, is not a passionate act of punishment or vengeance on the part of God. It is the re-establishment of the balance between God and man, which is disturbed by man's elevation against God.[1]

When there is great distress in our land that comes from natural causes, it seems that corporately we refuse to recognize the hand of God, yet the

207

Scriptures warn: "Those who go down to the sea in ships, who do business on great waters; they have seen the works of the LORD and His wonders in the deep. He spoke and raised up a stormy wind, which lifted up the waves of the sea. They rose up to the heavens, they went down to the depths; their soul melted away in their misery" (Ps. 107:23–26 NASB).

When things are relatively quiet, we forget that our God is all-powerful and that all the forces of nature obey His command. But when we see the ocean begin to churn and the earth move, we can know that it is God who is in control.

Listen to the conclusion of this passage in Psalm 107: "They reeled and staggered like a drunken man and were at their wits' end. Then they cried to the Lord in their trouble, and He brought them out of their distresses. He caused the storm to be still" (vv. 27–29 NASB).

My friend, we may not ever see our nation turn to God as an entire people. It may be too late. But let it be said of you and me that we know where the power of the universe resides . . . in the hands of our all-powerful God.

WEEK 44 — TUESDAY
GOD'S INTERRUPTIONS

Interruptions are often irritating. And one of the *most* irritating are salespeople on the telephone!

I feel for them. I know they have a job to do. But their calls never come at a convenient time, and I consider their sales pitch an intrusion into my daily routine.

I know of one woman, however, who sees such calls as divine appointments. Using her own special style of witnessing, she has led five or six telephone salesmen to the Lord.

Jesus, too, was never troubled by interruptions. These words in *The Quest for Serenity,* by G. H. Morling, are disturbingly convicting: "Consider the self-oblivious gentleness of our Lord's responses to the demands of men— always seeing in the tiresome claims of others the overruling claim of God."[2]

In the hundred interruptions of our lives, is it possible that there really could be a divine purpose? Could God actually be saying something to us?

Let these words sink in: "A valuable study of the Gospels could be made noticing how many times Jesus gave some of his greatest teachings in circumstances where he had simply been interrupted. How different this is from us; we hate to be interrupted. To Jesus, the importance seemed to lie in the person whose path had crossed his own. Things don't just 'happen' in the providence of God. The interruption may well be our highest task at that very moment."[3]

Think about the potential interruptions that may change your plans today. It may be from one of your children who pulls a stunt to get your attention. It may be from a neighbor who drops in unannounced, but in deep need of your concern. It may be from someone you see at the mall, a total stranger, or from the person who works beside you. How will you respond? How will you handle the change in your plans?

I pray that you and I will have the spiritual sensitivity to view the interruptions of our lives as if God Himself were knocking on the door of our hearts!

WEEK 44 — WEDNESDAY
"CALL ON ME"

Do you know what it means to "call on the name of the Lord"?

For too many people, calling on the name of the Lord is a form of slang—"O Lord!" this or "O Lord!" that—uttered in a moment of intense anxiety or frustration. God never intended for His children to be so cavalier about His name. He intended for us to take Him and the process of calling on His name seriously.

The Hebrew word for *call* implies addressing a specific person with a specific request. Rarely was God's name used in a random outcry. In fact, for the Old Testament saint, calling on the name of the Lord was the reverent act of summoning aid from Jehovah God, Yahweh, the God whose name they would not dare speak aloud.

The first recorded mention of this kind of invocation is found in Genesis 4:26, after Seth's son, Enosh, is born: "At that time men began to call on the name of the Lord." Up until this time, people had made sacrifices in worship to Him, but had not asked Him for anything.

This event signaled a whole new concept in communication with the God of creation: "This poor man called, and the LORD heard him; he saved him out of all his troubles" (Ps. 34:6). "In your distress you called and I rescued you, I answered you out of a thundercloud" (81:7). "Seek the Lord while he may be found; call on him while he is near" (Isa. 55:6).

Calling for help is not foreign to us. In some circles we are encouraged to admit helplessness and to ask for assistance. Even the Yellow Pages of the telephone directory are set up for that purpose. But in the area of spiritual matters, the great dilemma comes in deciding whom to call.

As the "new age" philosophy escalates, people are being urged to call on "god as you know him . . . or her" or to appeal to "your higher power." The Bible makes it very clear that there is only one Source of legitimate help—the Lord God of heaven and earth. And there is a good reason why it is so specific.

Recently I heard an interview with a television personality whose lifestyle gives no indication that she knows or serves God. When a certain tabloid newspaper printed a story maligning her and her husband, she said the two of them just gave the whole situation over to their "higher power." As a result, the next day a man came to their house with enough dirt on that particular tabloid to sue them for "millions and millions of dollars."

This person who makes no claim of knowing the God of the Scriptures says she chooses to trust in "god as she knows him," and she got an answer when she called on him. But who answered?

My friend, we are living in dangerous times. The great God of the universe invites: "Call to me and I will answer you and tell you great and unsearchable things you do not know" (Jer. 33:3). What more do we need?

WEEK 44 — THURSDAY
FUTURE SHOCK

The future is a scary place. None of us has been there. We don't know anything about it or what we will find when we get there. But we seem to spend an inordinate amount of time thinking about it.

Are you single, keeping your life on hold until that mate (you just know is coming) shows up?

Are you in school, worrying about what you will do when you graduate?

Are you married and dissatisfied with your spouse, hoping that things will improve . . . someday?

Are you in debt, wondering how you are going to dig yourself out, in a shaky economy?

For many of us, the unknown is our greatest source of fear. But there is One who can put our fears to rest.

In his book, the *The Quest for Serenity,* G. H. Morling writes:

Paul speaks of a peace of God that "passes understanding," by which he means a peace that extends beyond the point of human "minding" or planning. Very properly we make provision for the future, financial and otherwise, but we cannot provide against everything and, in any case, our "minding" is necessarily confined to time. God's minding for us, however, foresees everything and reaches into eternity, so for those who live in the world of God, there are no uncertainties.[4]

If God is omniscient—all-knowing—and if He is omnipresent—present everywhere—then He has already experienced the future. He knows about it and He is present in it.

If you are apprehensive about the future, try making a list of your concerns. In Column A, list those things you can do something about. These might include saving some money, starting an exercise program, teaching your kids about the perils of drugs. In Column B, list the things over which you have no control, such as widowhood, children leaving home, or job loss. These belong to the part of the future that is not your problem.

Now symbolically present the concerns in Column B to God and thank Him for being in control. Since there is not a thing you can do to influence those potential circumstances, decide to leave them in His loving and capable hands.

In the words of G. H. Morling: "We can live very restfully when we have left the future quietly to the Father who knows all that will come to us and has already provided for it."

WEEK 44 — FRIDAY
TRY BENDING YOUR ATTITUDE

In the book, *A Touch of Wonder,* by Arthur Gordon, I read a story entitled, "If You Can't Change Facts, Try Bending Your Attitudes":

Without doubt, the bleakest period of my life so far was the winter of 1942–43. I was with the English Air Force in England. Our bomber bases, hacked out of the sodden English country-side, were seas of mud. On the ground, people were cold, miserable, homesick. In the air, people were getting shot. Replacements were few, morale was low.

But there was one sergeant—a crew chief—who was always cheerful, always good-humored, always smiling. I watched him one day, in a freezing rain, struggle to salvage a fortress that had skidded off the runway into an apparently bottomless mire. He was whistling like a lark.

"Sergeant," I said to him sourly, "how can you whistle in a mess like this?"

He gave me a mud-caked grin. "Lieutenant," he said. "When the facts won't budge, you have to bend your attitude to fit them, that's all!"[5]

The idea of bending my attitude to fit the events of the day is intriguing. I don't even know what is going to happen today, and neither do you. Oh, we may have a hint. Someone may be facing tests at the hospital, or a conference with a rebellious son's principal, or a job review with a difficult boss. You could be going to an audit with your Internal Revenue Service agent. I don't know what this day holds, but there is one thing sure: Our attitude—how we view the people and situations we will encounter—will determine how the day goes.

Paul gives some practical advice for bending our attitude: "May you always be joyful in your union with the Lord. I say it again: rejoice! Show a gentle attitude toward everyone. The Lord is coming soon. Don't worry about anything, but in all your prayers ask God for what you need, always asking him with a thankful heart. And God's peace, which is far beyond human understanding, will keep your hearts and minds safe in union with Christ Jesus" (Phil. 4:4–7 TEV).

I have had to apply this principle more than once lately. When the reviews began coming in on my second book, *Please Don't Say You Need Me: Biblical Answers for Codependency*, I was elated. It's exciting to read a glowing report. But when the reviewer is less than positive, it is hard to keep a great attitude. I can only conclude that he or she has missed the whole point or has read with some preconceived idea!

I can worry about what people think, and be irritated at the incompetence of some reviewers, or I can simply say, "Thanks, Lord. You're in control and You know the truth." That gives my attitude the kick in the seat it needs, and I can move on, if not cheerfully, at least without grumbling, complaining and rehearsing the unfairness of it all.

Bending our attitudes to fit the facts will promote quiet thoughts and restful spirits as we "trust in Christ Jesus."

WEEK 45 — MONDAY
DON'T BE AFRAID

I'm not a "fraidy cat." But there are a few things that evoke fear in me. Being in close places is one of them.

I have found that I'm not the only one who fears being confined. A friend of mine told me of her experience in a local sauna. After accompanying her husband to the athletic club one evening, they separated to go into adjoining rooms—she, to the woman's sauna; he, to the men's. When she had had enough heat, she pushed against the door of the small booth, but it wouldn't budge. Soon she was beating on the door frantically, yelling for her husband.

He, of course, couldn't come to her rescue, since the entrance led through the women's dressing room. Eventually, however, she noticed that the door pulled open easily, and she got out without further trouble. Though she was never in any danger, my friend's irrational fear blinded her to the truth.

When we are afraid, we need Someone who is greater and more powerful to come to our rescue. "Fear not, for I have redeemed you; I have summoned you by name; you are mine. . . . Do not be afraid, for I am with you" (Isa. 43:1, 5).

Consider these words by Amy Carmichael:

> I am more and more impressed as I read the Bible, by the reiterated "Fear not." There are so many promises, that it would not be strange if there were no "fear not"; the promises are enough to rest upon. We should not need to be told not to be afraid, and yet there it is over and over again, in one form or another, this strong, loving, encouraging "Fear not" of our God. "Fear not, nor be afraid"; neither be cowardly [it is good sometimes to face the truth that yielding to fear is cowardice]. It is the Lord your God that advances with thee in the midst of thee, neither will he by any means forsake thee, nor desert thee . . . And the Lord that goes with thee shall not forsake thee nor abandon thee."
>
> It seems to be God's plan to allow all sorts of things to happen that would naturally cause fear, but to forestall them by the assurance of His presence.[1]

How precious of the Lord that, knowing our human tendency to be afraid, He continually reassures us and calms our fears. Let's memorize some of those "Fear not" passages today, and simply rest in His many promises that He will never leave us nor forsake us.

WEEK 45 — TUESDAY
THE UNEQUAL MADE EQUAL

"It is only in love that the unequal can be made equal." These words, from a parable told by the theologian Kirkegaard, will encourage you:

Phillip Yancey paraphrases the story in his book, *Disappointment With God:*

> Suppose there was a king who loved a humble maiden. The king was like no other king. Every statesman trembled before his power. No one dared breathe a word against him, for he had the strength to crush all opponents. And yet, this mighty king was melted by love for a humble maiden.
>
> How would he declare his love for her? In an odd sort of way, his very kingliness tied his hands. If he brought her to the palace and crowned her head with jewels and clothed her body in royal robes, she would surely not resist—no one dared resist him. But would she love him?
>
> She would say she loved him, of course, but would she truly? Or would she live with him in fear, nursing a private grief for the life she had left behind? Would she be happy at his side? How could he know?
>
> If he rode to her forest cottage in his royal carriage, with an armed escort waving bright banners, that too would overwhelm her. He did not want a cringing subject. He wanted a lover, an

equal. He wanted her to forget that he was a king and she was a humble maiden and to let shared love cross over the gulf between them.

For it is only in love that the unequal can be made equal. The king, convinced he could not elevate the maiden without crushing her freedom, resolved to descend. He clothed himself as a beggar and approached her cottage incognito, with a work cloak fluttering loosely about him. It was no mere disguise, but a new identity he took on. He renounced the throne to win her hand.[2]

The picture is repeated in these words from Philippians 2: "Who, although he existed in the form of God, did not regard equality with God a thing to be grasped, but emptied Himself, taking the form of a bond-servant, and being made in the likeness of men. And being found in appearance as a man, He humbled Himself by becoming obedient to the point of death—even death on a cross" (vv. 6–8 NASB).

The whole thing boggles my mind! That God would "empty Himself," give up everything—His position, His possessions, His power . . . for us! And as if that were not enough, that He would "humble Himself," becoming a servant, then dying as a common criminal . . . for us! He who was equal with God lowered Himself to become equal with mankind.

In spite of all this, He has not forced His love on us. He has left us free to take it or leave it. But before you "leave it," consider what it cost Him to buy your salvation and what that says about His great love for you. Jesus Christ thought you were worth the effort!

If you have lost sight of just how much you are loved, draw hope and encouragement from these words. Remember that God went "incognito," taking on the identity of humanity to win your heart! How can you resist Him?

WEEK 45 — WEDNESDAY
WORKING TOGETHER FOR GOOD

Do a little heavy-duty thinking with me about a verse we Christians use to comfort one another at least once a week: "And we know that in all things God works for the good of those who love him, who have been called according to his purpose" (Rom. 8:28).

Paul could have stopped after the words, "All things work together for good," but he specified that the recipients of "good" would be "those who love him." The qualifying clause makes all the difference.

Barclay makes this comment:

> If a man loves God and trusts God and accepts God, if a man feels and knows and is convinced that God is the all-wise and all-loving Father, then he can humbly accept all that God sends to him. A man may go to a physician or a surgeon, and the physician or surgeon may prescribe a course of treatment which at the time is unpleasant or even painful; but the man trusts the wisdom of the man of skill and accepts the thing that is laid upon him.
>
> It is so with us if we love God. But if a man does not love and trust God, he may well resent what happens to him; he may well fight against the will of God; he may well find that the pains and

the sorrows and the trials of life move him to anger and rebellion. It is only to the man who loves and trusts that all things do work together for good, for to him they come from a Father who in perfect wisdom, love and power is working ever for the best.[3]

Let's go back to this verse that evokes either acceptance or rebellion. We can believe that God causes all things to work together for good, but our definition of the word *good* will determine whether or not we accept His sovereign intervention in our affairs.

Most of us assume that *good* implies "satisfying and pleasing, beautiful in appearance, making a good impression directly on those who come in contact with it." But the Greek word translated as *good* in Romans 8:28 means something quite different: "inwardly good, appealing to the moral sense. Good in result and worthy of admiration and respect."

The truth of this definition was demonstrated recently in a restaurant where I encountered a man whose face had been horribly disfigured, presumably by fire. My first thought was, *Oh God, how could he stand to go on living with his face burned away?* There was nothing good or satisfying or beautiful in his appearance. But, of course, as a casual bystander, I could not possibly have evaluated the inner good, the good that is worthy of admiration in that man's spirit.

I took another look. I noticed that he was carrying a small baby in his arms and was surrounded by other family members. To the casual observer, there was nothing good about the man's appearance. But to those who knew and loved him, there were limitless possibilities for living happily despite the scars.

If we learn how to define *good* as God defines it, we might be amazed at the beauty He is able to bring out of the deep hurts and injuries in our lives.

WEEK 45 — THURSDAY
GOING FOR THE GOLD

In Alabama, a new product offering high energy and other healthful benefits has been introduced to the elderly population. It's called "Jogging in a Jug." The manufacturers claim that all a person has to do is drink it, and he or she will instantly experience all the strength and power of jogging regularly!

Few of us, either senior or junior citizens, will ever compete in the Olympics, but all of us long for the feeling of well-being and the glow that accompanies successful participation, whether in a contest or in life. While I cannot attest to the claims of this health product, I do know that God's grace gives believers the power to run a winning race . . . without all the effort.

In 1 Corinthians 9:24, the apostle Paul writes, "Do you not know that in a race all the runners run, but only one gets the prize? Run in such a way as to get the prize. Everyone who competes in the games goes into strict training. They do it to get a crown that will not last; but we do it to get a crown that will last forever."

I have always been a strong competitor, but early in my Christian life, I had a tough time trying to run the race. I struggled and failed repeatedly with my bad attitudes and with my habit of speaking before I think. I knew I was called to a different lifestyle than I had lived before, and that, as a Christian, I now had a new Master and new goals for my life. But I never seemed to measure up. I was barely staying in the race, much less going for the prize!

One of the most encouraging dimensions of my new life was the idea of God's grace. He gives grace for the race, and once we realize that life-giving power is ours, we will not be content simply to sit on the sidelines and watch others run, but we'll go for the gold.

Having God's grace means we don't have to use our energy at all, nor do we have to be concerned with all the times we've stumbled and fallen previously. All we need to do is accept His grace—the favor we don't deserve—and receive the strength to turn in a winning performance.

This effortless competition seems too good to be true. Yet 1 John 3:1 tells us: "How great is the love the Father has lavished on us, that we should be called children of God! And that is what we are!" The Greek word for *how great a love* is really "what a foreign kind of love." What a peculiar kind of love that doesn't require love in return, that doesn't expect a particular behavior, that sets no conditions except that it be received. That is grace!

As if this were not enough, our heavenly Father has also set aside a prize for those who persevere in the race. While the world may confer gold medals and blue ribbons, our reward is "a crown that will last."

Even if you have always been an armchair athlete in the race of life, decide to accept God's grace. He will enable you to stay with the contest until you are ready to receive His reward for a race well run.

WEEK 45 — FRIDAY
THE STRONG-WILLED CHRISTIAN

Are you a go-getter who gets things done while others are still standing around scratching their collective heads? Or do you stubbornly insist on your own way in spite of evidence to the contrary?

A strong will can be either an asset or a liability as Clara Barton, founder of the American Red Cross, learned:

> She could not sit idly by when she saw Civil War soldiers suffering for want of supplies for medical care and in some cases needlessly sacrificing their lives when they could have gone on to contribute further to the war effort. She began collecting supplies and opened a warehouse for distribution. So successful was she that the surgeon-general permitted her free travel to the front lines to carry out her service.
>
> Following the war she traveled abroad and learned about the International Red Cross and was determined to have it started in America. She wrote and lectured on the topic at a time when many people were far more interested in getting their lives back together and earning money. But her stubborn persistence paid off. Despite bouts of sickness, she continued campaigning in this one-woman struggle until at last, in 1882, she won. The American Red Cross came into being, with Clara Barton as its president.
>
> But the stubborn persistence that was an asset in founding the organization was a liability in keeping it going. Miss Barton, still determined to be boss, insisted on managing everything in the organization. Problems developed and those under her com-

plained about her management. At the age of eighty-three, after an investigation by a special commission, she was forced to resign, and she departed, still fully convinced that she was in the right and everyone else was wrong.[4]

If Clara Barton had known and applied this Scripture verse—"Submit to one another out of reverence for Christ" (Eph. 5:21)—she might have avoided the sad conclusion to her story. But a strong will coupled with a sense of mission sometimes leads to conflict with others who desire to come alongside and help perpetuate the vision.

To submit to the Father is to be willing to be in submission to those around you. If you have been given a responsibility, God has also placed strategic people in your life to bring balance and harmony.

There is a fine line between being responsible and being stubborn. If you find that the people around you are questioning your decisions, perhaps it would be wise to remember that there is wisdom in many counselors and there is blessing in a submissive heart.

WEEK 46 — MONDAY
WOUNDED LOVER

While reading Philip Yancey's book, *Disappointment with God,* I came across a very interesting image of God. Yancey brings the metaphor to life as he puts words in God's mouth:

I'll tell you how I feel! I feel like a jilted lover. I found my lover thin and wasted, abused, but I brought her home and made her beauty shine. She is my precious one, the most beautiful woman in the world to me, and I lavish on her gifts and love. And yet she forsakes me. She pants after my best friends, my enemies— anyone. She stands by a highway and under every spreading tree and, worse than a prostitute, she *pays* people to have sex with her. I feel betrayed, abandoned, cuckolded.[1]

God knows the pain and frustrated anger of a broken heart. The tragedy is that, we, like faithless Israel, are responsible for it.

One of my very favorite books of the Bible is the book of Hosea. The cycle of love, broken vows, forgiveness, and reconciliation is the story of God's love affair with the human race. We can see it played out in the lives of Hosea and his wife, Gomer, who betrays her husband time after time, falling for first one man and then another. Each time, against all odds, God instructs Hosea to take her back. Finally, when Gomer's youth and beauty are gone and she has become a public spectacle, Hosea buys her back, out of the depths of depravity to which she has fallen.

"What can I do with you, Ephraim? What can I do with you, Judah? Your love is like the morning mist, like the early dew that disappears. . . . Like Adam, they have broken the covenant—they were unfaithful to me" (Hos. 6: 4, 7).

God's own wounded heart speaks through this story. What is He going to do with people who insist on running after other lovers? Our faithlessness, too, may be demonstrated, not in physical adultery, but in lusting for power and position, manipulation and control, or worldly possessions. Anything we yearn for as a substitute for God may be as seductive to us as Gomer was to her lovers.

But God is faithful. He says, " 'Therefore I am now going to allure her; I will lead her into the desert and speak tenderly to her. There I will give her back her vineyards, and will make the Valley of Achor a door of hope. There she will sing as in the days of her youth. . . . In that day,' declares the LORD, 'you will call me "my husband" . . . and I will betroth you to me forever' " (2:14–16, 19).

If you are a believer, consider renewing your vows to God today. Let Him know that, with His help, no person, goal, or thing will ever seduce you from your devotion to Him. If you are not a believer, read the book of Hosea and see just how much God loves you!

WEEK 46 — TUESDAY
THY KINGDOM COME

"Our Father, who art in Heaven, hallowed be thy name. Thy Kingdom come, thy will be done on earth as it is in Heaven."

Lately I have been doing a lot of thinking about God's kingdom because it seems to me that the differences between the citizens of His kingdom and the kingdoms of this world are growing increasingly pronounced.

When we pray, "Thy kingdom come, thy will be done," we are asking God to bring about His reign as sovereign Lord over this universe and to do it His way.

Carroll Simcox writes:

Wherever Christ's will is done, God's will is done, and the kingdom appears then and there. Such appearances of the kingdom in this present world actually occur, but they are only sporadic. They are the exception, not the rule. St. Paul's way of putting it, "He must reign till he hath put all enemies under his feet," exactly describes things as they now are in Christ's kingdom on earth. A soldier lays down his life that his countrymen might live: there is the kingdom. A woman slanders her neighbor at a bridge party: there the kingdom is defied and set at naught. A churchman forgoes luxuries for a month so that he will have more money to give for famine relief: there is the kingdom. An auto mechanic charges a customer for work he did not do: there the kingdom is defied and rejected. All human works and ways, thoughts, words and deeds, are either manifestations—acceptances—of the kingdom and rule of Christ, or denials and defiances of it; and Christ must reign till he has put all enemies—rebel wills—under his feet.[2]

What's going on in your world? Is it really your sincere desire to see evidence of the kingdom of God? If so, it may be costly. Worse still, the only observers may be those in the invisible kingdom, and you may never receive credit for your sacrifice.

Will you snap back at an irritable co-worker, or use a soft answer? Will you be kind to a critical mate? Will you keep your mouth shut about another's wrong when there would be no eternal value in bringing it up? Will you take the time to listen to your child although you have a thousand things that have to be done before bedtime?

If you are willing to think first about the kingdom, the place where God's will is done, then you have an opportunity to be part of a powerful force here on the earth—the power of God triumphing over our natural tendencies. Those natural inclinations that fit easily in the kingdom of this world will never make it in God's kingdom.

Remember these words today and ask God to give you a real consciousness of His kingdom here on earth: "The kingdom of God is not a matter of eating and drinking, but of righteousness, peace and joy in the Holy Spirit" (Rom. 14:17).

WEEK 46 — WEDNESDAY
COUNTING THE DAYS

This is the year I hit the midway mark of life. In a few weeks, I will be halfway to ninety, and as I look in the mirror, I think, *Oh, my . . . I never thought I would be a middle-aged woman. But that's exactly what I am!*

Life is so brief. Sometimes I am really saddened when thinking about the things I haven't done and the people I haven't loved as I should and the opportunities I could have seized and didn't.

Psalm 90:12 gives us a word of wisdom: "Teach us to number our days aright, that we may gain a heart of wisdom." Or, as it is translated in the Living Bible, "Teach us to number our days and recognize how few they are; help us to spend them as we should."

I like that reminder. "Help us to spend them as we should."

Since there is no use in crying over spilt milk, we can decide to begin today to seize the moments as they come. One of the areas in which time often robs us of great opportunities is in relationships. Things happen. Quarrels erupt. Difficulties and misunderstandings undermine feelings. And the years tick by while nothing is done to right old wrongs.

Phillips Brooks says it this way:

You who are letting miserable misunderstandings run on from year to year, meaning to clear them up some day; you who are keeping wretched quarrels alive because you cannot quite make up your minds that now is the day to sacrifice your pride and kill them; you who are letting your neighbor starve—until you hear he is dying of starvation; or letting your friend's heart ache for a word of appreciation or sympathy, which you mean to give him someday; if you could only know and see and feel all of a sudden that time is short, how it would break the spell! How you would go instantly and do the thing which you might never have another chance to do![3]

My friend, why not take a look in the mirror today? Instead of looking for new wrinkles or a gray hair or two, ask the Lord to show you who you are and where you have fallen short. Ask Him to point out where you need to mend fences or forgive.

There is no hoarding time. We can't stash it away like money for the proverbial rainy day. We can't hold it in reserve. When it is gone, it is gone . . . and there are no savings accounts or insurance policies to provide more.

We have this moment and this moment alone. What will you do with it? Spend it well.

WEEK 46 — THURSDAY
JOSEPH—MAN OF MANY MOODS

When I think of Joseph, images from childhood Bible stories come quickly to mind—his coat of many colors, his dreams, and the betrayal by his wicked stepbrothers.

But a deeper study of Joseph's life reveals a much more interesting and complex character. Despite his father's favoritism, Joseph grew up to be a man of great integrity, wisdom, and discernment, as well as sensitivity and deep emotion. I think it is his emotional intensity that attracts me most to Joseph and helps me see him as a human being with whom I can relate.

As the child of his father's most beloved wife, Joseph was the apple of his eye. How he escaped being completely insufferable, I can't imagine, though we know that his brothers perceived him as a spoiled brat whose interpretation of dreams always cast himself in a favorable light.

To get rid of this interloper to their father's affections, the brothers decided to kill him in the desert. But the eldest brother, moved by his cries for help, sold him into slavery instead, ripping away his splendid coat in the process.

Years later, when Joseph's brothers stood before him in Egypt, they failed to recognize him, and Joseph "turned away from them and began to weep" (Gen. 42:24).

When his younger brother, Benjamin, was brought to him, Joseph was deeply moved. He hurried out of the room, looking for a place to weep. He went into his private room and wept there. After he had washed his face, he came out, and in a controlled voice, he ordered the servants to wait on his family (43:30–31).

In a third encounter with his brothers, Joseph "wept so loudly that the Egyptians heard him" (45:2).

Joseph's journey from the pit to the palace is paved with tears—not for himself, but for lost relationships. While he is listed among the heroes of the faith cataloged in Hebrews 11, we may forget how he got there. Strong faith is built by adverse circumstances, and pain produces tears.

There was another who wept for others. Jesus' tears were shed for the sins of the world. Like Joseph to his brothers who had sinned against him, Jesus could say to His executioners: "You intended to harm me, but God intended it for good to accomplish what is now being done, the saving of many lives" (50:20).

WEEK 46 — FRIDAY
A BLESSED DEFEAT

When you think of brokenness, do you have the mental picture of a broken vessel or of someone who has been beaten into subjection? Brokenness is much more. Brokenness is the "willing submission of one to the will and wisdom of another who has the right to own, to control, to master."

219

Consider the wild horse, running free. He is beautiful to see, but useful for nothing. He does no work nor does he provide pleasure for anyone but himself.

But for the horse who has been broken to the bit by his owner, there is a wonderful sense of controlled and usable strength. His value soars because he is now a source of satisfaction and joy.

C. S. Lewis writes of the ultimate brokenness: "Every story of conversion is the story of a blessed defeat." Brokenness begins at the point of conversion, when one's will is surrendered to the will of Christ.

When David prayed his prayer for pardon, he spoke for all of us who have ever sinned: "The sacrifices of God are a broken spirit; a broken and contrite heart, O God, you will not despise" (Ps. 51:17).

That initial surrender is only the beginning. There are ongoing breakings that have to take place because we continue to live in these bodies of flesh that struggle to rise up and have the preeminence, even when we have given the reins of our lives to our Lord and Master.

As Roy Hession, author of *The Calvary Road,* a classic work on brokenness, writes: "Every humiliation, every one who tries and vexes us, is God's way of breaking us, so that there is a yet deeper channel in us for the Life of Christ."[4]

It is only as that part of us that is capable and strong and defensive comes down that the life of the Lord Jesus can be seen. It is a choice we are each called on to make in so many small ways.

If you really want the Life of Christ to be seen in you today, there is a display window that no one can miss—the place where your relationships are lived out. Have I overlooked my husband's thoughtless action toward me? Have I chosen to let my friend's tacky remark go unanswered? Have I let a slight plass without comment?

Our daily lives showcase our yieldedness to the Master who owns and controls us.

WEEK 47 — MONDAY
DEALING WITH HUMILIATION

If you have ever been humiliated—painfully embarrassed to the point of feeling loss of self-respect—you can probably name the date, the time, the place, and every minute detail!

Nancy Friday, in her book, *My Mother, My Self,* gives valuable insight on this common emotion:

> In time we forget feelings of passion, the faces of people we've loved. We laugh at old angers and rages, time heals the memory of even physical pain. But old humiliations stay with us for life. They wake us out of the deepest sleep and flush our face with shame and anger even when we are alone.
>
> "Patients with problems of humiliation," says Dr. Robertiello, "are the most difficult to treat." Humiliation is so powerful it can make us wish for our own annihilation: our very ego shrinks and wills itself for the moment no longer to exist. How can we best respond to humiliation? As difficult as it is, it is essential to remember that we are not alone in experiencing this emotion and

220

that, while our humiliation is consuming us . . . others may be entirely oblivious to it.[1]

If you have been humiliated at the hands of another, or even by something you yourself have done, one essential step is necessary. That is to forgive, to give up your right to punish, to give up the power you might have to humiliate in return. When you are willing to lay down that right, the healing process can begin.

Just this past year I went through a humiliating experience. I doubt that many people knew my feelings, but in my heart, I felt as if the whole world were watching. This miserable state continued until I decided to give up my right to punish the individual who had humiliated me.

I asked the Lord to show me how He felt about my experience. It was the neatest thing when He reminded me that He had been humiliated, too: "They stripped [me] and put a scarlet robe on [me], and then twisted together a crown of thorns and set it on [my] head. They put a staff in [my] right hand and knelt in front of [me] and mocked [me]: 'Hail, King of the Jews!' they said. They spit on [me], and . . . struck [me] on the head again and again" (Matt. 27:28-29).

His words of encouragement were to "leave it to God who judges righteously." My humiliation would be safe in the hands of the One who balances the scales. So I laid down all the weapons I could have used to get even.

So when the feelings of embarrassment, of having been made to look the fool come back to haunt me, I mentally take myself back through the process and remind myself that I have given up my right to retaliate, that it has been given over to God who judges righteously.

My friend, if you are dealing with humiliation, I pray you will find the path to healing so that you can be free of that strangling emotion.

WEEK 47 — TUESDAY
PUFFED UP WITH PRIDE

When was the last time you acknowledged that every material blessing you have is from God? When did you last thank Him for your job? When did you last give Him credit for the work that is being done in your church? Have you recently examined yourself to determine whether or not there is any hidden pride and that you must humble yourself before God takes things into His own hands?

The matter of pride is an issue with which believers must grapple all the time. It is such a subtle thing. In fact, the root for the biblical word for pride means, "wrapped in smoke . . . having to do with being puffed up with nothing!"

Pride shows itself in the inconsequential things it takes to make us feel important—the right car, the right clothes, the right friends. If these are important to you, then you are in danger of being prideful about *nothing*. There is a little smoke in your Christian walk, but no real substance, though the puff may allow you to maintain an exalted view of yourself.

Nebuchadnezzar was the greatest ruler who ever lived, but his arrogance in defying God led to his being reduced to the state of an animal. "Seven times will pass by for you," said Daniel, the prophet, "until you acknowledge that the

Most High is sovereign over the kingdoms of men and gives them to anyone he wishes" (Dan. 4:25).

As God had ordained, this mighty king was driven away to live with the wild animals. He ate grass like cattle, his hair grew like the feathers of an eagle, and his nails like the claws of a bird. This condition persisted for seven years, as Daniel had prophesied, until at last Nebuchadnezzar said: "I . . . raised my eyes toward heaven, and my sanity was restored. Then I praised the Most High; I honored and glorified him who lives forever" (v. 34).

Fortunately, the ending to Nebuchadnezzar's story is a happy one. He learned a painful lesson. But pride can ruin everything.

Peter warns: "Clothe yourselves with humility toward one another, because God opposes the proud but gives grace to the humble. Humble yourselves, therefore, under God's mighty hand, that he may lift you up in due time" (1 Peter 5:5–6).

When the Scriptures say that God is opposed to the proud, it means He pulls out all the armaments of heaven to bring low the person who disregards His laws or ignores His sovereignty. Nebuchadnezzar felt God's mighty hand of chastening and finally responded correctly, but not before a humiliating experience.

Check yourself today. Choose to humble yourself . . . or you will one day find yourself humbled by Him!

WEEK 47 — WEDNESDAY
TIME ALONE

Not long ago I was confined to bed due to an illness. At first I relished the delicious freedom from my demanding schedule. I rested, read, prayed. Then I flipped the TV from channel to channel. About two days of that enforced solitude and I was stir-crazy, bordering on depression.

I talk with many people who claim that their greatest pain is loneliness and, consequently, they try to avoid being alone at all costs. I have even heard "aloneness" used as an excuse for pursuing illicit sexual relationships, for murmuring and complaining against God, and even for contemplating suicide.

Being alone can be frightening, but I am convinced that the constructive use of these times can be one of the best helps you will find for combatting loneliness.

Jesus Christ used aloneness to advantage. The Scriptures say repeatedly that He "often withdrew to lonely places and prayed" (Luke 5:16). He deliberately made time to be alone, when in reality He could have been surrounded by people constantly.

If you often find yourself alone against your will, you may be caught by surprise at the feeling of panic and emptiness. The busier people are, the harder it is to adjust to aloneness. But if you plan your alone times, you can view the time as a gift rather than a curse.

Try these practical suggestions for spending time alone:

1. *Write out your prayers.* Take the time to pour out your heart to God on paper. You'll be amazed at what that will do for you when you come back to it the next day or the next month. This record of your conversation with God may motivate you to communicate more often with Him. And it will be exciting to see how He responds.

2. *Read.* There are some powerful books now available that can change your life. Go to a Christian bookstore or library and get a book you have wanted to read. This is a good time to begin.
3. *Catch up on your correspondence.* Ask God to give you the pen of an encourager as you reach out to people you have been meaning to write.
4. *Complete that project you've put aside for a rainy day.* As you work, talk with God as if He were standing by your elbow. Invite Him to speak to you in the still, small voice that can only be heard when you are quiet . . . and alone.

When you are back in circulation, you will feel refreshed and better able to meet the challenges of your busy life.

WEEK 47 — THURSDAY
NOWHERE TO GO BUT UP

The story is told of a woman who enrolled in a basic acting class during her first term at UCLA:

> For her first assignment, she performed a monologue from "The Madwoman of Chaillot," playing the lead part, the maid. Although she "memorized and crammed like crazy," she was nervous, especially after she had seen her classmates perform so well.
> "It was my turn. I was the only one left. I didn't feel so okay anymore. The stage in the tiny classroom was about six inches high and I tripped stepping up on it. I turned around and introduced my presentation . . . I got it out, and I was word-perfect. My homework had paid off in that respect, and I had added a personal touch to the character of the little maid by making small circles in the air with a clenched fist, so it would look as if she were dusting something. I returned to my seat, with my heart in my ears, thankful to God it was all over. I don't recall any clapping."
> "But it wasn't all over. Now came the critiques . . . she skinned me alive. She wound up giving me a D minus. She explained to the class, 'I'm giving [this student] a D minus, because she at least had the piece memorized. However, it was an F performance.' She dismissed us with 'Now . . . choose new partners for your next scenes.' Everyone left but me. I felt as empty as the classroom. I could quit or stay. It was my choice. I decided to stay. I had nowhere to go but up."[2]

The student was Carol Burnett, who went on to become one of television's most beloved actresses and comedians. She used that embarrassing failure as a launching pad for future success.

Some of our biblical forebears knew how it felt to fail.

David, of course, failed miserably in his affair with Bathsheba. Maybe even worse than his adultery and murder of Uriah was his lack of conscience about his sin . . . until the prophet Nathan confronted him: "Thou art the

223

man." But David's contrition was genuine, and he went on to lead the nation of Israel to great heights.

Peter was another who dropped the ball at a crucial moment. Fearing for his life after Jesus' arrest, he flatly denied ever having known Him when questioned in the courtyard. It was Jesus' gentle rebuke that galvanized him into repentance and subsequent action as one of the most loyal of the Master's followers.

Giving up after failure is an option that seems to lurk in the shadows. But David and Peter didn't quit after their failures.

> Troubles without number surround me;
>   my sins have overtaken me, and I cannot see.
> They are more than the hairs of my head,
>   and my heart fails within me. . . .
>
> I waited patiently for the Lord;
>   he turned to me and heard my cry.
> He lifted me out of the slimy pit,
>   out of the mud and mire;
>
> He set my feet on a rock
>   and gave me a firm place to stand.
> He put a new song in my mouth,
>   a hymn of praise to our God.
>
> (Ps. 40:12, 1–3)

Jesus never gives up on us. Though we may and do fail, His love is unfailing and His mercies extend to all generations.

When there is nowhere to go but up, try prayer. Ask the Lord to convict you of any hindering sin, then confess and find the release of His forgiveness. Such grace is a motivating force to propel you on to achieve all the Lord has ordained for you.

WEEK 47 — FRIDAY
THE PRODIGAL

Letting go of someone we cherish is frightening and painful. When we are parted from loved ones by death, we somehow eventually learn how to cope. But when the parting is a deliberate attempt on the part of a child to put distance between himself and a parent, healing comes more slowly, particularly if his independence means a break with the traditions and beliefs you have tried to instill in him.

Barbara Johnson knows all about prodigals. In her book, *Fresh Elastic for Stretched-Out Moms,* she writes:

> The problem is that many parents try to play Holy Spirit to their kids. We try to bring conviction on them, but instead we bring condemnation. It is the job of the Holy Spirit to convict. That is why kids become resentful when parents try to force God on them. We have to give them to God, and then take our hands off.
>
> It is like wrapping a package up and putting on a label . . . but letting God put the address on the label, or on that life. Can you

love your child and pray for him and let God do with his life what He wants to do? Minus your instructions? Can you be content to train up your child and let him go? Your child is God's property, and God always goes after the prodigal.[3]

Barbara speaks from experience. It was her son who chose to leave home and embrace a gay lifestyle for eleven years. During that time, she lived out this poem:

> *She waited for the call*
> *that never came;*
> *searched every mail*
> *for a letter,*
> *or a note,*
> *or card,*
> *that bore his name;*
> *and on her knees*
> *at night,*
> *and on her feet*
> *all day,*
> *she stormed heaven's gate*
> *in his behalf;*
> *She pled for him*
> *in heaven's high court.*
> *"Be still and wait,"*
> *the word He gave*
> *and so she knew*
> *He would*
> *do in, and for,*
> *and with him,*
> *that which she never could.*
> *Double ignored,*
> *she went about her chores*
> *with joy;*
> *knowing, though spurned,*
> *His word was true.*
> *The prodigal had not returned*
> *but God was God,*
> *And there was work to do.[4]*

> —Ruth Bell Graham

If you are asking where you went wrong, this is the time to find sweet comfort in the Word of God: "So take a new grip with your tired hands, stand firm on your shaky legs, and mark out a straight, smooth path for your feet so that those who follow you, though weak and lame, will not fall and hurt themselves, but become strong" (Heb. 12:12 LB).

God has promised that the prodigals will return. Take comfort in knowing that things are not always what they seem.

WEEK 48 — MONDAY
WHY DOES IT HAVE TO HURT?

Even though believers understand, at least theoretically, that God can cause our pain to work for good, a question from childhood often surfaces: "Why does it have to hurt?"

225

These words, written by a woman who obviously knows what it means to experience pain, express the searching and finding of her own heart:

PAIN

Why must I be hurt?
Suffering and despair,
Cowardice and cruelty,
Envy and injustice,
All of these hurt.
Grief and terror,
Loneliness and betrayal
And the agony of loss or death—
All these things hurt.
Why? Why must life hurt?
Why must those who love generously,
Live honorably, feel deeply
All that is good—and beautiful
Be so hurt,
While selfish creatures
Go unscathed?
That is why—
Because they can feel.
Hurt is the price to pay for feeling.
Pain is not an accident,
Nor punishment, nor mockery
By some savage god.
Pain is part of growth.
The more we grow
The more we feel
The more we feel—the more we suffer;
For if we are able to feel beauty,
We must also feel the lack of it—
Those who glimpse heaven
Are bound to sight hell.
To have felt deeply is worth
Anything it cost.
To have felt Love and Honor,
Courage and Ecstasy
Is worth—any price.
And so—since hurt is the price
Of larger living, I will not
Hate pain, nor try to escape it.
Instead I will try to meet it
Bravely, bear it proudly:
Not as a cross, or a misfortune, but an
Opportunity, a privilege, a challenge—to the God
     that gropes within me.[1]

—Elsie Robinson

The "God who gropes within" also calls you and me to discover the riches of His glory: "Dear friends, do not be surprised at the painful trial you are suffering, as though something strange were happening to you. But rejoice

226

that you participate in the sufferings of Christ, so that you may be overjoyed when his glory is revealed" (1 Peter 4:12-13).

Why does it have to hurt? Because if you never experience pain, then you will never experience joy. It's as simple as that.

WEEK 48 — TUESDAY
GIVING AN EXCUSE

No matter how wrong someone may be, if you fail to respond in the right way, you give him an excuse for his sin.

Several years ago I watched a taped speech by a young woman whose father was a drug addict. Although she was very young, she was also very wise. She said, "I have learned not to react to his bad behavior, because it only gives him an excuse for his addiction. If we come at him with outbursts of anger, he says, 'If you weren't mad at me, I wouldn't have to take drugs.' "

Under the circumstances, this young woman could easily have become defensive or fought back. She could have been tempted to fight fire with fire. After all, when someone is insensitive and unwilling to change, we naturally want to punish them.

Roy Hession, in his book *The Calvary Road*, talks about taking the splinter out of someone's eye while we still have a beam in our own eye.

> Without doubt, there is a wrong in the other person, but our reaction to that is wrong, too. The mote in him has provoked in us resentment, or coldness, or criticism, or bitterness, or evil speaking, or ill will—all of them variants of the basic ill, unlove.
>
> And that, says the Lord Jesus, is far, far worse than the tiny wrong (sometimes quite unconscious) that provoked it. A mote means in the Greek a little splinter, whereas a beam means a rafter. And the Lord Jesus means by this comparison to tell us that our unloving reaction to the other's wrong is what a great rafter is to a little splinter.[2]

Every time we point one of our fingers at another and say, "It's your fault," three fingers are pointing back at us. God have mercy on us when in our hypocrisy we have pointed out another person's fault, all the while hiding a far worse sin in our own hearts.

What exactly is a "beam in our eye"? It is not necessarily a violent reaction on our part. The beginnings of resentment, the first flickers of an unkind thought, or the merest suggestion of unloving criticism can all be beams.

Beams—our own sins—distort our vision. They prevent us from seeing our brothers and sisters as beloved children of God. With hardened eyes we look at them, and unsoftened and unchanged by love, they return our steely gaze.

If you really want to see another person change, then you yourself have to be right with God. If you try to change him or her by force, criticism, harshness, coldness, sarcasm, or rejection, then God cannot help you, no matter how wrong the other person has been.

Once we are aware of our own sin—the beam in our own eye—then we can remove it and see better how to remove the mote out of our neighbor's eye.

WEEK 48 — WEDNESDAY
FORGIVENESS

Sometimes forgiveness is a tedious chore. It requires constant choice to give it no matter what.

I wonder if you are like I am. Some days, I feel very benevolent and forgiving. Without question, I choose to forgive whoever has offended me. On other days, forgiveness is a tedious process that I would rather not go through. When I have forgiven and forgiven and forgiven, it makes me tired to keep on forgiving.

I think my friend the apostle Peter must have felt the same way when he confidently asked Jesus, "Lord, how many times shall I forgive my brother when he sins against me? Up to seven times?" (Matt. 18:21). Do you know what Jesus answered? "I tell you, not seven times, but seventy-seven times" (Matt. 18:22).

It's easy to apply this principle when a person asks for forgiveness, but what about the person who refuses to admit he has done anything wrong and defies your forgiveness?

Corrie ten Boom and her family had hidden Jews from the Nazis during World War II. But when two of her fellow citizens tipped off the German police, she and her whole family were arrested and sent to concentration camps, where several of them died. But there is more to Corrie's story:

> After the war was over, the two Dutchmen who had betrayed her family were taken into custody and put on trial. That they were getting what they deserved would have been the natural response, but not so. [Corrie said,] "My sister Nollie . . . heard of the trial of these two men who told the Gestapo about us, and she wrote a letter to both of them. She told them that through their betrayal they had caused the death of our father, our brother and his son, and our sister. She said we had suffered much, although both of us had come out of prison alive. She told them that we had forgiven them and that we could do this because of Jesus, who is in our hearts."
>
> Both men responded. One wrote: "I have received Jesus as my Savior. When he can give such ability to forgive to people like Corrie ten Boom and her sister, then there is hope for me. I brought my sins to Him." The other letter gave an opposite viewpoint: "I know what I have done to your family, that I have caused the death of several of you who have saved Jews, and above that I have helped to kill many hundreds of Jewish people. The only thing I regret is that I have not been able to kill more of your kind."[3]

Corrie ten Boom still forgave, even after her betrayer refused to acknowledge his sin. She knew that the only true freedom came when she forgave and forgave and forgave, no matter how many times the face of that

228

man appeared before her mind's eye. She had to make the choice to forgive, no matter how many times were required.

Seventy-seven times means we are to forgive an infinite number of times. We are to forgive in spite of the severity of the wrongdoing. Jesus forgave those who crucified him even while he was still on the cross.

WEEK 48 — THURSDAY
OVERWHELMED WITH GUILT

"One tiny nut left unturned." A mistake that any aviation mechanic could potentially make, especially if his attention were momentarily distracted by what seemed to be a more pressing concern. Yet that little mistake resulted in the crash of a twin engine Piper Aztec in New Guinea in 1972.

Seven people died in that fiery crash, including the chief pilot for JAARS, the jungle aviation arm of Wycliffe Bible Translators, and Darlene Bee, a brilliant linguist and Bible translator. The mechanic was left with crushing guilt. As Ruth Tucker writes in her book, *Sacred Stories:*

> An inspection of the wreckage at the crash site indicated that the mid-air explosion had resulted from a fine spray of gasoline escaping where a nut had not been properly tightened. The individual responsible for tightening that B-nut on the fuel line was a mechanic who was reaching remote villagers with the gospel of Christ. Indeed, he had made great sacrifices to serve in the disease-infested jungle of New Guinea.
>
> For this guilt-ridden JAARS mechanic—the pain was almost unbearable. "The funeral was a ghastly ordeal," he confessed. "The sight of those caskets lined up in the little open-sided tropical church hit me like a blow to the stomach. I wanted nothing but to get out of there. How could I face my friends? How could I face myself? I was overwhelmed with guilt. I was overwhelmed with failure."[4]

There was a man in Scripture who, like the JAARS mechanic, was utterly devastated by guilt: "My guilt has overwhelmed me like a burden too heavy to bear. My wounds fester and are loathsome because of my sinful folly. I am bowed down and brought very low; all day long I go about mourning. My back is filled with searing pain; there is no health in my body. I am feeble and utterly crushed; I groan in anguish of heart. All my longings lie open before you, O Lord; my sighing is not hidden from you" (Ps. 38:4–9).

Guilt is an awesome emotion. To know that you have failed miserably and that other people have suffered because of it is a burden that can seem almost too heavy to bear.

Maybe you wonder how it was possible for a man responsible for the deaths of seven people to recover. But he did. He explains how: "I felt forgiveness from everyone around me—my co-workers and most importantly, the pilots who continued to entrust themselves to my skill and workmanship. I knew their total, loving acceptance.

"Except for God's grace," he later wrote, "I'd be somewhere cowering in a corner in guilt-ridden despair—the eighth fatality of that Aztec crash. . . . Praise God it isn't so."

Two thoughts give guidance to our lives today. First, forgiveness is the most effective antidote to guilt available. If someone has failed, your forgiveness could make the difference between his going on or succumbing to despair. Second, if you are the one needing forgiveness, you can remember God's grace—His unmerited favor—for you.

WEEK 48 — FRIDAY
TOO DAMAGED TO BE OF VALUE?

If you see yourself as too old, too young, too wounded, too sick, too broke, too unsuccessful for the Lord to use in His kingdom's work, then read these words: "For men are not cast off by the Lord forever. Though he brings grief, he will show compassion, so great is his unfailing love. For he does not willingly bring affliction or grief to the children of men" (Lam. 3:31–33).

William Cowper, the hymn writer, also struggled with feelings of unworthiness:

Cowper was a well-educated, cultured, affluent gentleman who eagerly became involved in lay ministry. But his desire to serve God was marred by his bouts of despair. On one occasion John Newton was called to Cowper's home only to find that he had made an unsuccessful attempt to commit suicide by cutting his throat with a knife. He was utterly convinced that God had rejected him.[5]

On another occasion, when Cowper was suicidal, Newton brought him to his own home and kept him under surveillance for several months.

During this period when Cowper's mental health was at its worst, John Newton's burden was heavy. Cowper's condition demanded almost constant attention. In his fits of depression, Cowper insisted God had marked him for eternal damnation, that he had been cut off from mercy and was hopelessly undone. For months Cowper's obsession that God had cast him off persisted despite all Newton's best efforts to convince him otherwise. His despair and woe were beyond words to describe.

Finally under John's leadership, prayer groups were formed to pray for Cowper's mental health. As these groups continued to pray, his condition began to slowly improve. After many months, the gloom finally began to lift from his spirit, and William Cowper became his normal self. It was during this time that he wrote "There Is a Fountain Filled With Blood."[6]

The words he penned reveal the depth of the man's spiritual victory:

There is a fountain filled with blood
Drawn from Immanuel's veins.
And sinners plunged beneath that flood.
Lose all their guilty stains.

God never cast him away, nor did his friends. Their steadfast belief in him helped him weather the storm of serious depression. Though it seems so hopeless, God will not allow this or any other malady to rob His children of their usefulness.

If you are close to someone who is depressed today, I encourage you to persevere. Even if they resist all your efforts, reassure them that they are precious to you and to the Lord who loves them with an unfailing love.

If you are the victim of despair, believe this: The very condition which now cripples you can be the inspiration for the "song" you will one day sing to the world!

WEEK 49 — MONDAY
LISTENING

How are you as a listener? Are you able to be quiet, lock in with your eyes, and communicate, "You matter to me?"

I can hear some of you saying, "Listen? I can barely get a word in edgewise at my house!" If you often find yourself caught in lopsided conversations, you may be developing patterns of poor conversation as you try to block everyone out.

If you come from a family where people talked *at* one another instead of *to* one another, you probably developed some defensive listening patterns that enabled you to look as if you were listening, but left you free to daydream all you wanted. That worked then, but now when your mate or your child wants your ear, you find it hard to really listen.

When it comes to listening, breaking bad habits is as important as developing good habits. I believe good listening is 90% of effective counseling. You can have all the wisdom in the world, but unless and until another person believes you have heard them, your good counsel will fall on deaf ears.

If you are going to interact with people on a level where you will be heard, you have to know where they are coming from. Rarely do the first few minutes of any conversation give you all you need to know to respond to a person.

First Thessalonians 5:14 says, "And we urge you, brothers, warn those who are idle, encourage the timid, help the weak, be patient with everyone." If you are going to be helpful to people as a friend, teacher, parent, or counselor, you have to know whether you are dealing with someone who is unruly or just excited, someone fainthearted or soft spoken, someone fearful or just weak. And you'll never know these things unless you learn to listen, really listen.

Webster says that listening means "to give close attention to in order to hear." Obviously, attention is an important element of listening. Whenever I counsel families, one of the first things I notice is whether they pay attention to one another or whether everyone gives his or her opinion without really hearing what the other person is saying.

Listening is something you have to learn to do even when the time is inopportune. Your family members usually don't make appointments to tell you what's on their minds. They speak whenever something is on their hearts.

You can also learn a lot by listening to what your family says to others. Often they will tell other people things in your presence that they might not say to you directly. When your teen or your mate has other people around, listen carefully.

When you are with others, resist the urge to dominate the conversation with your scintillating personality. Unless the people in the group are your

231

intimate friends, it is best to let someone else be charming, while you listen and try to learn what you might need to know.

These are simple guidelines that you probably already know. But sometimes it's good to be reminded that listening is an art to be developed with care.

WEEK 49 — TUESDAY
DIFFICULT PEOPLE

You just don't like her. You have tried to like her, but somehow you just can't make yourself warm up to her. She is a difficult person.

There is at least one person like that in every life. Someone who invariably rubs us the wrong way, who has a knack for saying the wrong thing at the wrong time, for misunderstanding motives, for hovering like a black cloud on the horizon of all our days.

Not long ago I read the fascinating story of a missionary who was attempting to deal with a difficult person. While she encouraged her students to love, she herself struggled to get along with an impossible co-worker. Finally, an elderly African woman challenged her, pointing out that the missionary was not showing the love she preached.

What a blow that must have been! How embarrassing, when we have worked to develop the right attitude toward a difficult person, only to betray our true feelings at an unguarded moment.

But the missionary was not to be defeated. As Ruth Tucker writes in *Sacred Stories:* "She determined that for one year she would read the love chapter, 1 Corinthians 13, each day and live with those verses fresh on her mind as she carried out every task that was before her. It became a pattern that changed the course of her life, and the Africans were the first to notice the change not only in her but also in her [difficult] colleague."

Read these life-changing words from that familiar passage:

> If I had the gift of being able to speak in other languages without learning them, and could speak in every language there is in all of heaven and earth, but didn't love others, I would only be making noise. If I had the gift of prophecy and knew all about what is going to happen in the future, knew everything about *everything,* but didn't love others, what good would it do? Even if I had the gift of faith so that I could speak to a mountain and make it move, I would still be worth nothing at all without love. If I gave everything I have to poor people and if I were burned alive for preaching the Gospel but didn't love others, it would be of no value whatever.
>
> Love is very patient and kind, never jealous or envious, never boastful or proud, never haughty or selfish or rude. Love does not demand its own way. It is not irritable or touchy. It does not hold grudges and will hardly even notice when others do it wrong. It is never glad about injustice, but rejoices whenever truth wins out. If you love someone you will be loyal to him no matter what the cost. You will always believe in him, always expect the best of him, and always stand your ground in defending him (1 Cor. 13:1–7 LB).

232

What a difference it would make if we could love as simply as this. Love is a choice we make. It is not based on how we feel or on another's behavior, but on the fact that God has told us to do it. If we don't have love, He says, then all the other things we do are worthless.

Love is the ingredient that gives substance even to the hard words of a prophet. If a message, a warning, or a word of advice is not given in love, it will probably miss its target.

My goal for the new year is to demonstrate a love that is equal to my message. I plan to keep a copy of 1 Corinthians 13 in front of me at all times, and when I encounter an "irregular person," I will be reminded that my ministry is only as effective as my ability to love him or her!

WEEK 49 — WEDNESDAY
THE HEART OF A CHILD

The heart of a child is a fragile thing. It must be handled with care. But let's face it. No one prepares us for all that parenthood entails.

I remember a day when unexpected company from out of town arrived at my house. With a two-year-old and a new baby, there had been little time to clean or entertain. I had been trying all day to get a moment to change the sheets on the bed and finish the laundry I had stacked in piles all over the kitchen floor.

I still remember the knowing smile of the woman, a mother of four grown children, as she took in the chaos. She cooed understanding words, took the baby and rocked him, while I gathered up the laundry and put on the coffee. Knowing that someone had been there before me was some comfort, but it took me a long time to adjust to the demands of small children.

Still, we can take so seriously the responsibility of rearing children that we forget to enjoy them, to laugh with them, to experience special events with them, to let them know we're glad they are in our family.

I have seen the bonding that takes place when parents and children enjoy one another, and I have seen that bonding hold through stressful events that would shred the hardiest of families if there had not been a bankful of joyous memories upon which to draw.

Often I am disbelieving when I hear of parents who are so insensitive that they make jokes at the expense of their children. A friend of mine tells of a cruel trick played by her parents when she asked for a car as a teenager. At Christmas, there was a box under the tree with a car key in it and a note with instructions to go to the garage. My friend jumped up and ran to the garage where she found a toy Volkswagen with her name on it. They laughed at their little joke while she held back the tears and determined she would never ask for anything from them again. Needless to say, as an adult, her relationship to her parents is rocky at best.

As parents we are there to direct, to correct, to love, to challenge, to pray, and to give joy to the children God has given. Why so many of us miss it, I don't know. Maybe we just need a reminder through the eyes of a child:

TRAGEDY

I always wanted a red balloon,
It only cost a dime,
But Ma said it was risky,

They broke so quickly,
And besides, she didn't have time;
And even if she did, she didn't
Think they were worth a dime.

We lived on a farm, and I only went
To one circus and fair,
And all the balloons I ever saw
Were there.

There were yellow ones and blue ones,
But the kind I liked best
Were red, and I don't see why
She couldn't have stopped and said
That maybe I could have one—
But she didn't—I suppose that now
You can buy them anywhere,
And that they still sell red ones
At circuses and fairs.
I got a little money saved;
I got a lot of time,
I got no one to tell me how to spend my dime;
Plenty of balloons—but somehow
There's something died inside of me,
And I don't want one—now.[1]

—Jill Spargur

My friend, take time today to appreciate the children God has placed in your care and to nurture the bond you share. Let them know they matter to you.

WEEK 49 — THURSDAY
HOW WELL DO YOU KNOW GOD?

All over the world the people of God have seen His hand, and even in the midst of incredible tragedy and chaotic change, are keenly aware that He is in control.

In fact, God's Word teaches it is in the midst of the greatest turmoil that "the people who know their God shall stand firm and take action" (Dan. 11:32 RSV).

In her book *Sacred Stories,* Ruth Tucker relates the story of Ken and Barbara Williams, missionaries to Guatemala, who, in 1970, were preparing to leave the Chuj people and move on to begin work on the translation of God's Word into another language.

It was a painful departure—"such incredible wrenching and tearing feelings," demonstrated by tears streaming down the faces of men who had never cried before. Ken had agonized over the decision to leave. Many of the people were Christians, but were they mature enough to stand alone? Then he remembered Paul's words to the Ephesian church leaders, "Now I commit you to God

234

and to the word of his grace." He would trust the Holy Spirit to lead them in his absence.

In the years that followed the Chuj people endured painful struggles. "Guerrilla warfare swept through their region like a searing fire. For three years no word got in or out because guerrillas had killed the bus drivers and burned the buses and trucks. The area was completely cut off." Finally, when word did reach Ken and Barbara, the message was, "We are bones." Crops and homes had been destroyed and the people were utterly impoverished.

Finally in 1986, it was once again safe enough for Ken and Barbara to return. Fearing that the church might not survive such devastation, they were astonished at how the church had grown. They were moved by the testimonies of courage, and by the numbers of people who had given their lives rather than deny their faith. Four pastors who had teamed up to share the gospel at a refugee camp had been brutally murdered by the guerrillas; others had been terrorized. Yet, the church grew to the point that half the Chuj people—nearly sixteen thousand people—had professed faith in Christ. Even more remarkable was the news that the Chuj church had sent out seven of their own families as cross-cultural missionaries.[2]

How well do you know God? As well as the Chuj people must have known Him? Well enough to trust Him not only with your death, but with your life?

Some of the stiff-necked Israelites came to know the Lord well only after many years of rebellion and failure. They were instructed to remind each other constantly of God's great and mighty works in their behalf—their deliverance from plagues, their safe exodus from Egypt, the crossing of the Red Sea on dry land, the miraculous provision in the wilderness.

Can you point to His grace in your life—not your salvation only, but incidents of healing, protection, material blessings, answered prayer? If so, you will be strong in the face of the toughest challenges and can act with confidence to accomplish His purposes.

When circumstances seem the most impossible, remind yourself of God's unchanging nature. Think of specific incidents in the past when He abundantly met your need. Trust Him to do it again today!

WEEK 49 — FRIDAY
ETERNALLY UNDISMAYED

We are living in incredible times!

We are seeing historic changes taking place around the world. Nations aligning themselves with former enemies to oppose aggression. World governments toppling. Walls of division crumbling. Kings and other heads of state being deposed. Economic boom and recession. Instability. War. Terrorism. But through it all—a cry for freedom!

It is the God-ordained right of people to be free. With the collapse of the Berlin Wall, even the media actually began to take note that the movement for freedom originated in the church. They can't explain away or ignore the fact that people who acknowledge God have been quietly standing for freedom for a long time. Through persecution and tyranny, believers have been planting the seeds that are now coming into bloom.

Yet it is this very freedom to pursue one's own course that allows us to mistreat each other and even to shake our fists at God and stubbornly insist on having our own way.

Cyrus Mitchell has written some prophetic words:

> *The soul of Jesus is restless today;*
> *Christ is trampling through the spirit-world,*
> *Compassion in His heart for the fainting millions;*
> *He trudges through China, through Poland,*
> *Through Russia, Austria, Germany, Armenia;*
> *Patiently He pleads with the Church,*
> *Tenderly He woos her.*
> *The wounds of His body are bleeding afresh for the sorrows*
> *   of His shepherdless people.*
> *We beseige Him with selfish petitions,*
> *We weary Him with our petty ambitions,*
> *From the needy we bury him in piles of carven stone,*
> *We obscure Him in the smoke of stuffy incense,*
> *We drown Him in the needs and sorrows of the exploited—*
> *   "least of His brethren."*
> *The soul of Jesus is restless today,*
> *But eternally undismayed.*[3]

Jesus must get really tired of our world crises, our clamoring demands, our religiosity. Still, He is "eternally undismayed"—unflinching, unswerving, undisturbed. No matter how we may conduct our history, or abuse our rights and privileges, or commit sins against our fellow human beings, He is undeterred from His great purpose.

Sometimes I think this world surely has no room for any more insanity, that the abuse of freedom and the exaltation of licentiousness could not possibly get worse. It helps to see Jesus standing in our midst, calm and "eternally undismayed."

WEEK 50 — MONDAY
AFTER YOU HAVE SUFFERED

Many people have asked, "How did you get into the kind of ministry you are in?" For those of you who still don't know what I do, perhaps I should explain that I am a conference speaker, an author, and a radio broadcaster. The truth is that this is the last thing on earth I ever thought I would be doing!

In college, I was studying for a career as an English teacher, until God intervened and took me on a different path. I never looked for a ministry, or sought a place to minister. I simply followed the progressive revelation of God's will in my life. But I have found that every time God gets ready to move me to a broader scope of ministry, He usually takes me through some deep

236

waters where I would declare that I would surely drown if He had not been there!

I love the story that G. Campbell Morgan tells: "A young fellow entered the ministry, and had remarkable success, and great blessing has attended his life and work. At the time he was a young man fresh from college, a brilliant preacher even then. He preached in my church in Birmingham, and I went home after the sermon and said to Mrs. Morgan, "Was that not wonderful?" She quietly remarked, "Yes, but it will be more wonderful when he has suffered."

I have discovered that through the years and with the experiences of suffering God has allowed, my own ministry had deepened and grown "more wonderful."

Peter must have had something like this in mind when he wrote: "The God of all grace, who called you to his eternal glory in Christ, after you have suffered a little while, will himself restore you and make you strong, firm and steadfast" (1 Peter 5:10).

Over a year ago I received a note in the mail from a person I don't even know. On a crudely trimmed piece of paper were these words by Chuck Swindoll: "You who have endured the stinging experiences make the choicest counselors God can use." I framed that quote and it is in my office where every day I can be reminded that the "stinging experiences" only make me more valuable to the One I long to serve.

Corrie ten Boom has said, "When we deepen our message, then God will expand our ministry." It's as simple as that. A heart for God must be broken before it really beats for Him.

If you long to be used and wonder why others seem to be God's chosen instruments, maybe you need to stop and consider how you have responded to the "stinging experiences." Do you fight them? Have you allowed them to make you bitter? Do you feel life is unfair? If so, you are undoubtedly sitting on the sidelines of ministry.

But if you have embraced your struggles as friends and your trials as trainers, then you know the joy of a deepening ministry. You can take comfort in the fact that the suffering lasts only "a little while," before the God of all grace Himself will restore you, and make you strong and steadfast!

WEEK 50 — TUESDAY
LISTENING TO THE LORD

"Blessed is the man who listens to me, watching daily at my doors, waiting at my doorway. For whoever finds me finds life and receives favor from the LORD" (Prov. 8:34–35).

Listening to the Lord can mean the difference between life and death.

When I was a little girl I would walk downtown with my daddy. He held my hand and everything felt secure. But when I got older I wanted to walk by myself. Often I would run ahead of him, and he would call for me to stop. I always did, but there were times I got right to the curb of a busy street before I slowed down. I can still remember my dad saying, "You have got to learn: When I tell you to stop, stop! Don't be so bull-headed. Someday it could save your life."

Sometimes we listen to the Lord like I listened to my dad. We rush headlong into situations that could have been avoided if we had just listened.

Listen in the Old Testament means to hear intelligently with the intent to obey. It is not the kind of listening that says, "Maybe I'll do what you say, maybe not." It is the kind of listening that says, "I'll do whatever you say, no questions asked."

What has your heavenly Father been speaking to you about? Have you been thinking that you are too grown up to listen to Him?

Has he been speaking to you about your marriage? Have you gotten into a rut? Have you hardened your heart against living obediently because you just don't like the principles He's calling you to follow?

What about finances? Has He asked you to give a certain amount of money for a specific situation, but for some reason you haven't yet given it?

Maybe He has spoken to you about sharing your faith with someone you work with. His instruction has been clear, but because you are uncomfortable with being that bold, you really haven't listened with the intent to obey.

If you are a poor listener sometimes, I understand. There are days when I feel as if I'm in a fog, and I can't hear anything. I think we all have "foggy" days, but not every day is like that. And if you and I intend to be people whom God can trust, we have to be people who listen.

In Psalm 81:11–14 God says:

> "But my people would not listen to me;
>   Israel would not submit to me.
> So I gave them over to their stubborn hearts
>   to follow their own devices.
> If my people would but listen to me,
>   if Israel would follow my ways,
> how quickly would I subdue their enemies
>   and turn my hand against their foes!"

God desires us to listen to Him. When he speaks he doesn't roar; he just gently reminds us over and over in the clearest way possible—through every route possible—"Listen to me. I love you; listen to me."

Remember, my friend, that God says if you listen to Him you will acquire understanding. There is no need to be in the dark. God simply says, "Listen."

WEEK 50 — WEDNESDAY
THE GUARANTEE OF HEAVEN

I have often been amazed at "on-the-street interviews" in which people are asked if they believe in life after death. Most answer with a wistful "I hope so" or an evasive "I doubt it." But Christians usually reply with a confidence that borders on holy boldness: "Yes! There is life after death!"

Paul explained to the Corinthian skeptics that true believers would someday have a new body: "Now we know that if the earthly tent [body] we live in is destroyed, we have a building from God, an eternal house in heaven, not built by human hands. . . . For while we are in this tent, we groan and are burdened, because we do not wish to be unclothed but to be clothed with our heavenly dwelling, so that what is mortal may be swallowed up by life. Now it is God who has made us for this very purpose and has given us the Spirit as a deposit, guaranteeing what is to come" (2 Cor. 5:1, 4–5).

When I read those verses in Corinthians, it was as if God Himself spoke and said, "When you know that you know that you know, despite all of the skeptics and mockers, it is because my Holy Spirit is a reassuring presence, a guarantee that can not be revoked—that there is a life to come."

It has become fashionable for people who have been clinically dead to come back and tell of their out-of-body experiences. While they report some very similar details, the differences are equally significant. So, if we are to know there is life after death, these reports are hardly authoritative.

There is further reliable documentation, however. We have the witness of the Scriptures that tell us that it is preferable "to be away from the body and at home with the Lord" (2 Cor. 5:8). Jesus Himself told us that He has gone "to prepare a place" for us so that where He is, there we may be also (John 14:2–3). The book of Revelation gives us a glimpse of the physical surroundings of heaven, but until we are there, at home with the Lord, we will never know the reality of heaven. In addition, God has placed within each of His children a guarantee, a down payment that guarantees us that the rest of the payments are coming. Our most eloquent witness is within ourselves!

If you are a believer, then the Scriptures and the Holy Spirit within you have already assured your heart that the joy and the comfort is true . . . and it is for you!

WEEK 50 — THURSDAY
IS IT PROPER TO CRY?

Seventeen years ago, having given birth to two healthy baby boys, I was shocked when we suddenly lost our third child in a miscarriage. But more than shock, I felt grief.

At that time, however, very little was said about miscarriage. It was just something that happened, and which you were expected to endure with no more emotion than having a tooth extracted. The physical pain lasted a day or two, then it was back to business as usual, never to mention the loss again.

Now we are beginning to realize that "even if your child died so early that his tiny body was barely formed, the loss of who that little one was to you may be mourned deeply, and rightly so."[1]

As we see the tragedy of children being purposely aborted at the same point in their lives that many miscarriages occur, I think it begins to dawn on us that the grief we feel is for a real person with all the potential of whole life locked within him at the moment of conception. We can't always know what goes wrong. But we do know that there is a feeling of acute loss.

One grieving father asks:

"IS IT PROPER TO CRY?"

Is it proper to cry
For a baby too small
For a coffin?
Does Jesus have
My too-small baby
In His tender arms?
Yes, I think He does.
There is so much I do not know
About you, my child—
He, she? quiet or restless?

239

Will I recognize
Someone I knew so little about
Yet loved so much?
Yes, I think I will.
Can we say
We loved you any less
Because we never held you?
No, I think not.
Ah, sweet, small child,
Can I say that loving you is like loving God?
Loving—yet not seeing.
Holding—yet not touching.
Caressing—yet separated by the chasm of time.
No tombstone marks your sojourn
And only God recorded your name.
I had neither opportunity
Nor capability
To say goodbye.
Not saying goodbye
Is just as hard
As saying goodbye.
The preparations are halted,
The royal guest was called away.
The banquet was canceled.
Just moved. Just moved.
Yet a tear remains
Where baby should have been.
Dedicated to my baby
this September 17, 1983
Age: —6 months
Sex: Unknown
Weight: Unknown
Color of eyes: Unknown
Loved: by the Father, Son and
Holy Spirit and by Mommy
and Daddy.[2]

—Bob Neudorf

When we weep for our children, no matter how small or incomplete, you can be sure that you have a heavenly Father who weeps with you.

WEEK 50 — FRIDAY
THE PEOPLE OF THE BOOK

About five years ago, a statement grabbed my heart and refused to let go: "If the people of the Book are like you, then read from the Book to me."

At the time, I was sitting at the table with two old friends who profoundly influenced my life when I was a child. One was a woman who had loved me, accepted me, and been very kind to me. As a social worker for a home mission board, I had seen her sacrifice a great part of her life as she poured herself out for disadvantaged people. The qualities that drew me to her eventually caused me to want to be like the Christ she served.

The other, the woman who shared these memorable words with me, was Mercy JayRaja Rao, from the southern tip of India. Though I had never spent a great deal of time with her, she impacted my life powerfully.

When I was about twelve years old, Mercy spent Christmas with my family. We picked her up early in the morning and, after enjoying the day together, we returned to her apartment where I was to stay overnight with her. Before we went to bed, we knelt, and Mercy began to pray. I'll never forget that prayer. She asked the Lord to be gracious to the little boy we had seen on the sidewalk early that morning and prayed for two homeless men who had been huddled by a fire. One by one, she asked the Lord to meet the needs of every single person we had encountered that day! My childish brain was over-whelmed by her memory and concern for people to whom I had given only passing interest.

Now, sitting across the table from these two great women of faith, I stared into the black eyes and the gray eyes and thanked God that they had been people of the Book, giving me a glimpse of what His people are supposed to be . . . how they are to behave . . . how deeply they are to care.

Since then, the words Mercy shared with me that day have come back many times as I have struggled to become a person of "the Book":

"You are the light of the world. A city on a hill cannot be hidden. Neither do people light a lamp and put it under a bowl. Instead they put it on its stand, and it gives light to everyone in the house. In the same way, let your light shine before men, that they may see your good deeds and praise your Father in heaven." (Matt. 5:14–16)

I pray that you and I will become people who so reflect the Lord we serve that someday we may hear, "If the people of the Book are like you, then read from the Book to me."

WEEK 51 — MONDAY
GIVERS OR TAKERS?

Kevin Leman, an internationally known psychologist and author, makes some interesting comparisons between givers and takers:

Givers understand reality and human need.	Takers prefer fantasy and meeting their own needs.
Givers realize they may have to wait to get what they want or even do without.	Takers live by the law of instant gratification.
Givers look out for their families.	Takers look out for themselves.[1]

Bringing up children to be givers instead of takers is a challenge all parents face. Unfortunately, there are a couple of factors in our society that work against us. One is our affluence. Separated from the raw realities of life by our suburban fortresses, in which we possess the best of both city and country, our children are rarely exposed to personal deprivation among their friends.

The second is that we ourselves may feel uncomfortable with direct

241

contact with the poor. It is easier to launder the whole process by giving money and letting someone else administer it.

Yet, we must find ways to bring down the barriers that separate us from the issue. One way is to involve our children at an early age in the hands-on process of giving.

I can remember going with my mother to take a basket of food to a poor family in the Washington, D. C., area when I was about six or seven. I still can see the long, narrow, dingy stairs we climbed on the way to the second-floor, two-room apartment. The gaunt mother met us at the door. She thanked us for the food, then asked if we wanted to see her new baby. Showing us past several beds that were lined up, side by side, we came to the last one. There, bundled in blankets, was the smallest baby I had ever seen. I remember wondering why there were no sheets.

After talking with the woman for a while, we were suddenly swarmed by several dirty-faced children, seemingly appearing out of nowhere. They all looked as malnourished as their mother. We finally said goodbye and, as we made our way back down the stairs, I remember the feeling of profound relief when we walked back out on the street and got in the warm car where my daddy was waiting. The memory of that moment is sealed in my heart.

I can't say that this experience made me a giver, but it certainly opened my eyes to the fact that not everyone lived in the comfort I enjoyed. If our children can see the need, however, I believe their natural compassion will surface, though it may take their salvation to give from the proper motive.

Proverbs 22:9 is a rich promise: "A generous man will himself be blessed, for he shares his food with the poor." Because our society is so segmented, we may have to make a conscious effort to model giving before our children. As we do so, we can encourage them with this word of hope and blessing.

WEEK 51 — TUESDAY
GOD CAN DO ANYTHING

We serve an able God. In the Old and New Testaments, that word for *able* is related to the word *power*. Our God is powerful, mighty, able to deliver. He can get the job done!

In the familiar story of the fiery furnace, the three young men— Shadrach, Meshach and Abednego—were told that they would either have to worship the gods of Nebuchadnezzar or suffer the consequences. The king told them: "If you do not worship [the image I made], you will be thrown immediately into a blazing furnace. Then what god will be able to rescue you from my hand?'

"Shadrach, Meshach and Abednego replied to the king, 'O Nebuchadnezzar, we do not need to defend ourselves before you in this matter. If we are thrown into the blazing furnace, the God we serve is able to save us from it, and he will rescue us from your hand, O king. But even if he does not, we want you to know, O king, that we will not serve your gods or worship the image of gold you have set up'" (Dan. 3:15–18).

Shadrach and his friends were in a tough spot! But they made a choice based on one fact: They knew that God was able to deliver them. One way or the other, they believed He would not leave them in peril without an all-sufficient hand to support them. So they took their stand. They would not worship the pagan gods . . . *even if He did not choose to deliver them!*

Of course, God intervened in the lives of the three young Jewish men, and He let them live, proving to King Nebuchadnezzar and all the world that His power transcends that of gods and men.

One lesson we might learn from this experience is that we should not waste time talking about the impossible circumstances we face or the Enemy who desires to thwart God's plans. The more we focus on the difficulties, the weaker our faith and the smaller our God seems to become. Rather, we should focus on God's *ableness* to overcome all obstacles in this natural world order and in the invisible world of powers and principalities.

If Shadrach, Meshach, and Abednego had begun to panic when they felt the heat of the fire, what kind of testimony would they have presented to those unbelievers looking on? Instead, they stood firm and steady, believing that God could deliver them if He chose to do so.

Even Nebuchadnezzar was impressed. And when the three stepped out of the furnace, unruffled and unsinged, he acknowledged the Lord: "Praise be to the God of Shadrach, Meshach and Abednego, who has sent his angel and rescued his servants! They trusted in him and defied the king's command and were willing to give up their lives rather than serve or worship any god except their own God" (v. 28).

My friend, you may be in a fiery furnace of your own today. As you walk through the experience, focus on the *ableness* of God, confess His greatness to those around you, and place your faith in His power to deliver you . . . *even if He does not.* Your testimony will bless others as you walk in confidence. Then, when you receive deliverance, they will be able to join you in praising the Lord!

WEEK 51 — WEDNESDAY
THE PERFECT GIFT

Every year, as the busiest week of the season approaches, I resolve to be ready, having planned ahead, shopped early, and mailed my greeting cards to friends and relatives by the first of December. And every year, I find myself at the eleventh hour, racing the Christmas clock!

But God never hurries. He waits for just the right moment to unwrap His most precious gifts. "When the time had fully come, God sent his Son" (Gal. 4:4).

Jesus is the perfect Gift for a world that is sick and tired. He came to bring healing and rest and the peace that passes understanding. And He came to fill time with new meaning. "I have come that [you] may have life and have it to the full" (John 10:10).

But Jesus is also coming again. We are living between the First and the Second Advent. We look back with gratitude and thanksgiving—"Joy to the world, the Lord is come, let earth receive her King!" We look forward in hope to His coming again, when all the struggle will make sense and all the questions will be answered.

In his book, *Knowing the Face of God,* Tim Stafford suggests that much of Jesus' teaching emphasized the "view from the end." When it's all over, we will be able to understand how all of history came together. Pain and sorrow will also be transformed by this perspective.

If we walk through a hospital, we can encounter a practical example of this. There is one particular ward where moans are most likely to assault our ears. Young women writhe in severe and helpless pain. Their problem is obvious to the eye: their stomachs have swelled to the size of beach balls. The taut skin glistens. As the hours pass, the women's faces grow increasingly worn with pain. If they were there with any other diagnosis, say cancer, the scene would cut our hearts.

Instead, we feel great joy in a maternity ward. The women there may be feeling as much pain as women with stomach cancer, but they look confidently toward a different end—a joyful end. Later, they will not even remember much of the process. How often have we heard a mother say, "Isn't it strange how you can't remember how much it hurt?" The pain that seemed so terrible has faded away because it came to its proper end: she holds her baby.[2]

What a perfect Gift! Jesus' coming puts everything into perspective. He is born; He is *already* here. He is coming again; He *will be* here, perhaps at any minute, but right on time. We bow before His manger throne in anticipation of seeing Him face to face!

WEEK 51 — THURSDAY
WRONG WORDS

Learning to listen will keep you from saying the wrong thing at the wrong time.

I know that seems like a simple statement that should be obvious to all, but I wonder if it really is that obvious. Often we end up in relational difficulties because we aren't listening to what another person is saying. We assume we know the problem and therefore we have no need to really listen. This is particularly true if you have lived with that person for a long time. It is tempting to believe that you *know* what that other person is saying just because you have experience with them.

Preconceived ideas or careless listening can get you in a lot of trouble. I have seen this happen with parents and teenagers. The things you laughed about with your ten-year-old may offend your thirteen-year-old. All along your child has been warning you, "I'm growing up; don't say those things in front of my friends," but because you haven't listened, you blunder and embarrass your child.

The Bible encourages us over and over to speak appropriately:

The tongue has the power of life and death. (Prov. 18:21)

An anxious heart weighs a man down, but a kind word cheers him up. (Prov. 12:25)

The tongue that brings healing is a tree of life. (Prov. 15:4)

Pleasant words are a honeycomb, sweet to the soul and healing to the bones. (Prov. 16:24)

A word aptly spoken is like apples of gold in settings of silver. (Prov. 25:11)

The Scriptures also say that bouncing in with inappropriately cheerful words is "like one who takes away a garment on a cold day" (Prov. 25:20). Words that don't fit the occasion or the individual usually come when you haven't listened—when you haven't keyed in to what is really going on in another's life.

Here are some thoughts on listening that may be helpful to you today. Ask the Lord to prick your heart in the areas where you need help in order to be a better listener.

1. Do you stop what you are doing while you listen?
2. Do you give eye contact?
3. Do you verbally respond to let the other person know you have heard him and to encourage him to continue?
4. Do you allow time for the other person to think about his words? Sometimes we are too quick to fill in the gaps when someone is groping for specific words. This can frustrate a person who is insecure about talking with you anyway.
5. If the conversation grows stressful, do you remain calm and non-defensive? Nothing is to be gained by a quick, self-protective answer.
6. When a conversation ends, do you summarize to say, "This is what I have heard. Do I understand you correctly?" Most people talk to those whom they believe will try to understand. If you can communicate "I understand," then you have successfully listened.

We have a great High Priest who understands our weaknesses. His name is the Lord Jesus Christ. If the King of the Universe can listen to our simplest cry, surely we can listen to one another.

WEEK 51 — FRIDAY
OUR KEEPER

I travel quite a bit and frequently stay in the hotel where I will be addressing a conference or seminar. When I check in at the front desk, I usually see a sign that tells me that the safest place to keep my valuables is in the hotel safe. If I want to be sure my jewelry and cash are not stolen, I will turn them over to the hotel security system.

A long time ago, I decided that everything on this earth that is dear to me needs to be placed in God's safekeeping. He is able to protect from the prying, thieving Enemy who has come to kill, steal, and destroy. His message to all His children is: Leave your valuables with Me!

Jesus has given us a wonderful promise: "My sheep listen to my voice; I know them, and they follow me. I give them eternal life, and they shall never perish; no one can snatch them out of my hand. My Father, who has given them to me, is greater than all; no one can snatch them out of my Father's hand" (John 10:27–29).

God does not take our trust lightly. He never allows anyone who has been entrusted to Him to be touched by anything that will not ultimately result in good. Our problem is that we want to be on the advisory committee to tell Him how to accomplish that!

Have you committed a mate to God's keeping, only to see him or her pursuing an increasingly disastrous course—alcohol, drugs, infidelity? If God has not brought healing and deliverance, are you tempted to wonder if He is really keeping the trust?

Did you give your children to the Lord as babies, yet now that they are older, you see them straying from the path, and you wonder if God is being a little careless with the ones you love?

God says He is able to keep . . . and sometimes that means letting them go as far as they can go under His watchful eye.

If you have just about given up trusting God with your loved ones, wait a while! We cannot see the unseen hand that is holding, protecting, and working in and through every situation. Don't stop believing. God delights in the person who will trust Him to keep that which has been committed, especially when it's too dark to see what He's doing!

WEEK 52 — MONDAY
STRANGERS IN THE WORLD

If ever there were a time we could describe our world as a world gone mad, it is now. I feel real pain when I see families disrupted by famine and war and disaster. But these problems only compound personal problems faced by people all over the world. Everywhere, they are beginning to ask, "How can we live in a world gone mad?"

There was another time and place when it seemed as if the whole world had gone mad. On July 19, in A.D. 64, fire broke out in the great city of Rome. The Emperor Nero, who had had his eye on some land, set fire to some ramshackle apartments on the property. As a result the city was ablaze for three days and three nights. Roman soldiers were ordered to hinder anyone who tried to put out the fires, and when they had died down, Rome was a "helpless brotherhood of wretchedness."

The people turned their fury on Nero. To defuse their wrath, he blamed the Christians, who were an easy target. Though up until this time Rome had been fairly benevolent and objective in protecting them, that changed overnight. Now, Nero accused believers of gathering at secret Lord's suppers to kill and eat Jews. Later, he added Gentiles and babies to the menu. We have only to read recorded history to realize that hearsay and pure slander have been some of the greatest weapons against Christians ever since.

Peter, the crude fisherman who got off to such a rocky start in his Christian walk, wrote to the believers who had scattered for their own survival, comforting them with these words: "Peter, an apostle of Jesus Christ, to God's elect, strangers in the world, scattered throughout Pontus, Galatia, Cappadocia, Asia and Bithynia, who have been chosen according to the foreknowledge of God the Father. . . . In this you greatly rejoice, though now for a little while you may have had to suffer grief in all kinds of trials. These have come so that your faith—of greater worth than gold, which perishes even though refined by fire—may be proved genuine and may result in praise, glory and honor when Jesus Christ is revealed" (1 Peter 1:1–2, 6–7).

My friend, it does seem as if trials are upon us. Maybe they will become more and more like those that afflicted our Christian brothers and sisters that night in July so long ago. We're beginning to feel more and more like strangers in the world.

But God is faithful. He has promised to limit the time of our trials on earth. He also guarantees that our faith, once tried, will prove genuine when we stand before the Lord. We won't be strangers anymore.

WEEK 52 — TUESDAY
STRETCH OUT YOUR LOVE

As we look at the instructions the apostle Peter gave to the Christians who had scattered to live among strangers, we find this guideline: "Above all, keep fervent in your love for one another, because love covers a multitude of sins" (1 Peter 4:8 NASB).

When Peter said, "Keep fervent in your love," he was using a term that meant "keep on being stretched out in your love with great intensity." But great pressure places demands on love, and it is not always easy to respond properly.

Our nation is now in great distress, with delicate international relations compounding internal problems of economics and corruption in government. Our support for our leadership is strong at the moment, but how long will it last if the tension drags on and on? There is the danger that love will be lost in the upheaval, and that the people who need to stand together won't be able to hold out.

Tragedy can either draw people together or tear them apart. I have seen families separate when there is the loss of a child or a critical illness. At the time when they most needed to be supportive to one another, someone lost their courage.

Peter understood this tendency of human nature, and knew that the Christians who had been cruelly persecuted by Nero after the great fire that destroyed Rome would need to be strong for one another. They were in constant turmoil and danger, and the great trial of their faith was bound to take its toll on relationships, both in families and in the body of believers.

In his book, *How Can It Be All Right When Everything Is All Wrong?* Lewis Smedes writes about suffering and marriage, the place where love is so easily destroyed:

> Anybody's marriage is a harvest of suffering. Romantic lotus-eaters may tell you marriage was designed to be a pleasure-dome for erotic spirits to frolic in self-fulfilling relations. But they play you false. Your marriage vow was a promise to suffer. Yes, to suffer. I will not take it back. You promised only to suffer *with*, however. You get your share of suffering *from* willy-nilly thrown at you. It made sense because the person you married was likely to get hurt along the route, sooner or later, more or less, but hurt he or she was bound to get. And you promised to hurt with your spouse. Marriage is a life of shared pain.[1]

God has said that "everyone who wants to live a godly life in Christ Jesus will be persecuted" (2 Tim. 3:12). We may even have to die to some hope or expectation that can never be realized. But the apostle Peter said, "Keep fervent in your love . . . *especially* when you are suffering."

My friend, if you are just about to buckle under suffering and stress, "stretch out your love" and see how it covers "a multitude of sins."

WEEK 52 — WEDNESDAY
THE PURE MILK OF THE WORD

Recently, while en route by plane to a speaking engagement, I sat near a crying baby. The mother offered every distraction she could think of—water, juice, little bits of cracker—but the baby obviously wanted something else. Only when a flight attendant brought milk to refill the bottle was the infant satisfied.

As I watched that little scene unfold, I was reminded of the words of Peter to the believers suffering terrible hardship and persecution: "Therefore, putting aside all malice and all guile and hypocrisy and envy and all slander, like newborn babes, long for the pure milk of the word, that by it you may grow in respect to salvation, if you have tasted the kindness of the Lord" (1 Peter 2:1–3 NASB).

The word Peter used for *malice* means to "put aside all the evil things you are thinking." Yes, it's true that life seems unfair and you are suffering, but dwelling on these things will only destroy you. Instead, long for [strongly desire] the unadulterated nourishment of God's Word.

"When you are in tough, trying circumstances," Peter was saying, "the tendency is to think maliciously. But I tell you that there is a way to grow even in this situation—by taking in the Word, just like a baby who won't be satisfied with anything else but a bottle!"

The alternative to throwing a "pity party" is making the effort to read the Word of God, asking for understanding as you read. God has said that His Word is living and powerful. Saints down through the years have recognized that when they were most vulnerable, it was the Word of God that sustained them.

Peter knew this when he told his Christian brothers and sisters to "long for the word." David knew this when he wrote: "I am laid low in the dust; preserve my life according to your word. I recounted my ways and you answered me; teach me your decrees. Let me understand the teaching of your precepts. . . . My soul is weary with sorrow; strengthen me according to your word" (Ps. 119:25–28).

It may seem simplistic at times to tell someone who is suffering to read the Bible. Are you sometimes embarrassed to offer that counsel? Or have you been burned by some unanswered prayer, so have dismissed the fact that there could be any help in the Word? It's true that we may occasionally need human encouragement to get past pain. But the foundation for all healing is found in the Word of God!

If you are tempted to entertain such thoughts as "This isn't fair!" or "I hate what has happened!" or "Why me?" then I encourage you to give yourself a gift. Take fifteen minutes to read through the Psalms. You won't have to read far before your heart will be nourished, renewed, and strengthened.

WEEK 52 — THURSDAY
AN AWESOME GOD

The Hubble telescope is receiving a lot of media attention these days. Recently I heard one of the scientists say, "We want to go to the limits of the universe and see what is beyond. We want to find out where earth came from, and how and why."

As I listened to him, I thought to myself, "It would be ironic, wouldn't it, if that telescope roared to the edge of space and beamed back a picture of the throne room of God, where we could hear the voice of God booming out with the authority, power, and dominion that belong to Him alone: "In the beginning I created the heavens and the earth . . . case closed!"

Our God is an awesome God! He is "able to do immeasurably more [exceedingly abundantly] than all we ask or imagine, according to his power that is at work within us" (Eph. 3:20).

What do you need for God to do for you today?

Do you need resources to meet the needs of someone who has crossed your path? Don't sit around worrying about it. Simply remind God that He "is able to make all grace abound to you, so that in all things at all times, having all that you need, you will abound in every good work" (2 Cor. 9:8).

Do you need courage? He will give you power, love, and a sound mind.

Do you need wisdom? He says all you have to do is ask, and you will have wisdom from above, gentle and pure.

Do you need patience? God says His Spirit will invade your life if you let Him in.

Do you need strength in time of weakness? God says His strength is perfected in your weakness. In other words, your weakness displays His power and might.

He doesn't promise to heal all our illnesses or take away all our pain. There is purpose in adversity. But He does promise that even if we walk right down through the middle of the Valley of the Shadow of Death, He will be with us, and all comfort, power, and strength will surround and enfold us.

We will miss His awesome power if we look only at the tangible provisions—the things we can hear, see, touch. Some of His greatest gifts can only be discerned by the Spirit. Ask God to reveal His awesome abundance!

WEEK 52 — FRIDAY
DO YOU KNOW WHAT TIME IT IS?

The year is dying. Another twelve months have ticked by, forever engraved on our memories in the form of meaningful events—birthdays, anniversaries, a seminar, a hunting trip, summer vacation, Thanksgiving, Christmas . . .

And now the new year stretches ahead—365 days of unwritten pages, unsung songs, unclaimed blessings. There is something about "newness" that is strangely stirring. I'm curious about the future. I want to get there, find out what it holds, turn the pages, live it!

In his book, *Living on the Ragged Edge,* author Charles Swindoll said much the same thing:

> God has not only put things into perspective by having a timetable in which events run their course, He has also put within every human being's heart a curiosity about tomorrow . . . an eternal capacity that prompts me to probe, to be intrigued, to search. That explains why your child—just about the time that little fella or gal starts to run around the house and talk—begins to ask questions about tomorrow, about life, and about life beyond. Children can ask the most profound questions. And when

they grow up, they don't stop asking questions. It's the way God made human beings. God has not put eternity in the hearts of animals, only into the hearts of men and women. And since that is true, since we will not find out about tomorrow without God, our pursuit must be of Him.

Meaning what? Meaning you and I are not really ready to handle life until we are ready to face death. When we get eternity securely in place, it's remarkable what it will do to time.[2]

God set it all in motion. "He has also set eternity in the hearts of men; yet they cannot fathom what God has done from beginning to end" (Eccl. 3:11).

Beginnings and endings are created to capture time, to make it usable to us. But in eternity, time will be no more. We won't need it since we will be living in the eternal present. There will be no stress factor, no schedules, no timetables, no deadlines . . . only the neverending now.

The interesting thing is that eternity begins now! We are actually living in it. And if we are, then we can begin our celestial agenda—praising God, spending time with Him, loving Him, basking in His presence, exalting His name:

> Praise the Lord, O heavens!
> Praise him from the skies!
> Praise him, all his angels, all the armies of heaven.
> Praise him, sun and moon, and all you twinkling stars.
> Praise him, skies above.
> Praise him, vapors high above the clouds.
> Let everything he has made give praise to him.
> For he issued his command, and they came into being;
> he established them forever and forever.
> His orders will never be revoked.
> And praise him down here on earth,
> you creatures of the ocean depths.
> Let fire and hail, snow, rain, wind and weather,
> all obey.
> Let the mountains and hills,
> the fruit trees and cedars,
> the wild animals and cattle,
> the snakes and birds,
> the kings and all the people,
> with their rulers and their judges,
> young men and maidens,
> old men and children—
> all praise the Lord together.
> For he alone is worthy.
> His glory is far greater than all of earth and heaven.
> He has made his people strong,
> honoring his godly ones—
> the people of Israel, the people closest to him.
> Hallelujah! Yes, praise the Lord!

(Ps. 148 LB)

250

NOTES

Week 1

¹ Ruth Harms Calkin, *Lord, Don't You Love Me Anymore?* (Wheaton, Ill.: Tyndale, 1988).
²Amy Carmichael, *Edges of His Ways* (Fort Washington, Penn.: Christian Literature Crusade, 1955).
³Quoted in Barbara Johnson, *Fresh Elastic for Stretched-Out Moms* (Old Tappan, N.J.: Revell, 1985).
⁴Ted Engstrom, *The Pursuit of Excellence* (Grand Rapids: Zondervan, 1982).

Week 2

¹Carroll Simcox, *Three Thousand Quotations on Christian Themes* (Grand Rapids: Baker Book House, 1988).

Week 3

¹Kathryn Stechert, *On Your Own Terms: A Woman's Guide to Working with Men* (New York: Random House, 1987).

Week 4

¹Wayne Martindale and Jerry Root, *The Quotable Lewis* (Wheaton, Ill.: Tyndale House, 1989).
²Carroll Simcox, *Three Thousand Quotations on Christian Themes* (Grand Rapids: Baker Book House, 1988).
³Quoted in Barbara Johnson, *Fresh Elastic for Stretched-Out Moms* (Old Tappan, N.J.: Revell, 1985).
⁴Ibid.

Week 8

¹Mrs. Charles E. Cowman, *Streams in the Desert* (Grand Rapids: Zondervan, 1925, 1953, 1965).
²Marie Chapian, *His Thoughts Toward Me* (Minneapolis: Bethany House, 1987).

Week 10

¹Elisabeth Elliot, *Table Talk* (1989).

Week 11

¹Hannah Whitall Smith, *God Is Enough* (Grand Rapids: Zondervan, 1986).

Week 12

[1]Max Lucado, *On the Anvil* (Wheaton, Ill.: Tyndale House, 1985).

Week 14

[1]Amy Carmichael, *Edges of His Ways* (Fort Washington, Penn.: Christian Literature Crusade, 1955).

[2]Max Lucado, *On the Anvil* (Wheaton, Ill.: Tyndale House, 1985).

Week 15

[1]Amy Carmichael, *The Gold Cord* (Fort Washington, Penn.: Christian Literature Crusade, 1883), 91.

Week 16

[1]William Barclay, *Daily Study Bible: Letters to the Galatians and Ephesians* (Philadelphia: Westminister, 1976).

Week 17

[1]Walter B. Knight, *Knight's Master Book of New Illustrations* (Grand Rapids: Eerdmans, 1956).

Week 18

[1]William Barclay, *Daily Study Bible: Letters to the Galatians and Ephesians* (Philadelphia: Westminister, 1976).

Week 19

[1]William Barclay, *Daily Study Bible: Letters to the Galatians and Ephesians* (Philadelphia: Westminister, 1976).

Week 20

[1]Paul Lee Tan, *Encyclopedia of 7700 Illustrations* (Rockville, Md.: Assurance Publishers, 1979).

Week 23

[1]Max Lucado, *On the Anvil* (Wheaton, Ill.: Tyndale House, 1985).

[2]Amy Carmichael, *Edges of His Ways* (Fort Washington, Penn.: Christian Literature Crusade, 1955).

[3]William Barclay, *Daily Study Bible: Letters to the Galatians and Ephesians* (Philadelphia: Westminister, 1976).

Week 24

[1]Amy Carmichael, *Candles in the Dark* (Fort Washington, Penn.: Christian Literature Crusade, 1981).

Week 25

[1]Amy Carmichael, *Edges of His Ways* (Fort Washington, Penn.: Christian Literature Crusade, 1955).

Week 28

[1]Catherine Marshall, *A Closer Walk* (Old Tappan, N.J.: Revell, 1985).

Week 29

[1]Sarah Hornsby, *At the Name of Jesus* (Old Tappan, N.J.: Revell, 1986).

Week 30

[1]Amy Carmichael, *Candles in the Dark* (Fort Washington, Penn.: Christian Literature Crusade, 1981).

Week 31

[1]Richard Shelly Taylor, *The Disciplined Life* (Minneapolis: Bethany House, 1974).
[2]Ruth Harms Calkin, *Marriage Is So Much More, Lord* (Wheaton, Ill.: Tyndale House, 1986).
[3]Marie Chapian, *Staying Happy in an Unhappy World* (New York: Bantam Books, 1989).

Week 32

[1]Robert Bretall, *A Kierkegaard Anthology* (Princeton, N.J.: Princeton University Press, 1948), 108.

Week 33

[1]Amy Harwell and Kristine Tomasik, *When Your Friend Gets Cancer* (Wheaton, Ill.: Harold Shaw, 1987).
[2]Amy Carmichael, *Edges of His Ways* (Fort Washington, Penn.: Christian Literature Crusade, 1955).
[3]Ibid.

Week 36

[1]Gary Inrig, *Quality Friendship* (Chicago: Moody Press, 1981).
[2]Letty Pogrebim, *Among Friends* (New York: McGraw-Hill, 1986).
[3]Corrie ten Boom, *Each New Day* (Old Tappan, N.J.: Revell, 1977).
[4]Corrie ten Boom, *Clippings from My Notebook* (Minneapolis: World Wide Publications, 1982).

Week 37

[1]Amy Carmichael, *If* (Fort Washington, Penn.: Christian Literature Crusade, 1966).
[2]Ibid.
[3]Ibid.

Week 40

[1]Paul Lee Tan, *Encyclopedia of 7700 Illustrations* (Rockville, Md.: Assurance Publishers, 1979).

Week 41

[1]Arthur Gordon, *A Touch of Wonder* (Old Tappan, N.J.: Revell, 1984).
[2]Ibid.
[3]A. L. Alexander, *Poems That Touch the Heart* (New York: Doubleday, 1941).
[4]Ibid.

Week 42

[1]Roy Hession, *The Calvary Road* (Fort Washington, Penn.: Christian Literature Crusade, 1964).

[2]Kevin Leman, *Why Women Get Stressed Out and What They Can Do About It* (Old Tappan, N.J.: Revell, 1987).

[3]Dolores Curran, *Traits of a Happy Family* (Minneapolis: Winston Press, 1983).

[4]A. L. Alexander, *Poems That Touch the Heart* (New York: Doubleday, 1941).

Week 43

[1]Wayne Martindale and Jerry Root, *The Quotable Lewis* (Wheaton, Ill.: Tyndale House, 1989).

[2]A. L. Alexander, *Poems That Touch the Heart* (New York: Doubleday, 1941).

Week 44

[1]From Carroll Simcox, *Three Thousand Quotations on Christian Themes* (Grand Rapids: Baker Book House, 1988).

[2]G. H. Morling and Ruth Bell Graham, *The Quest for Serenity* (Waco, Tex.: Word, 1989).

[3]Ibid.

[4]Ibid.

[5]Arthur Gordon, *A Touch of Wonder* (Old Tappan, N.J.: Revell, 1984).

Week 45

[1]Amy Carmichael, *Edges of His Ways* (Fort Washington, Penn.: Christian Literature Crusade, 1955).

[2]Philip Yancey, *Disappointment with God* (Grand Rapids: Zondervan, 1988).

[3]William Barclay, *Daily Study Bible: Letter to the Romans* (Philadelphia: Westminster, 1975).

[4]Emily Hahn, *Once Upon a Pedestal* (New York: Crowell, 1974), 160–61.

Week 46

[1]Philip Yancey, *Disappointment with God* (Grand Rapids: Zondervan, 1988).

[2]Carroll Simcox, *Three Thousand Quotations on Christian Themes* (Grand Rapids: Baker Book House, 1988).

[3]Ibid.

[4]Roy Hession, *The Calvary Road* (Fort Washington, Penn.: Christian Literature Crusade, 1964).

Week 47

[1]Nancy Friday, *My Mother, My Self* (New York: Dell, 1987).

[2]Carol Burnett, *One More Time* (New York: Random House, 1986), 186.

[3]Barbara Johnson, *Fresh Elastic for Stretched-Out Moms* (Old Tappan, N.J.: Revell, 1985).

[4]Ruth Bell Graham, *Sitting by My Laughing Fire* (Dallas, Tex.: Word, 1977).

Week 48

[1]A. L. Alexander, *Poems That Touch the Heart* (New York: Doubleday, 1941).
[2]Roy Hession, *The Calvary Road* (Fort Washington, Penn.: Christian Literature Crusade, 1964).
[3]Ruth Tucker, *Sacred Stories* (Grand Rapids: Zondervan, 1989).
[4]Ibid.
[5]Ibid.
[6]Ibid.

Week 49

[1]Quoted in Barbara Johnson, *Fresh Elastic for Stretched-Out Moms* (Old Tappan, N.J.: Revell, 1985).
[2]Ruth Tucker, *Sacred Stories* (Grand Rapids: Zondervan, 1989).
[3]Lorraine Eitel, editor, *Treasury of Christian Poetry* (Old Tappan, N.J.: Revell).

Week 50

[1]Maureen Rink, *Free to Grieve* (Minneapolis: Bethany House, 1985).
[2]Bob Neudorf, "Is It Proper to Cry?" *Alliance Life* (September 16, 1987): 14.

Week 51

[1]Kevin Leman, *Why Women Get Stressed Out and What They Can Do About It* (Old Tappan, N.J.: Revell, 1987).
[2]Tim Stafford, *Knowing the Face of God* (Grand Rapids: Zondervan, 1989).

Week 52

[1]Lewis Smedes, *How Can It Be All Right When Everything Is All Wrong?* (San Francisco: Harper & Row, 1982).
[2]Charles Swindoll, *Living on the Ragged Edge* (Waco, Tex.: Word, 1990).

TOPICAL INDEX